Cuban Missile Crisis

Cuban Missile Crisis

The Essential Reference Guide

Priscilla Roberts, Editor

ABC-CLIO

Santa Barbara, California • Denver, Colorado • Oxford, England

Copyright 2012 by ABC-CLIO, LLC

Library of Congress Cataloging-in-Publication Data

Roberts, Priscilla Mary.
    Cuban Missile Crisis : the essential reference guide / Priscilla Roberts.
        p. cm.
    Includes bibliographical references and index.
    ISBN 978-1-61069-065-2 (hardcopy : acid-free paper) —
ISBN 978-1-61069-066-9 (ebook)   1. Cuban Missile Crisis, 1962.   2. Cuban Missile Crisis, 1962—Sources.   3. Cuban Missile Crisis, 1962—Chronology.
I. Title.
    E841.R55   2012
    972.9106'4—dc23   2011051907

ISBN: 978-1-61069-065-2
EISBN: 978-1-61069-066-9

16 15 14 13 12   1 2 3 4 5

This book is also available on the World Wide Web as an eBook.
Visit www.abc-clio.com for details.

ABC-CLIO, LLC
130 Cremona Drive, P.O. Box 1911
Santa Barbara, California 93116-1911

This book is printed on acid-free paper ∞

Manufactured in the United States of America

Remembering Des Robinson
(1937–2012)
Spectacular Athlete
Inspiring Teacher
Most Splendid of Friends

Contents

List of Entries

Introduction:
The Cuban Missile Crisis

Priscilla Roberts

Causes

The October 1962 Cuban Missile Crisis was the closest the two Cold War superpowers, the United States and the Soviet Union, ever came to full-scale nuclear war. It represented the convergence of several trends in U.S. foreign policy: the long-time assumption of a hegemonic role in the Western Hemisphere (first enunciated in the Monroe Doctrine); the Cold War policy of containing global communism enshrined in the 1947 Truman Doctrine declaration; post–World War II U.S.-Soviet competition for the loyalties of the developing world; and the nuclear rivalry between the United States and the Soviet Union.

From the early 19th century, successive U.S. governments held it almost axiomatic that their country should rightfully be predominant over the rest of the Western Hemisphere. The Monroe Doctrine was an 1823 declaration that no other power should acquire any further colonies in the Americas nor seek to regain colonies that had become independent. In 1904 President Theodore Roosevelt took this still further, announcing, in what he termed the Roosevelt Corollary to the Monroe Doctrine, that the United States had the right to intervene to restore order in any Latin American nation that failed to conduct its affairs to U.S. satisfaction. U.S. officials treated Latin America as a de facto sphere of influence. Six years earlier, Roosevelt had been among the strongest advocates of war against Spain to end continuing unrest and rebellion in Cuba, then a Spanish colony. In 1898 the United States finally declared war on Spain, winning a quick victory over the European power. At the end of the year, Spain ceded Cuba, together with the Philippines, Guam, and Puerto Rico, to the United States.

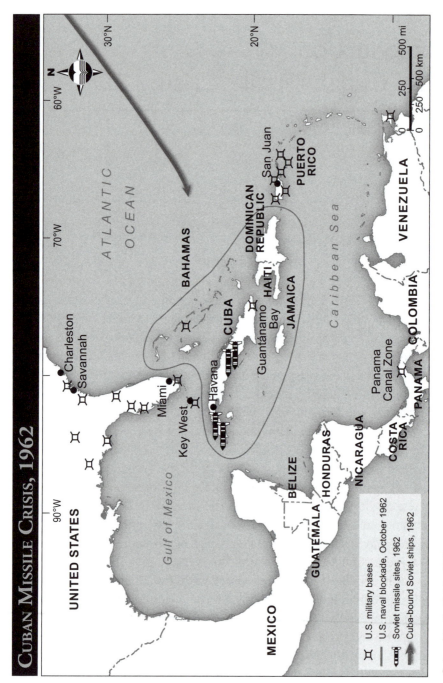

Cuban Missile Crisis, 1962

After four years of U.S. occupation, in 1902 Cuba received independence, with some qualifications. The U.S. Navy obtained a permanent lease on a base at Guantánamo Bay in Cuba. Cuba was also forced to accept the Platt Amendment, whereby the United States retained the right to intervene in Cuba's economic, military, and political affairs should the U.S. government disapprove of Cuban conduct of these. American troops returned again in 1906 for three years, and once more in 1912 to suppress domestic unrest. In 1933 the new government of Ramón Grau, brought to power by a military coup, nullified the Platt Amendment, whereupon U.S. president Franklin D. Roosevelt denied diplomatic recognition to Cuba for a year. Gen. Fulgencio Batista, the military strongman who dominated the new regime and served as president from 1940 to 1944 and again from 1952 to 1958, quickly became a reliable U.S. client, aligning himself with U.S. policies in both World War II and the Cold War. Throughout, Cuba remained heavily commercially and financially dependent on the United States, and American-owned firms dominated the Cuban economy.

From the late 1940s onward, U.S. foreign policy was dominated by the global competition between the United States, the standard-bearer of liberal, democratic, and capitalist values, and the Soviet Union, the world's foremost communist power. In 1947 the Truman Doctrine made containment, the effort to prevent any additional nations becoming communist, the guiding principle of U.S. foreign policy. By the 1950s, the Soviet Union and the United States each possessed horrifically destructive thermonuclear weapons, which meant that unless they exercised great caution conflicts between them had the potential to spiral into devastating war. Rather than confronting each other directly, Soviet and U.S. leaders sought to win the loyalties of developing countries in what was termed the Third World, supporting political groups they considered broadly sympathetic to their own ideological viewpoint. Across Asia, Latin America, and the Middle East, in such countries as Guatemala, Iran, and Vietnam, successive U.S. administrations opposed and tried to overthrow leftist governments while supporting political regimes, however authoritarian, that professed themselves reliably anticommunist.

In 1958 an indigenous revolutionary movement led by Fidel Castro seized power from Batista. Although Castro initially declared that he was not a communist, from spring 1959 he covertly sought Soviet aid and military protection. American economic pressure and boycotts quickly impelled him to move openly into the Soviet camp. In response, the U.S. Central Intelligence Agency (CIA) planned to assist Cuban exiles to attack the island and overthrow Castro. Initiated under President Dwight D.

Eisenhower and inherited by his successor, John F. Kennedy, the April 1961 Bay of Pigs invasion attempt proved a humiliating fiasco for the United States. Kennedy and Secretary of Defense Robert S. McNamara continued to develop plans for invasion, and their CIA and military advisers also devised various ingenious, if often implausible, schemes to overthrow or assassinate Castro, who not unnaturally sought further Soviet aid.

In mid-1961, as the concurrent Berlin Crisis intensified and culminated in the building of the Berlin Wall, military hard-liners in the Kremlin, frustrated for several years, succeeded in implementing a 34-percent increase in spending on conventional forces. Both the Bay of Pigs and Kennedy's bellicose inauguration rhetoric that his country would "pay any price, bear any burden, meet any hardship, support any friend, oppose any foe, in order to assure the survival and the success of liberty," may have energized them. Despite claims of a missile gap between the Soviet Union and the United States, in practice the strategic missile imbalance greatly advantaged the United States, which had at least eight times as many nuclear warheads as its rival. Even U.S. leaders were unaware of just how lopsidedly the nuclear situation favored them, believing the ratio to be only about three to one.

The 1961–1962 U.S. deployment of 15 intermediate-range Jupiter missiles in Turkey, directly threatening Soviet territory, further angered Soviet premier Nikita Khrushchev, making him eager to redress the balance. It seems that Khrushchev also hoped to pressure the United States into making concessions on Berlin. Additionally, installing missiles on Cuba rebutted charges from the People's Republic of China, increasingly the Soviet Union's ideological rival within the communist world, that the Soviets were only paper tigers, unwilling to take concrete action to advance the cause of international revolution. Khrushchev, moreover, apparently felt a romantic sense of solidarity with the new Cuban state, whose emergence reassured him and other old communists that their movement still possessed international vitality.

Early in 1962, Khrushchev offered Soviet nuclear-capable missiles, controlled by Soviet technicians and troops, to Castro, who accepted and oversaw their secret installation. Khrushchev apparently believed that these would deter U.S. plans to invade Cuba. Rather optimistically, he calculated that once the missiles were in place Kennedy and his advisers would find the prospect of nuclear war over them so horrifying that, despite their chagrin, they would accept their presence in Cuba. The Bay of Pigs fiasco, followed by Khrushchev's June 1961 summit meeting with Kennedy at Vienna, apparently convinced the Soviet leader that Kennedy was weak and could easily be intimidated. So confident was Khrushchev that when Kennedy administration officials warned from July to September 1962 that the United States would respond strongly should the Soviets deploy nuclear or other offensive weaponry in Cuba, he implicitly denied any intention of doing so. Admittedly, by this time the missiles had already been secretly dispatched and their installation was at least a partial fait accompli. At this stage of his career, moreover, Khrushchev's behavior tended to be somewhat erratic. In any case, he miscalculated. Instead of treating the Cuban missiles as deterrent weapons, the Kennedy administration regarded them as evidence of Soviet aggressiveness and refused to tolerate their presence.

Course

On October 16, 1962, Kennedy was provided with photographic evidence, obtained by U-2 reconnaissance planes, that Soviet officials had installed intermediate-range nuclear-capable weapons in Cuba. In response, the president summoned a secret Executive Committee (ExComm) of 18 top advisers, among them Joint Chiefs of Staff chairman Maxwell D. Taylor, CIA Director John McCone, Secretary of State Dean Rusk, Secretary of Defense Robert S. McNamara, national security adviser McGeorge Bundy, Vice President Lyndon B. Johnson, Treasury Secretary C. Douglas Dillon, and the president's brother and closest adviser, Attorney General Robert F. Kennedy, to decide on a course of action. President Kennedy also included senior members of the broader foreign policy establishment, including former secretary of defense Robert A. Lovett and former secretary of state Dean Acheson. Other top officials, such as Adlai Stevenson, U.S. ambassador to the United Nations, and John J. McCloy, Kennedy's disarmament adviser, occasionally joined its deliberations. Technically a committee of the National Security Council, for 13 days ExComm debated how best to respond to Khrushchev's secretive tactic.

Whatever the logical justification for Khrushchev's behavior, politically it would have been almost impossible for any U.S. president to accept the situation. Hard-line Republicans in Congress, such as Senator Barry Goldwater, a potential presidential candidate, were eager to attack Kennedy should he show himself weak on Soviet or communist expansion, especially so close to U.S. shores. The U.S. military calculated that the missiles would increase Soviet nuclear striking force against the continental United States by 50 percent. (In reality the missiles would have doubled or even tripled Soviet striking capabilities, reducing the existing U.S. numerical advantage to a ratio of merely two or three to one.) Kennedy, however, considered the missiles less a genuine military threat than a test of his credibility and leadership. Taylor, speaking for the U.S. military, initially favored launching air strikes to destroy the missile installations— a scenario that would almost certainly have killed substantial numbers of Soviet troops, was unlikely to eliminate all the missiles, and might well have provoked nuclear war. An invasion of Cuba by U.S. ground forces might also provoke a full-scale war. Discussions continued for several days. Eventually, on October 22, Kennedy publicly announced the presence of the missiles in Cuba, demanded that the Soviet Union remove them, and proclaimed the imposition of a naval blockade around the island, a measure intended to prevent the delivery of any further Soviet weaponry or military personnel to Cuba.

Several tense days ensued, during which (on October 27) Soviet antiaircraft batteries on Cuba shot down—without specific authorization from Kremlin leaders, whom this episode greatly alarmed—a U.S. U-2 reconnaissance plane. Seeking to avoid further escalation, Kennedy rejected Taylor's advice to retaliate militarily and he deliberately refrained from action. After some hesitation, Khrushchev decided not to challenge the naval quarantine and acquiesced in the removal of the missiles. Simultaneously, his ambassador in Washington, Anatoly Dobrynin, secretly obtained an unpublicized pledge from Robert Kennedy that his brother would shortly remove Jupiter missiles in Turkey and Italy. Provided that the Soviet missiles departed and were not replaced, the United States also promised not to mount another invasion of Cuba.

Recently released tapes of conversations among President Kennedy and his advisers reveal that to avoid nuclear war, he was prepared to make even greater concessions to the Soviets, including taking the issue to the United Nations and openly trading Turkish missiles for those in Cuba. In so doing, he parted company with some of his more hard-line advisers. Showing considerable statesmanship, Kennedy deliberately refrained from emphasizing Khrushchev's humiliation, although other administration officials were privately less diplomatic and celebrated their victory to the press.

Newly opened Soviet documentary evidence has demonstrated that the Cuban situation was even more menacing than most involved then realized. Forty-two thousand well-equipped Soviet soldiers were already on the island, far more than the 10,000 troops that U.S. officials had estimated. Moreover, although Kennedy's advisers believed that some of the missiles might already be armed, they failed to realize that no less than 158 short- and intermediate-range warheads on the island, whose use Castro urged should the United States invade, were already operational and that 42 of these could have reached U.S. territory. The bellicose Castro also hoped to shoot down additional U-2 planes and provoke a major confrontation. The potential for a trigger-happy military officer to spark a full-scale nuclear conflagration almost certainly existed, retrospectively chilling evidence of the dangers inherent in these weapons.

Consequences

The Cuban Missile Crisis had a sobering impact on its protagonists. On Kennedy it had a certain salutary maturing effect, making the once-brash young president a strong advocate of disarmament in the final months before his untimely death in November 1963. His stance induced the Soviet leadership to agree to establish a hotline between Moscow and Washington to facilitate communications and ease tensions during international crises. The two powers also finally reached agreement in 1963 on the Partial Test Ban Treaty (PTBT), which halted nuclear testing in the atmosphere, under water, and in space. From then onward both superpowers exercised great caution in dealing with each other, and subsequently they never again came so close to nuclear war.

Soviet officials felt that they had come dangerously near to losing control of the actual employment of nuclear-capable weapons in Cuba, either to their own military commanders on the ground or even potentially to Castro's forces. Humiliation at U.S. hands was among the factors that propelled Soviet leaders into an expensive major nuclear buildup to achieve parity with the United States, which they reached in 1970. The historian John Lewis Gaddis has even argued that one result of the Cuban Missile Crisis was that the possession of massively destructive nuclear weapons enabled the Soviet Union to command international respect as a superpower for many years longer than it might have otherwise, given the country's increasingly lackluster economic performance.

Khrushchev's fall from power in 1964 was at least partly due to the missile crisis. Politburo colleagues criticized him for recklessness in originally installing the missiles and weakness in subsequently yielding to U.S. pressure. Kennedy's Cuban policies may also have indirectly caused his own assassination. The man arrested for Kennedy's murder, Lee Harvey Oswald, was an unpredictable leftist who had spent some time in the Soviet

Union, sympathized strongly with Castro's Cuba, and opposed Kennedy's efforts to overthrow Castro. Others have suggested that Cuban exiles who resented Kennedy's failure to do more to assist them may have been involved in his death.

The Cuban Missile Crisis tested and perhaps weakened the Western alliance. Western European political leaders, including British prime minister Harold Macmillan, Federal Republic of Germany (FRG) (West German) chancellor Konrad Adenauer, and most notably French president Charles de Gaulle, felt some discomfort that although Kennedy dispatched former secretary of state Dean Acheson to brief them on the crisis, they had not been consulted on decisions of great importance to the survival of their own countries, which were likely to be prime targets for Soviet nuclear missiles in any major war. The Kennedy administration was equally high-handed in ignoring the North Atlantic Council when deciding to remove Jupiter missiles from Italy and Turkey, even though these weapons were supposedly under NATO control. Such behavior on the part of the U.S. government probably confirmed de Gaulle in his decision to take a highly independent foreign policy line in subsequent years.

Although the U.S.-Soviet settlement effectively ensured his regime's survival, Castro, meanwhile, felt deeply humiliated and resentful that the superpowers had settled matters between themselves without consulting him. Before Khrushchev's fall from power, though, the two men were reconciled, and Cuban-Soviet relations remained close until the end of the Cold War. To the chagrin of successive U.S. presidents, most of whom would have welcomed his overthrow, the durable Castro remained in power into the 21st century, eventually becoming the doyen among world political leaders before finally retiring in 2008.

For decades after the Cuban Missile Crisis, new evidence on almost every aspect of these events continued to surface. Robert Kennedy's memoir *Thirteen Days,* posthumously released in 1969, a year after his assassination in June 1968, for the first time confirmed rumors of a U.S.-Soviet understanding on the removal of missiles from Turkey. Aging Kennedy administration officials gradually released new information, greatly qualifying the initial depiction of the crisis as published early on in works by such Kennedy associates as Arthur M. Schlesinger, Jr., and Theodore Sorensen. The release of secret tapes of the deliberations of ExComm, made without the knowledge of any participants except the two Kennedy brothers, demonstrated that to avoid nuclear war President Kennedy was willing to be far more conciliatory than earlier accounts had suggested and also highlighted inaccuracies in the recollections of other participants.

Equally fruitfully, the ending of the Cold War and the consequent relaxation of tensions with the communist world opened the floodgates of recollections from the other side. From the late 1980s onward, several international conferences bringing together Cuban, American, and Soviet participants in the crisis took place in the United States and Cuba. Attendees let slip much new information, including details of just how many Soviet troops and nuclear-capable missiles were already installed on Cuba in October 1962 and accounts of at least one dramatic confrontation between U.S. warships and a nuclear-armed Soviet submarine. Additional documentary evidence released from both Soviet and U.S. archives continued to fill in missing information on aspects of the Soviet-U.S.-Cuban imbroglio, giving historians a far fuller, accurate, and more nuanced understanding of Soviet dealings with Cuba and of the actions of Khrushchev and other Soviet officials before and during the crisis. More is also becoming available from the archives of Western European allies of the United States, illuminating once-obscure episodes and correcting earlier assertions and assumptions on these nations' contributions to the crisis. Undoubtedly, some areas still remain and perhaps always will be murky. Fifty years after the Cuban Missile Crisis, however, our understanding of this terrifying and spectacular international confrontation demonstrates that in hindsight it was even more complex and possessed wider ramifications than appreciated at the time.

A

Acheson, Dean Gooderham (1893–1971)

U.S. secretary of state (1949–1953) and chief architect of U.S. foreign policy in the Cold War's formative years. Born on April 11, 1893, in Middletown, Connecticut, to British parents, Dean Acheson attended the prestigious Groton School, Yale University, and Harvard Law School. In 1921 Acheson joined a Washington, D.C., law firm. He entered public life in 1933 when President Franklin D. Roosevelt named him undersecretary of the treasury. Acheson resigned soon thereafter, however, over a disagreement concerning gold and currency policies. In 1940 he authored a key legal opinion that led to the Lend-Lease program. He became assistant secretary of state in 1941 and then undersecretary of state in 1945. In 1949 President Harry S. Truman appointed him secretary of state, a position he held until 1953.

The possessor of a brilliant legal mind, a regal bearing, and a biting wit, Acheson initially favored a policy of postwar cooperation with the Soviet Union, but he quickly reversed his view and, along with Russian specialist George F. Kennan, became one of the chief proponents of the Cold War containment policy. Unlike Kennan, who believed that the contest with the Soviet Union was primarily political in nature, Acheson stressed the military dimension. Sobered by the failure of democratic nations to halt the Axis powers in the 1930s, Acheson advocated a policy of developing military strength before negotiating with the Soviet Union. Acheson also played a critical role in implementing major Cold War initiatives in Europe, including the Truman Doctrine program of assistance to Greece and Turkey, the Marshall Plan (a program of economic aid to Western Europe), and the North Atlantic Treaty Organization (NATO) security pact.

Acheson retired from public life in 1953 but soon became the main Democratic critic of President Dwight D. Eisenhower's foreign policy. When the Eisenhower administration committed itself to a policy of massive retaliation that emphasized nuclear responses over conventional responses to crises, the former secretary of state reacted with utter disbelief to what he termed "defense on the cheap."

In the 1960s, Acheson returned to public life as the head of NATO task forces, special envoy, diplomatic troubleshooter, and foreign policy adviser for presidents John F. Kennedy and Lyndon B. Johnson. Told by Kennedy in early 1961 of the projected Bay of Pigs invasion of Cuba, an alarmed Acheson hoped, he later recalled, that the president was not "serious" and warned him that "1,500 Cubans weren't as good as 25,000 Cubans." His advice tended to the hawkish. In the 1961 Berlin Crisis, he counseled Kennedy to take a firm stand, and he privately believed that Kennedy should have dismantled the Berlin Wall.

During the Cuban Missile Crisis, Acheson's advice was equally forceful. Included in ExComm's discussions, he invariably advocated air strikes against the missile installations, brushing aside the fears of Attorney General Robert F. Kennedy, the president's brother, that bombing them without warning would constitute another Pearl Harbor. On October 21 President Kennedy dispatched Acheson to Europe to brief President Charles de Gaulle of France, Chancellor Konrad Adenauer of West Germany (FRG), and the North Atlantic Council on the situation. Returning after the implementation of the U.S. naval blockade of Cuba, when the ultimate outcome still hung in the balance, Acheson again advocated air strikes against the missiles. When the confrontation was resolved, Acheson privately felt that President Kennedy had been "out of his depth," disorganized, and insufficiently forceful in handling the crisis and termed his success "homage to plain dumb luck," criticisms he made public in 1969, when Robert F. Kennedy's own account was published. Acheson died of a heart attack on October 12, 1971, in Sandy Spring, Maryland.

Caryn E. Neumann

See also: Bay of Pigs Invasion; Berlin Crises; Containment, Doctrine and Course of; Kennedy, Robert Francis; U.S. Allies

References

Beisner, Robert L. *Dean Acheson: A Life in the Cold War.* New York: Oxford University Press, 2006.

Brinkley, Douglas. *Dean Acheson: The Cold War Years, 1953–71.* New Haven, CT: Yale University Press, 1992.

Chace, James. *Acheson: The Secretary of State Who Created the American World.* New York: Simon and Schuster, 1998.

Isaacson, Walter, and Evan Thomas. *The Wise Men: Six Friends and the World They Made.* New York: Simon and Schuster, 1986.

McMahon, Robert J. *Dean Acheson and the Creation of an American World Order.* Washington, DC: Potomac Books, 2009.

Alekseev (Shitov), Aleksandr Ivanovich (1913–2001)

Soviet diplomat and KGB intelligence officer, Soviet ambassador to Cuba, June 12, 1962–January 15, 1968. Alekseev was born Aleksandr Shitov on January 8, 1913, in Russia's western Komstromskoi Oblast. After studying French and Spanish at Moscow State University, he joined the Soviet intelligence service, the KGB, in 1941. Later that year, as German forces pushed into Soviet territory, the Moscow-based Shitov took the cover name Alekseev, planning to remain in Moscow as an espionage operative should German forces capture the city. From 1941 to 1943 he worked in the Soviet mission in Tehran, Iran; from 1944 to 1951 in French North Africa and in the Soviet embassy in Paris, returning to Moscow in 1951 to work for the Soviet Information Bureau. From 1954 Alekseev was based in Buenos Aires, where, supposedly working as a correspondent for TASS, the Soviet news agency, he was actually recruiting for the KGB. Recalled to Moscow in 1958, he worked on Latin American propaganda activities in the Commission of Cultural Affairs of the Central Committee of the Soviet Communist Party.

On January 10, 1959, the Soviet Union recognized the new radical government of Cuba established under Prime Minister Fidel Castro nine days earlier. Alekseev requested assignment to Havana to establish contact with the new Cuban leaders. The first Russian granted a visa to Cuba, Alekseev arrived on October 1, 1959. Working with covert members of the Cuban Communist Party within the Cuban government, notably Castro's brother Raúl and the Argentinian revolutionary Ernesto "Che" Guevara, Alekseev sought to steer the new regime in a pro-Soviet direction. As Castro initiated radical land reform and nationalized U.S. property in Cuba during 1959 and 1960, Cuban relations with the United States deteriorated. On September 2, 1960, Fidel Castro made a major public proclamation of radical principles, the Declaration of Havana. The following month, the United States imposed a complete economic embargo. In early January 1961, the United States broke all diplomatic relations with Cuba.

These circumstances facilitated Alekseev's efforts to broker a rapprochement between Cuban leaders and the Soviet Union. At his urging, in February 1960 Anastas Mikoyan, a top Soviet Presidium member, visited Cuba and concluded a Soviet-Cuban trade agreement, whereby the Soviet Union purchased Cuban sugar in exchange for oil and other goods. In May the two countries agreed to resume diplomatic relations. The Soviet embassy in Havana reopened its doors on July 8, 1960, and the following month Ambassador Sergei Mikhailovich Kudryatsev took up his post, with Alekseev as cultural attaché. Kudryatsev never developed good relations with the Cuban revolutionaries. In September 1960 Castro told the ambassador that Alekseev should handle all meetings with top Cuban leaders.

Fearing that the United States was planning military intervention, Castro also turned to Alekseev in a quest for Soviet arms, to supplement existing Cuban purchases from Czechoslovakia and several Western European countries. In July 1960, Soviet premier Nikita Khrushchev publicly stated that if necessary his country would intervene with nuclear weapons to protect Cuba. The Soviet Union gave Cuba increasing quantities of weapons, announcing a major military aid program, including tanks, rifles, and artillery, during Raúl Castro's July 1960 visit to Moscow. Soon afterward, as rumors of a forthcoming U.S. invasion attempt on Cuba circulated internationally, a total of 41 military aircraft (MiG-19 and MiG-15 fighter jets and reconnaissance planes) were promised to Cuba, together with enhanced quantities of other weapons. The Soviet Union also began training 17 Cuban intelligence operatives for espionage against the United States and the Cuban émigré community. After the U.S.-backed April 1961 Bay of Pigs invasion attempt on Cuba, Fidel Castro moved even closer to the Soviet Union in his search for protection, requesting additional KGB operatives and assistance in training Cuban intelligence agents, a request Alekseev supported. On April 16, 1961, Castro announced that he himself was a communist, and on December 1, 1961, he confirmed his adherence to Marxism-Leninism.

Alekseev had little if any input into the Soviet decision to base nuclear-capable missiles in Cuba. In early May 1962, Khrushchev and the KGB summoned him to Moscow and informed him that he was to be appointed ambassador to the island, to supervise the deployment of substantial Soviet forces equipped with conventional weapons. Later in May, Khrushchev enhanced this plan by including substantial numbers of short-, medium-, and intermediate-range nuclear-capable missiles and warheads, together with a nuclear-armed submarine squadron. Alekseev unavailingly suggested that Castro would refuse the offer of such armaments, reminding Khrushchev that the Cuban leader sought to expel the Americans from their Cuban base of Guantánamo Bay by demanding the removal of all foreign outposts in Latin America.

As the Cuban Missile Crisis escalated, especially after President John F. Kennedy's October 22 public statement, Alekseev served as Castro's principal Russian confidant, warning Khrushchev early on October 27 that Castro believed U.S. intervention to be inevitable and translating a cable from the Cuban leader to Khrushchev that apparently urged a nuclear first strike against the United States. The same day the Kremlin, in turn, sought to use Alekseev's privileged access to Castro to persuade Cuba's prime minister to endorse publicly Khrushchev's proposal that the United States trade Turkish for Cuban missile bases and assure the United Nations that all work on Soviet missile installations in Cuba had ceased. On October 28, Alekseev was instructed to deliver a letter from Khrushchev to Castro, explaining the Soviet position, but Castro refused to meet him. In the following days Alekseev, a textbook example of an ambassador who had gone native, largely embraced Castro's defiant attitude toward both superpowers, questioning the good faith of Washington's pledge not to invade Cuba and warning his Kremlin superiors not to pressure or irritate the volatile Cuban leader.

Hardly surprisingly, Alekseev survived the October 1962 debacle. His cordial relationship with Cuban officials, Castro included, made him too valuable to sacrifice to political expediency. In spring 1963, Alekseev successfully encouraged Castro to visit the Soviet Union and repair his relations with Khrushchev and others. Weathering Khrushchev's fall 1964 ouster by Leonid Brezhnev, Alekseev remained ambassador to Cuba until January 1968. He subsequently served as an adviser to the leftist President Salvador Allende of Chile, who died following a military coup in 1973. Alekseev retired in 1980 and then became an official adviser to the Soviet embassy in Cuba. In 1992 he attended a major conference in Havana marking the 40th anniversary of the missile crisis, where 30 prominent Cuban, Soviet, and U.S. official participants in the crisis pooled their recollections. Alekseev died in 1998.

Priscilla Roberts

See also: ANADYR, Operation; Castro, Fidel; Castro, Raúl; Guantánamo Bay Naval Base; Guevara de la Serna, Ernesto "Che"; Khrushchev, Nikita Sergeyevich; Mikoyan, Anastas Ivanovich

References

Andrew, Christopher, and Vasili Mitrokhin. *The World Was Going Our Way: The KGB and the Battle for the Third World.* New York: Basic Books, 2005.

Dobbs, Michael. *One Minute to Midnight: Kennedy, Khrushchev, and Castro on the Brink of Nuclear War.* New York: Knopf, 2008.

Fursenko, Aleksandr, and Timothy Naftali. *One Hell of a Gamble: Khrushchev, Castro, and Kennedy, 1958–1964.* New York: Norton, 1997.

Polmar, Norman, and John D. Gresham. *DEFCON-2: Standing on the Brink of Nuclear War during the Cuban Missile Crisis.* New York: John Wiley, 2006.

Alliance for Progress

A financial aid program devised by the United States in March 1961 to promote social reform in Latin America. The program's architects hoped to curb violence and prevent communist-inspired revolutions in the region. When dealing with Latin America after World War II, the United States generally emphasized security imperatives at the expense of social and economic concerns. Rejecting the region's pleas for a Latin American plan similar to the 1947 Marshall Plan that revived the Western European economies, the United States had endorsed private investment and free trade as the keys to Latin America's socioeconomic development. While this approach meshed well with President Dwight Eisenhower's efforts to eschew direct aid, it often conflicted with the prevailing economic climate in Latin America.

Two events in the late 1950s demonstrated the risks in this course. First, in May 1958 Vice President Richard M. Nixon's goodwill tour of South America provoked hostile demonstrations and major rioting in the cities of Caracas in Venezuela and Lima in Peru. Second, Fidel Castro seized control of Cuba's government in January 1959, and by 1960 he was becoming increasingly anti-American and pro-Soviet.

In the late 1950s, therefore, the Eisenhower administration began to direct more attention to Latin America's economic and social problems. Latin Americans had long sought U.S. support for a regional development bank. In August 1958 the United States dropped its long-standing opposition to the bank and in October 1960 supported the establishment of the Inter-American Development Bank. This shift in U.S. policy continued at Bogotá, Colombia, in September 1960 at a special meeting called by the Council of the Organization of American States (OAS) to study new measures for Pan-American economic cooperation. In signing the Act of Bogotá, the Eisenhower administration laid the groundwork for the Alliance for Progress by pledging $500 million for economic development and social reform in Latin America. In return the Latin American nations agreed to implement sound economic policies and to eliminate obstacles to social and economic progress.

During the U.S. presidential elections of 1960, Democratic nominee John F. Kennedy criticized the Eisenhower administration and Republican candidate Richard M. Nixon for "losing" Cuba and failing to align U.S. policy with Latin Americans' rising aspirations. Kennedy called for an "alliance for progress" between the United States and Latin America in his inaugural address.

In March 1961 the Kennedy administration formally committed itself to an Alliance for Progress with Latin America, a long-term program of U.S. aid linked to social and structural reforms, economic development, and democratization. That program took official form at the inter-American meeting at Punta del Este, Uruguay, in August 1961. The conference proclaimed a lengthy list of objectives for the program, including democratization, acceleration of social and economic development, promotion of education, fair wages and working conditions, health programs, tax reforms, agrarian reform, fiscal stability, and the stimulation of private enterprise. To achieve its goals, the program would need $100 billion during its first decade, $20 billion of which would come from external sources, with the United States pledging to provide a major part of that funding. The remaining $80 billion was expected to come from Latin American sources, both public and private. When launching this program, which was designed to provide peaceful, democratic alternatives to violent social revolution and a "second Cuba" in the hemisphere, the U.S. preoccupation with containing the communist threat was greatly in evidence.

The objectives of the Alliance for Progress soon collided with the harsh realities of international economics and growing domestic pressures in both Latin America and the United States. The program implicitly assumed that most Latin American elites would support reforms to avoid violent revolution. Many of the elites, however, were reluctant to implement major reform, realizing that such changes might strip them of power. With Latin America already experiencing high levels of political instability, U.S. officials hesitated to apply too much pressure for reform, fearing that this would only enhance regional political uncertainty. Should the program promote growth but not structural reforms, traditional elites would naturally reap most of the rewards of increased growth. Much Alliance for Progress aid went to pay off earlier loans rather than promoting social modernization and economic development. Rapid population growth in Latin America also undermined potential advances in social and economic reform.

Domestic U.S. politics also hindered the success of the Alliance for Progress program. Kennedy's assassination in 1963 removed the leader most closely connected to the program's fate. Projected funding for the program was based on capital needs for a decade, but the annual U.S. congressional appropriations process prevented presidents from guaranteeing long-term aid levels.

In the United States, from the mid-1960s onward a series of problems undercut the Alliance for Progress. Kennedy's successor, Lyndon B. Johnson, was primarily interested in domestic issues, while in foreign policy he became increasingly preoccupied with the deteriorating situation in Vietnam. The ability of the program to uplift Latin America was oversold from its inception. These exaggerated hopes for the program made later disillusionment with it all the easier. Latin American governments were often unwilling or unable to implement the program's structural reforms. The U.S. Congress cut funding for the program, which quickly lost its reform content and evolved into a conventional aid program. Although there was no officially declared ending of the Alliance for Progress, like many other programs of its time, it became subsumed by political pressures and broader Cold War imperatives and thus never fulfilled its original goals.

Don M. Coerver

See also: Eisenhower, Dwight David; Johnson, Lyndon Baines; Kennedy, John Fitzgerald; Mann, Thomas C.; Organization of American States

References

Kaufman, Burton I. *Trade and Aid: Eisenhower's Foreign Economic Policy, 1953–1961.* Baltimore, MD: Johns Hopkins University Press, 1982.

Levinson, Jerome, and Juan de Onis. *The Alliance That Lost Its Way: A Critical Report on the Alliance for Progress.* Chicago: Quadrangle Books, 1970.

Rabe, Stephen G. *The Most Dangerous Area in the World: John F. Kennedy Confronts Communist Revolution in Latin America.* Chapel Hill: University of North Carolina Press, 1999.

Taffet, Jeffrey F. *Foreign Aid as Foreign Policy: The Alliance for Progress in Latin America.* New York: Routledge, 2007.

ANADYR, Operation (1962)

Soviet initiative to base a large military and naval force, equipped with a wide range of conventional and nuclear-capable weapons, on Cuba. In late May 1962, Soviet premier Nikita Khrushchev decided that the best way of preventing the United States from overthrowing Prime Minister Fidel Castro's communist regime on Cuba was to station a large force of troops, with substantial numbers of nuclear-capable arms as well as conventional weapons, on the island. This would have the additional advantage of reducing the massive nuclear imbalance in strategic weapons the United States enjoyed over the Soviet Union. Khrushchev hoped, moreover, that an enhanced sense of nuclear vulnerability might make the United States more accommodating toward Soviet efforts to expel the Western powers from West Berlin. In mid-May, Castro also expressed concerns about Cuba's security from U.S. attack, indicating that he feared that the substantial conventional military assistance the Soviet Union had already offered him earlier that month was inadequate to meet the threat from the United States.

The U.S. destroyer *Barry* pulls alongside the Russian freighter *Anosov* in the Atlantic Ocean, November 10, 1962, to inspect cargo as a U.S. patrol plane flies overhead. The Soviet ship presumably carries a cargo of missiles being withdrawn from Cuba. The interception took place about 780 miles northeast of Puerto Rico. (AP/Wide World Photos)

In late May 1962, Khrushchev prevailed upon other Soviet Presidium members to endorse placing regiments equipped with nuclear-capable missiles on Cuba, even though some, especially Anastas Mikoyan—a senior Presidium member with close ties to Cuba—and Foreign Minister Andrei Gromyko, initially expressed misgivings. To inform Castro of this offer, Khrushchev dispatched a delegation to Cuba, one that included Aleksandr Alekseev, Sharaf R. Rashidov, an agricultural specialist and Presidium candidate member, and Marshal Sergei Biryuzov, head of Soviet Strategic Forces. Castro agreed to accept the proffered military units and equipment, all of which were to be moved to Cuba and installed under conditions of strict secrecy, while Rashidov and Biryuzov erroneously reported that Cuba's tropical forests provided ample cover to conceal the missile installations from U.S. U-2 surveillance overflights during their construction. In July 1962 Raúl Castro arrived in Moscow to negotiate a draft treaty between Cuba and the Soviet Union defining the terms on which Soviet troops would be based on the island. After lengthy negotiations and numerous modifications in Havana, in August 1962 Cuba's Interior Minister Ernesto "Che" Guevara came to Moscow and finalized the Treaty on National Cooperation for the Defense of the National Territory of Cuba in the Event of Aggression, an agreement that he and Soviet Defense Minister Rodion Malinovsky secretly initialed late that month. Fidel Castro wished to announce the treaty openly immediately, in which case he would have traveled to Moscow himself to sign it in August, but he deferred to Khrushchev's wishes. Khrushchev planned to visit Cuba in November 1962, after the politically sensitive U.S. midterm congressional elections, by which time he expected all the missiles to be installed and operational, and then publicly announce both the defense treaty and the presence of Soviet nuclear-capable weapons on Cuba.

By June 1962 the Soviet General Staff, following Malinovsky's instructions, had drawn up plans to send nearly 51,000 military personnel to Cuba. The group would include five nuclear missile regiments, three equipped with a total of 36 R-12 (SS-4) medium-range ballistic missiles (MRBMs) with a range of 1,100–1,400 miles, based at 24 launch sites, and two with 24 R-14 (SS-5) intermediate-range ballistic missiles (IRBMs) with a range up to 2,800 miles, based at 16 launch sites. The group would also comprise four motorized regiments of 2,500 troops each, two tank battalions with the latest T-55 tanks, one wing of MiG-21 fighter jets, 42 Il-28 light bombers, two cruise missile regiments with a total of 80 short-range FKR tactical nuclear warheads with a range around 100 miles, antiaircraft batteries, and 12 surface-to-air missile (SA-2) units with a total of 144 launchers. In addition, Soviet forces would have a substantial naval contingent of 2 cruisers; 4 destroyers, of which 2 would have missile launchers; 12 "Komar" ships with 2 conventional R-15 missiles apiece; and 11 submarines, 7 carrying nuclear-capable missiles. The presence of MRBMs and IRBMs in Cuba would double the number of Soviet warheads capable of reaching the continental United States.

Between June and October 1962, Soviet troops and equipment were shipped in great secrecy to Cuba, where, under the command of Army Gen. Issa Alexandrovich Pliyev, construction of the missile installations and other facilities began. Through Georgi Bolshakov, a Soviet military intelligence operative in Washington with close ties to Attorney General Robert Kennedy, the U.S. president's brother, Khrushchev requested that as a goodwill gesture U.S. aircraft should relax their surveillance and harassment of Soviet shipping, a move he hoped would minimize and deflect U.S. scrutiny. Despite Soviet claims that these forces were specialized agricultural and technical advisers, the massive buildup gave rise to intelligence reports from Cuba that attracted considerable press and political attention in the United States. On September 4, 1962, President John F. Kennedy warned publicly that the United States would not tolerate the presence of Soviet nuclear-capable weapons in Cuba. The Kremlin responded by seeking to accelerate the pace of construction. Khrushchev also added six Il-28s modified to carry atomic bombs, and three detachments of Luna short-range missiles, with a total of 12 two-kiloton warheads, to the forces destined for Cuba, but he canceled the naval squadron, apart from four Foxtrot submarines, each carrying 22 torpedoes. Soviet officials decided that one torpedo on each of these submarines should be nuclear-armed.

By late September, 114 of a projected 149 Soviet shipments had been dispatched to Cuba, 94 of which had already reached their destination. All loading was expected to be completed by October 20, and the final cargo would arrive by November 5. By the end of September all 36 R-12 missiles had arrived in Cuba. On October 4 the Soviet freighter *Indigirka* delivered 45 R-12 one-megaton nuclear warheads, 12 tactical warheads for the Luna weapons, six 12-kiloton bombs for the Il-28s, and thirty-six 12-kiloton warheads for the FKR cruise missiles. On October 22, when President Kennedy publicly announced that the United States would not tolerate the presence of Soviet nuclear-capable weaponry in Cuba, the R-12 MRBM sites had been completed, but those for R-14 IRBMs were still under construction. The Luna weapons and cruise missiles were already in Cuba. After Kennedy's speech, construction of missile sites continued at full speed, as did uncrating and assembly of Il-28s. One Soviet ship, the *Alexandrovsk,* carrying 24 nuclear warheads for R-14 IRBMs and 44 warheads for FKR land-based cruise missiles, reached Cuba on October 23, hours before the United States imposed a naval quarantine or blockade, though four other Soviet vessels carrying F-14 missiles turned back. By that time, around 41,900 Soviet military personnel were present on the island.

On October 16, Kennedy and most of his senior advisers learned of the presence of medium-range nuclear-capable missile installations on Cuba, and over the following two days U.S. reconnaissance planes also identified intermediate-range missile sites. U.S. officials initially assumed that the warheads had not yet reached the island, and throughout the crisis they remained unaware that short-range tactical nuclear-capable weapons and nuclear-armed Il-28s were deployed on Cuba. In addition, U.S. leaders estimated the number of Soviet troops on Cuba to be only around 10,000. While Khrushchev and Malinovsky in Moscow sought to maintain operational control over all the missiles, especially the R-12s and R-14s, which could be used to attack targets in the continental United States, until October 22 it seems that Pliyev had at least verbal authorization to use the tactical nuclear-capable weapons in combat situations without necessarily consulting Kremlin officials. Whether distant Soviet leaders in Moscow could have reined in military officers in Cuba from using these weapons under battlefield conditions when facing U.S. air strikes or invasion was never tested.

Khrushchev ultimately yielded to Kennedy's demands that the nuclear-capable missiles be withdrawn from Cuba, in exchange for an open promise that the United States would not invade the island and a private agreement that NATO missiles in Turkey would also be removed within six months. Despite efforts by Castro and Malinovsky to retain the cruise missiles and Il-28s, in November and December 1962 all the missiles were dismantled and returned to the Soviet Union. By February 1963 only around 18,000 Soviet troops, armed with conventional weapons, remained on Cuba. Khrushchev indicated to Kennedy administration officials that eventually he hoped to withdraw all Soviet military personnel, but Kennedy's assassination in November 1963 and Khrushchev's fall from power the following year aborted such plans. A substantial Soviet military contingent remained in Cuba until the late 1980s, when the reformist Soviet general secretary Mikhail Gorbachev drastically reduced his country's overseas commitments.

Priscilla Roberts

See also: Alekseev (Shitov), Aleksandr Ivanovich; Bolshakov, Georgi Nikitovich; Castro, Fidel; Castro, Raúl; Gribkov, Anatoli Ivanovich; Kennedy, Robert Francis; Khrushchev, Nikita Sergeyevich; Malinovsky,

Rodion Yakovlevich; Mikoyan, Anastas Ivanovich; Military Balance; Nuclear Arms Race; Pliyev, Issa Alexandrovich

References

Dobbs, Michael. *One Minute to Midnight: Kennedy, Khrushchev, and Castro on the Brink of Nuclear War.* New York: Knopf, 2008.

Fursenko, Aleksandr, and Timothy Naftali. *One Hell of a Gamble: Khrushchev, Castro, and Kennedy, 1958–1964.* New York: Norton, 1997.

Gribkov, Anatoli I., and William Y. Smith. *Operation ANADYR: U.S. and Soviet Generals Recount the Cuban Missile Crisis.* Edited by Alfred Friendly, Jr. Chicago, Berlin, Tokyo, and Moscow: edition q, 1994.

Polmar, Norman, and John D. Gresham. *DEFCON-2: Standing on the Brink of Nuclear War during the Cuban Missile Crisis.* New York: John Wiley, 2006.

Arkhipov, Vasili Alexandrovich (1926–1999)

Soviet naval officer. Vasili Arkhipov was born into a peasant family in the town of Staraya Kupavna, near Moscow, on January 30, 1926. Educated at the Pacific Higher Naval School, in August 1945 he served against Japan in a minesweeper. After graduating from the Caspian Higher Naval School in 1947, Arkhipov saw submarine service in the Soviet Black Sea, Northern, and Baltic fleets. In July 1961, as deputy commander of the Hotel-class submarine K-19, Arkhipov helped prevent a mutiny when there was a major problem with the submarine's nuclear reactor.

During the Cuban Missile Crisis, Arkhipov was second in command on B-59, one of four Foxtrot-class attack submarines ordered to Cuba from Murmansk on October 1, 1962. Each submarine had had its designation number scraped off its conning tower, to hamper identification, and each carried 22 torpedoes, one of which was nuclear-armed. On October 24, as the United States imposed a naval blockade (or quarantine, as it was called) around Cuba, U.S. officials informed their Soviet counterparts of their intention to drop practice depth charges to force submarines to surface. The Kremlin, however, failed to transmit this information to its submarine commanders.

On October 27, a group of 11 U.S. destroyers and the aircraft carrier USS *Randolph* enforcing the blockade located, harried, and trapped B-59 in the West Atlantic near the quarantine line, dropping practice depth charges to persuade the vessel, whose batteries were running low, to surface and identify itself. The submarine's captain, Valentin Grigorievitch Savitsky, concluding that war had already begun, wished to fire the nuclear torpedo against the attackers, but procedure required that the second in command (Arkhipov) and the political officer (Ivan Semonovich Maslennikov) agree to the action. In heated arguments Arkhipov refused to endorse the launch and eventually persuaded his comrades to surface the submarine and request further orders from Moscow. The U.S. naval vessels surrounding the submarine (the *Beale, Cony, Lowry,* and *Murray*) had been unaware it was carrying any nuclear-capable weapons. To indicate that their intentions were not hostile, the U.S. vessels had a jazz band playing on the deck of one ship when the Soviet submarine surfaced. The Americans suspected that B-59 was suffering some mechanical problems, but Savitsky declined their offer of assistance. B-59 eventually turned around, heading east, accompanied by U.S. naval vessels until it submerged late on October 29. The other three Foxtrot submarines received orders to also abort their voyages to the island.

The full implications of this episode were not generally known until a conference held in Havana in October 2002 to mark the 40th anniversary of the Cuban Missile Crisis. Its organizer, Professor Thomas Blanton of the Washington-based National Security Archive, stated, "a guy called Vasili Arkhipov saved the world."

Arkhipov remained in the Soviet Navy, rising to command first submarines and then submarine squadrons. Promoted in 1975 to rear admiral, when he became head of the Kirov Naval Academy, he rose to vice admiral in 1981, retiring in the mid-1980s. He died in Zheleznodorozhny, near Moscow, in 1999.

Priscilla Roberts

See also: ANADYR, Operation; Nuclear Arms Race

References

Burr, William, and Thomas S. Blanton, eds. *The Submarines of October: U.S. and Soviet Naval Encounters during the Cuban Missile Crisis.* National Security Archive Electronic Briefing Book No. 75. http://www.gwu.edu/~nsarchiv/NSAEBB/NSAEBB75/

Dobbs, Michael. *One Minute to Midnight: Kennedy, Khrushchev, and Castro on the Brink of Nuclear War.* New York: Knopf, 2008.

Huchthausen, Peter. *October Fury.* New York: John Wiley, 2002.

Mozgovoi, Aleksandr. *Kubinskaya Samba Kvarteta Fokstrotov* [Cuban Samba of the Foxtrot Quartet]. Moscow: Military Parade Publishing House, 2002.

Polmar, Norman, and John D. Gresham. *DEFCON-2: Standing on the Brink of Nuclear War during the Cuban Missile Crisis.* New York: John Wiley, 2006.

B

Ball, George Wildman (1909–1994)

International lawyer, undersecretary of state, 1961–1966. George Ball was born on December 21, 1909, in Des Moines, Iowa. He obtained bachelor's and law degrees from Northwestern University and, after a spell as a lawyer in the general counsel's office of the U.S. Treasury Department, practiced law in Chicago until the early 1940s as a lawyer in the general counsel's office of the U.S. Treasury Department. During World War II he took government positions with the Lend-Lease Administration and the Foreign Economic Administration. After the war Ball moved to Washington, where he helped found the international law firm of Cleary, Gottlieb, Steen, and Cox.

In the run-up to the 1960 presidential election, Ball prepared foreign policy position papers for the Democratic candidate, Sen. John F. Kennedy. Once elected, Kennedy made Ball undersecretary of state for economic affairs; in November 1961 Ball rose to undersecretary of state, second only to Secretary Dean Rusk within the State Department. Until November 1961, Ball's responsibilities were primarily economic. Excluded from top-level meetings on political and military strategy, Ball was not involved in planning the unsuccessful April 1961 Bay of Pigs invasion and had no foreknowledge of it. With hindsight, he hoped he would have opposed this enterprise but confessed himself uncertain whether he would have been sufficiently confident to do so.

During the Cuban Missile Crisis, Kennedy included Ball in the Executive Committee (ExComm) of senior officials who met regularly to discuss the U.S. response. Ball forcefully advised the imposition of a naval blockade or quarantine around Cuba, which he believed would give Soviet leaders time to reflect and back down, and he opposed the more drastic option of launching surprise air strikes against Cuba. He also strongly opposed any unannounced air strike against missile installations, arguing that this would jeopardize the United States' moral standing and alienate its allies. After the crisis, Ball wrote a legal justification for the Kennedy administration's position and made arrangements to inform U.S. allies of this.

Ball remained undersecretary until September 1966. Throughout his tenure, he argued forcefully but unavailingly against the steady expansion of U.S. commitments in Vietnam, first under Kennedy and then under President Lyndon B. Johnson. Weary of publicly defending policies he deplored, eventually he resigned and became a senior partner in Lehman Brothers, the New York investment bank, where he remained—with one three-month spell in 1968 as U.S. ambassador to the United Nations—until retiring in 1982. Ball continued to speak and write extensively on international issues. He died of abdominal cancer on May 26, 1994, in New York City.

Priscilla Roberts

See also: Bay of Pigs Invasion; Kennedy, John Fitzgerald; Rusk, Dean David; U.S. Allies

References

Ball, George W. *The Past Has Another Pattern: Memoirs.* New York: Norton, 1982.

Bill, James A. *George Ball: Behind the Scenes in U.S. Foreign Policy.* New Haven, CT: Yale University Press, 1997.

DiLeo, David L. *George Ball, Vietnam, and the Rethinking of Containment.* Chapel Hill: University of North Carolina Press, 1991.

Batista y Zaldívar, Fulgencio (1901–1973)

Authoritarian Cuban president (1940–1944, 1952–1958). Born in Banes, Cuba, on January 16, 1901, Fulgencio Batista joined the army in 1921, eventually becoming a military stenographer. He first emerged on the national scene during the 1933 revolution that deposed the dictator Gerardo Machado.

During the short-lived Ramón Grau San Martín government (September 1933–January 1934), Batista was the military strongman behind the scenes and was ultimately responsible for the government's collapse.

Batista was the true power figure behind successive puppet governments during 1934–1940. In 1940 he was elected president. His four-year term was noted for its progressive social reforms, links with the Communist Party, and support for the Allied side in World War II. Batista provided the United States with access to naval and air bases and sold it nearly all Cuba's sugar production.

Batista was succeeded by another democratically elected leader, Ramón Grau San Martín, the man he had helped overthrow in January 1934. The increasing corruption of the Grau government and its successor facilitated Batista's return to power in March 1952, when he and elements of the army seized power. The new regime suspended the constitution and declared its loyalty to the United States. Batista now largely repudiated his earlier reformism and consolidated his predecessors' anticommunist measures. In the mid-1950s, with support from the U.S. Federal Bureau of Investigation, Batista established a repressive anticommunist political police force.

Rapid successes by anti-Batista movements, especially among middle-class students and including Fidel Castro's July 26 Movement, brought Batista's fall in late 1958. On January 1, 1959, he fled Cuba for the Dominican Republic as Castro's forces closed in on Havana. Batista died on August 6, 1973, in Estoril, Portugal.

Barry Carr

See also: Castro, Fidel; Eisenhower, Dwight David

References

Argote-Freyre, Frank. *Fulgencio Batista: From Revolutionary to Strongman.* New Brunswick, NJ: Rutgers University Press, 2006.

Gellman, Irving. *Roosevelt and Batista: Good Neighbor Diplomacy in Cuba, 1933–1945.* Albuquerque: University of New Mexico Press, 1973.

Morley, Morris. *Imperial State and Revolution: The United States and Cuba, 1952–1986.* Cambridge: Cambridge University Press, 1987.

Bay of Pigs Invasion (April 15–19, 1961)

Abortive U.S.-backed invasion of Cuba whose failure contributed to the subsequent Cuban Missile Crisis.

On January 1, 1959, an indigenous revolutionary movement led by Fidel Castro seized power from Fulgencio Batista, dictator of Cuba since 1933 and a U.S. client. Although Castro initially declared that he was not a communist, from spring 1959 he covertly sought Soviet aid and military protection. U.S. economic pressure and boycotts quickly impelled him to move openly into the Soviet camp. In response, in March 1960 President Dwight D. Eisenhower authorized the Central Intelligence Agency (CIA) to devise a scheme to train Cuban exiles based in Guatemala to invade the island and overthrow Castro. Eisenhower had no schedule for such an invasion, but he did want a plan to be in place and ready to execute at his decision. In early January 1961, shortly before leaving office, Eisenhower took the measure of ending U.S. recognition of Castro's government.

Eisenhower's successor, John F. Kennedy, inherited this projected invasion operation. Perhaps fearing to appear soft on communism, despite lukewarm assessments from the Joint Chiefs of Staff (JCS) of the risk of failure and over Secretary of State Dean Rusk's misgivings, in March 1961 the newly elected president approved its implementation, with two important modifications. First, notwithstanding evidence that U.S. involvement in the training of Cuban exiles had become widely known throughout Latin America, seeking to maintain the deniability of any U.S. contribution to the operation, Kennedy insisted that no American troops or pilots participate. Second, in order to facilitate an unobtrusive clandestine night-time landing, the invasion site was moved a hundred miles west, from Trinidad, on Cuba's southern coast—which offered an escape route into the nearby Escambray Mountains, where the fighters could live as guerrillas if the operation failed—to the more vulnerable Bay of Pigs (Bahia de Cochinos), south of the city of Matanzas. These changes, unfortunately, jeopardized the invasion's chances of success. Although Kennedy wished the invasion force to recruit only liberal Cubans, their outlook anti-Castro but non-Batista, in practice it included many somewhat reactionary Batista supporters.

Initial air strikes against Cuba's air force bases launched on April 15, 1961, by exile Cuban pilots flying surplus U.S. B-26 bombers inflicted damage but failed to destroy the entire Cuban air force. Alarmed by news reports exposing the deceptive U.S. cover story that, as U.S. ambassador Adlai Stevenson publicly stated in the United Nations, defectors from Castro's military had flown these missions, Kennedy refused to authorize a scheduled second air strike, which had been expected to eliminate the remaining Cuban airplanes.

On April 17, 1961, 1,400 Cuban exiles, known as Brigade 2506, commenced their invasion. Some parachuted in; others used amphibious craft.

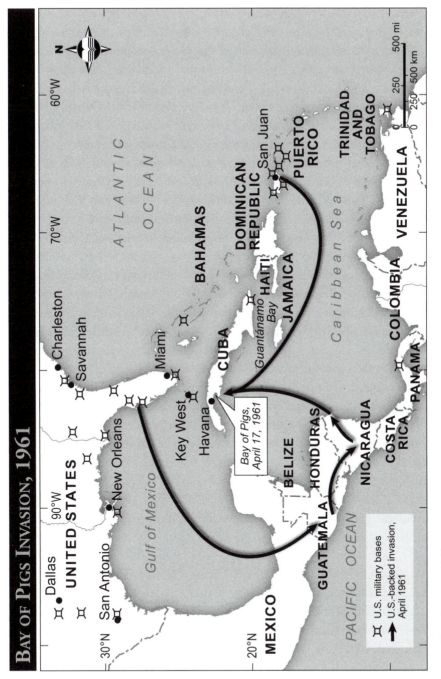

BAY OF PIGS INVASION, 1961

Bay of Pigs Invasion, 1961

Air attacks by Castro's forces slowed the process, destroying one transport carrying vital supplies, and ultimately led the invasion flotilla to put out to sea, while Cuban T-33 fighter jets proved unexpectedly successful in downing the exiles' B-26s. Castro's swift incarceration of one to two hundred thousand potential domestic opponents effectively precluded any internal uprising to support the invasion. Meanwhile, Cuban ground forces, tanks, and artillery wreaked havoc on the invaders. A few escaped by small boat to U.S. naval vessels nearby, but 114 were killed and 1,113 captured. Cuban losses were far greater: approximately 1,650 dead and two thousand wounded. With Kennedy administration backing, 18 months later private sources in the United States provided Cuba with $53 million of food and medicine in exchange for the imprisoned fighters.

The Bay of Pigs represented a humiliating international failure for the United States, vindicating those critics who considered that nation an overbearing, imperialist state that backed unpopular right-wing forces around the globe. Publicly, Kennedy took full responsibility for the operation; privately, he deeply resented what he perceived as CIA mismanagement, and the following year he replaced both Allen W. Dulles, the CIA's near-legendary director, and Richard Bissell, the head of its Clandestine Service. From then onward the CIA placed greater emphasis on intelligence collection as opposed to flamboyant but risky covert operations. Kennedy's reckless authorization and half-hearted implementation of this operation may have helped convince Soviet premier Nikita Khrushchev that he was a lightweight without the resolve to confront the Soviet Union. Undoubtedly, the botched invasion and fear of another subsequent attempt were major reasons impelling Khrushchev to offer and Castro and other leaders in Havana to accept the deployment in Cuba of those Soviet missiles whose presence provoked the Cuban Missile Crisis.

Priscilla Roberts

See also: Batista y Zaldívar, Fulgencio; Bissell, Richard Mervin, Jr.; Castro, Fidel; Central Intelligence Agency; Dulles, Allen Welsh; Eisenhower, Dwight David; Joint Chiefs of Staff; Kennedy, John Fitzgerald; Kennedy, Robert Francis; Khrushchev, Nikita Sergeyevich; Rusk, Dean David; Stevenson, Adlai Ewing II; United Nations

References

Bissell, Richard M., Jr.; with Jonathan E. Lewis and Francis Pudlo. *Reflections of a Cold Warrior: From Yalta to the Bay of Pigs.* New Haven, CT: Yale University Press, 1996.

Blight, James, and Peter Kornbluh, eds. *Politics of Illusion: The Bay of Pigs Invasion Reexamined.* Boulder, CO: Lynne Rienner, 1998.

Higgins, Trumbull. *The Perfect Failure: Kennedy, Eisenhower, and the CIA at the Bay of Pigs.* New York: Norton, 1987.

Jones, Howard. *The Bay of Pigs.* New York: Oxford University Press, 2008.

Kornbluh, Peter, ed. *Bay of Pigs Declassified: The Secret CIA Report on the Invasion of Cuba.* New York: New Press, 1998.

Paterson, Thomas G. *Contesting Castro: The United States and the Triumph of the Cuban Revolution.* New York: Oxford University Press, 1994.

Rabe, Stephen G. *The Most Dangerous Area in the World: John F. Kennedy Confronts Communist Revolution in Latin America.* Chapel Hill: University of North Carolina Press, 1999.

Rasenberger, Jim. *The Brilliant Disaster: JFK, Castro, and America's Doomed Invasion of the Bay of Pigs.* New York: Scribner, 2011.

Welch, Richard E., Jr. *Response to Revolution: The United States and the Cuban Revolution, 1959–1961.* Chapel Hill: University of North Carolina Press, 1985.

Berlin Crises (1958–1961)

Continual disagreement over the control of Berlin between the Soviet bloc and the Western Allies began in earnest in the late 1940s, culminating in the Berlin Blockade (1948–1949). Then, following a period of relative—if tense—calm, renewed Cold War tensions transformed the city into one of the world's potential flash points during 1958–1961.

With Soviet prestige dramatically boosted by the launch of *Sputnik 1* in 1957, Soviet premier Nikita Khrushchev decided to revive the issue of Berlin. On November 10, 1958, he sought to end the joint-occupation agreement in the city by demanding that Great Britain, France, and the United States withdraw their 10,000 troops from West Berlin. He also declared that the Soviet Union would unilaterally transfer its occupation authority in Berlin to the German Democratic Republic (GDR) (East Germany) if a peace treaty were not signed with both East and the Federal Republic of Germany (FRG) (West Germany) within six months. West Berlin would then become a free city. Khrushchev couched his demands by portraying West Berlin's proposed free-city status as a concession because it lay in East German territory and therefore properly belonged to the GDR. None of the Western powers, however, formally recognized East Germany, viewing it as a mere subsidiary of the Soviet Union.

President Dwight D. Eisenhower flatly rejected Khrushchev's demands, although other Western leaders initially tried to make some concessions by proposing an interim Berlin agreement that placed a limit on Western forces and curtailed some propagandistic West Berlin activities, such as radio broadcasts targeting East German audiences. These Allied proposals would have given the Soviets and East Germans some degree of power in West Berlin, a measure that many West Berliners considered a highly dangerous step toward neutralization and, ultimately, abandonment. In December 1958, the Allies issued a North Atlantic Treaty Organization (NATO) declaration rejecting Soviet demands and insisting that no state had the right to withdraw unilaterally from an international agreement.

Khrushchev gradually retreated from his hard-line stance on Berlin. U.S. overflights of the Soviet Union by U-2 reconnaissance planes indicated that the West had an accurate count of the comparatively small number of Soviet nuclear missiles, and the Soviet leader obviously feared starting a war that he could not win. The Soviets now envisioned a gradual crowding out of the Western powers without bloodshed. Meanwhile, East Germany's economic situation continued to deteriorate, with vast numbers of refugees continuing to flee to the West.

In 1961, the newly elected U.S. president, John F. Kennedy, abandoned the demand for German unification that had been U.S. policy since the 1940s, after his foreign policy team concluded that this position was not only impractical but might actually provoke a U.S.-Soviet war. Kennedy and his advisers decided that only three interests were worth risking nuclear war: the continued Allied presence in West Berlin, Allied access to West Berlin by land and by air, and the continued autonomous freedom of West Berlin. Realizing that a rather inconsequential event and a sequence of mutually threatening and unnecessary mobilizations had led to World War I in 1914, Kennedy worried constantly that a relatively minor incident in Germany could escalate into World War III.

Meanwhile, GDR leader Walter Ulbricht decided to close the East Berlin borders in an attempt to exercise control over all traffic to and from Berlin, including Allied military as well as German civilian travelers. On August 13, 1961, East German authorities began construction of the Berlin Wall, essentially sealing off East Berlin from West Berlin and permanently bisecting the city. Ulbricht sought to control both what went into East Berlin and what came out, including thousands of East Germans who sought refuge in West Berlin. The Soviets and the East Germans had wagered that the West would not react to the wall's construction. Kennedy, in accordance with his policy, offered little resistance. In a symbolic incident on

October 22, 1961, the Chief of the U.S. Mission in Berlin asserted the right of U.S. officials to travel freely between West and East Berlin and return, a stance backed up by U.S. tanks.

Throughout the Cuban Missile Crisis, U.S. leaders suspected that West Berlin was the real Soviet target and feared that, should they launch military action against Cuba, the Soviet Union would respond by forcibly seizing West Berlin. Research in Soviet archives has not substantiated these apprehensions. Khrushchev and other Soviet officials apparently had no wish to expand the confrontation by taking such action. On a broader level, the two crises were, it seems, closely connected. When deciding to offer to install missiles in Cuba, Khrushchev apparently hoped that, once these were in place, the Americans would be intimidated into abandoning West Berlin.

Caryn E. Neumann

See also: Eisenhower, Dwight David; Kennedy, John Fitzgerald; Khrushchev, Nikita Sergeyevich; Military Balance; U-2 Overflights; U.S. Allies; Warsaw Pact

References

Ausland, John C. *Kennedy, Khrushchev, and the Berlin-Cuba Crises, 1961–1964.* Oslo, Norway: Aschehoug Publishing House, 1996.

Flemming, Thomas. *Berlin in the Cold War: The Battle for the Divided City.* New York: Berlinica Publishing, 2010.

Harrison, Hope M. *Driving the Soviets up the Wall: Soviet-East German Relations, 1953–1961.* Princeton, NJ: Princeton University Press, 2003.

Kempe, Frederick. *Berlin 1961: Kennedy, Khrushchev, and the Most Dangerous Place on Earth.* New York: G. P. Putnam's Sons, 2011.

Murphy, David E., Sergei A. Kondrashev, and George Bailey. *Battleground Berlin: CIA vs. KGB in the Cold War.* New Haven, CT: Yale University Press, 1997.

Smyser, W. R. *From Yalta to Berlin: The Cold War Struggle over Germany.* New York: St. Martin's Press, 1999.

Taylor, Frederick. *The Berlin Wall: A World Divided.* New York: Harper, 2007.

Bissell, Richard Mervin, Jr. (1909–1994)

Head of the Central Intelligence Agency's (CIA) Directorate of Plans from 1958 to 1962. Born on September 18, 1909, in Hartford, Connecticut,

Richard Mervin Bissell, Jr. graduated from Yale University in 1932 with a BA in history, then studied at the London School of Economics before obtaining a doctorate of economics from Yale in 1939. During World War II, Bissell served in the Office of Strategic Services (OSS), beginning his career in intelligence. After working in the Department of War Mobilization and Reconversion and the Economic Cooperation Administration, in 1954 Bissell joined the CIA, becoming head of the Directorate of Plans (or covert operations) in 1958.

The operations of the Directorate of Plans were soon dubbed "Black Operations" for their clandestine mandate to eradicate world leaders unfriendly to the United States. Bissell and his deputy, Richard Helms, engineered the ouster of Guatemala's Jacobo Arbenz in 1954 and later became nearly obsessed with overthrowing Cuban leader Fidel Castro after his 1959 revolution. During Bissell's CIA tenure, he was also instrumental in developing the U-2 reconnaissance plane and the Corona spy satellite. It was, however, the unsuccessful 1961 Bay of Pigs invasion that won Bissell greatest notoriety.

In March 1960 CIA director Allen W. Dulles was tasked with devising a strategy to remove Castro from power, a mission he turned over to Bissell and Helms, who devised and organized a plan for a paramilitary invasion of Cuba involving nearly 400 CIA officers as well as some 1,400 Cuban exiles, who were to carry out the attack itself. The invasion force, trained and armed by the CIA, landed at Cuba's Bay of Pigs on April 17, 1961. Castro's forces quickly routed them, blowing the cover on the operation and greatly embarrassing the Kennedy administration. As the invasion attempt faced disaster at Cuban hands, Bissell begged Kennedy to allow intervention by U.S. airplanes and naval forces, but Kennedy refused. The Bay of Pigs fiasco effectively ended Bissell's CIA career, as he was forced to leave the agency in February 1962. He subsequently worked for a think tank and then held positions in a number of private corporations. Bissell died in Farmington, Connecticut, on February 7, 1994.

Valerie Adams

See also: Bay of Pigs Invasion; Castro, Fidel; Central Intelligence Agency; Containment, Doctrine and Course of; Dulles, Allen Welsh; Eisenhower, Dwight David; Kennedy, John Fitzgerald; U-2 Overflights

References

Bissell, Richard M., Jr. *Reflections of a Cold Warrior: From Yalta to the Bay of Pigs.* New Haven, CT: Yale University Press, 1996.

Thomas, Evan. *The Very Best Men: Four Who Dared: The Early Years of the CIA.* New York: Simon and Schuster, 1995.

Bohlen, Charles Eustis (1904–1974)

U.S. diplomat. Born in Clayton, New York, on August 30, 1904, Charles "Chip" Bohlen was educated at St. Paul's School in Concord, New Hampshire, and at Harvard University. He joined the U.S. Foreign Service in 1929, becoming one of the small initial group of U.S. diplomats trained as Soviet specialists. When the United States resumed diplomatic relations with the Soviet Union in 1933, Bohlen became one of three Russian-language officers in the U.S. embassy in Moscow.

In 1942 Bohlen became assistant chief of the Russian Section of the State Department's Division of European Affairs and in 1944 was promoted to chief. He attended the Moscow Conference of Foreign Ministers in 1943 and the Tehran and Yalta summits of the Allied leaders in 1944 and 1945. Although later criticized by Sen. Joseph McCarthy of Wisconsin for acquiescing in the decisions at Yalta, Bohlen in fact had reservations as to the wisdom of U.S. policies. Deeply suspicious of Soviet actions and intentions, he advocated firm diplomatic pressure in an effort to win Soviet concessions on Eastern Europe. Appointed political adviser to the secretary of state in 1946 and State Department counselor in 1947, Bohlen helped develop Cold War containment policy.

Bohlen spent 1953 to 1957 as U.S. ambassador to the Soviet Union, and two further years as ambassador to the Philippines. In 1959 he became special assistant to Secretary of State Christian A. Herter. Preparing for the June 1960 U.S.-Soviet Paris summit, Bohlen advised President Dwight D. Eisenhower to remain resolute over West Berlin, then under considerable Soviet pressure. Bohlen accompanied Eisenhower to this meeting, which was cut short by the U-2 Affair.

In their first 18 months in office, President John F. Kennedy and Secretary of State Dean Rusk relied heavily on Bohlen's expertise. In his administration's first weeks, Kennedy consulted Bohlen on plans inherited from the Eisenhower administration to mount an invasion of Cuba and overthrow the anti-American and pro-communist government of Fidel Castro, the leader of the recent revolution. To his subsequent regret, Bohlen did not inform Kennedy and other officials of his private reservations over this venture, misgivings that derived in part from his belief that revolutionary fervor in Cuba was still strong and the Cuban people were therefore unlikely to support the invasion. Instead, in response to specific queries Bohlen merely stated that, given the island's strategic insignificance to the Soviet Union, the Soviet Union was unlikely to intervene militarily, though it might provide Castro with arms and supplies and would undoubtedly exploit any invasion for propaganda purposes. His failure to oppose the invasion plan forthrightly, perhaps because he believed its momentum was now unstoppable, revealed the occasional limitations of Bohlen's belief that professional diplomats should function primarily as technical experts rather than policymakers.

In October 1962, when Soviet nuclear-capable missiles were discovered in Cuba, Kennedy consulted Bohlen, who counseled a mixture of firmness and restraint, suggesting that Kennedy first correspond sternly but privately with Soviet premier Nikita Khrushchev—advice the president ignored—and then declare a naval blockade of the island, the course ultimately chosen. Bohlen urged that an ultimatum demanding the removal of the missiles should precede any air strike, and he warned Kennedy in writing that an air strike "will inevitably lead to war." Bohlen was scheduled to leave for France, where Kennedy had appointed him ambassador, so attended only the first two days of meetings of the Executive Committee (ExComm) of senior advisers who handled the crisis, for fear that postponing his departure would alert the Soviets to the missiles' discovery.

Bohlen retired in 1969, warning President Richard M. Nixon not to try using China against the Soviet Union. Bohlen was publicly skeptical of both the emerging U.S. policy of détente and West German chancellor Willy Brandt's Ostpolitik opening to East Germany. He died of cancer in Washington, D.C., on January 1, 1974.

Priscilla Roberts

See also: Bay of Pigs Invasion; Castro, Fidel; Containment, Doctrine and Course of; Eisenhower, Dwight David; Kennedy, John Fitzgerald; Khrushchev, Nikita Sergeyevich; Rusk, Dean David; U-2 Overflights; U.S. Allies

References

Bohlen, Charles E. *Witness to History, 1929–69.* New York: Norton, 1973.

Isaacson, Walter, and Evan Thomas. *The Wise Men: Six Friends and the World They Made.* New York: Simon and Schuster, 1986. Mayers, David. *The Ambassadors and America's Soviet Policy.* New York: Oxford University Press, 1995.

Ruddy, T. Michael. *The Cautious Diplomat: Charles E. Bohlen and the Soviet Union, 1929–1969.* Kent, OH: Kent State University Press, 1986.

Bolshakov, Georgi Nikitovich (1922–1989)

Soviet military intelligence operative. From 1941 to 1943 Georgi Bolshakov, who was born in 1922, served in the Red Army as a Finnish-language interpreter and then a division-level intelligence officer on the northwest front. In 1943 he joined the GRU, the army intelligence service, spending three years at the General Staff High Intelligence School and four in the Soviet Army's Military-Diplomatic Academy. Graduating in 1950 with impressive English-language skills, in 1951 he went to Washington, D.C., on his first foreign assignment, remaining there for four years, ostensibly as a correspondent for the Soviet news agency, TASS. From 1955 to 1957 Bolshakov worked in Moscow as an officer for special missions on the staff of Marshal Georgi Zhukov, the Soviet defense minister, briefing him on intelligence information. Zhukov's dismissal temporarily derailed Bolshakov's career. Bolshakov's personal friendship with Aleksei Adzhubei, son-in-law of Soviet premier Nikita Khrushchev, rescued him from obscurity, and in fall 1959 he returned to Washington, supposedly a cultural attaché at the Soviet embassy. Outgoing and gregarious, unlike many of his colleagues Bolshakov socialized easily with Americans and had numerous personal contacts among the political, diplomatic, and media elite.

Through an intermediary in the press, in late April 1961 U.S. Attorney General Robert F. Kennedy, the brother of President John F. Kennedy, contacted Bolshakov. On more than 40 occasions over the next 15 months, Bolshakov served as a back-channel conduit for private messages between Khrushchev and the Kennedy administration, on the June 1961 Vienna summit meeting, the Berlin situation, and the terms of a possible nuclear test ban treaty. Seeking to conceal the dispatch of Soviet troops and weaponry to Cuba, in July 1962 the Soviet government used Bolshakov to transmit a request to the Kennedy administration to decrease its surveillance of Soviet shipping. When the Americans complied, in August Khrushchev sent thanks through Bolshakov and suggested their two countries should accelerate their efforts for a nuclear test ban treaty. As U.S. apprehensions over Soviet arms shipments to Cuba intensified throughout September and into October, on the Kremlin's instructions Bolshakov met Robert Kennedy on October 5, to assure him that the weapons the Soviet Union had dispatched were "only ... of a defensive character" and could not threaten the United States, a message he repeated to leading American journalists.

Despite Robert Kennedy's anger over this disinformation, on October 23, at the height of the crisis, he apparently contacted Bolshakov through emissaries to sound out Soviet officials on the possibility of re-moving NATO Jupiter nuclear missiles in Turkey and Italy, in exchange for the Soviet nuclear-capable weapons on Cuba, and to encourage the Soviets to halt further arms shipments to Cuba immediately. On November 9, when dismantling of nuclear-capable missiles was already in progress but the continued presence of Il-28 light bombers had become a sticking point, Robert Kennedy met Bolshakov in person, to request that the bombers leave Cuba in the near future, a message Kennedy repeated with harsh emphasis on November 18 when he encountered Bolshakov at a performance by the visiting Bolshoi ballet. Three days later Bolshakov delivered a message from Khrushchev that Soviet officials would remove the Il-28s.

After the Cuban Missile Crisis, the Kennedys blew Bolshakov's cover, allowing journalists friendly to them, in articles on the episode that they authorized, to reveal his role as a liaison with Khrushchev and a conduit for Soviet disinformation in October 1962. Khrushchev complained to U.S. officials that these leaks compromised his use of such channels. In December 1962, hostile embassy officials engineered Bolshakov's recall to Moscow. Relegated to a bureaucratic limbo of routine office chores, Bolshakov sought consolation in alcohol and the company of women. In a rather bizarre footnote to their relationship, after his brother's assassination Robert Kennedy sent a close family associate, William Walton, to meet with Bolshakov in Moscow. Walton told Bolshakov that the president's death was due to a right-wing plot by Americans who sought to undermine his policies of U.S.-Soviet détente and that Lyndon B. Johnson, the new president, lacked his predecessor's commitment to improving relations between their two countries, information that undercut Johnson's own efforts to reassure Soviet leaders that he would continue Kennedy's approach to international affairs. The convivial Bolshakov survived until 1989, but his career never regained its former momentum.

Priscilla Roberts

See also: ANADYR, Operation; Berlin Crises; Johnson, Lyndon Baines; Jupiter Missiles (Turkey and Italy); Kennedy, John Fitzgerald; Kennedy, Robert Francis; Khrushchev, Nikita Sergeyevich; Partial Test Ban Treaty; Vienna Conference

References

Fursenko, Aleksandr, and Timothy Naftali. *One Hell of a Gamble: Khrushchev, Castro, and Kennedy, 1958–1964.* New York: Norton, 1997.

Polmar, Norman, and John D. Gresham. *DEFCON-2: Standing on the Brink of Nuclear War during the Cuban Missile Crisis.* New York: John Wiley, 2006.

Bundy, McGeorge (1919–1996)

U.S. special assistant for national security affairs, 1961–1966. Born on March 30, 1919, in Boston, McGeorge Bundy came from a prominent Boston family with a strong tradition of public service. He excelled academically at Groton School, Connecticut, and Yale University. From 1941 to 1945 he served in the army. After helping former secretary of state and secretary of war Henry L. Stimson write his memoirs, *On Active Service in Peace and War* (1948), laying out that influential statesman's worldview for future generations, in 1950 Bundy began teaching government and international affairs at Harvard University, where in 1953 he became dean of Arts and Sciences.

In 1961 President John F. Kennedy, whom Bundy had advised during his presidential campaign, appointed him special assistant for national security affairs, a position in which he greatly overshadowed Secretary of State Dean Rusk. Bundy shared with Kennedy a strong faith in the centrality of U.S. power and the need to employ it. Bundy was known for intellectual brilliance, energy, swift assimilation of information, and wit, though critics subsequently suggested that as dean and public official these superficial qualities masked an absence of deeper reflection or any firm moral compass, and tendencies to accept prevailing conventional Cold War wisdom and accord overly high priority to pragmatic considerations of political expediency. Bundy thought it his function to be a competent manager, rather than an innovative formulator of policy; to ensure that the president was briefed on both sides of issues, he sometimes played devil's advocate. As Kennedy's gatekeeper on foreign affairs, Bundy controlled the access of both information and individuals to the president, prepared agendas for National Security Council meetings, and selected personnel for task forces Kennedy established to handle specific foreign policy problems.

A few weeks after taking power, Bundy voted for the disastrous April 1961 Bay of Pigs invasion attempt against Cuba, which brought international humiliation on the United States. Bundy proffered his resignation to Kennedy, which the president refused, and conducted postmortems on the abortive operation. During the Cuban Missile Crisis, when the U.S. government discovered Soviet nuclear-capable missiles in Cuba and demanded their withdrawal, it was Bundy who informed Kennedy that U.S. overflights had detected the presence of these weapons. Surprisingly indecisive, in Executive Committee (ExComm) meetings of Kennedy's top advisers, Bundy initially supported air strikes to destroy the missiles, subsequently endorsed the naval quarantine option Kennedy eventually selected, yet then switched once more to air strikes. When Soviet premier Nikita Khrushchev sent two somewhat contradictory responses to Kennedy's ultimatum on Cuba on October 26 and 27, it was Bundy who suggested replying only to the first, less confrontational message. Reflecting later on this crisis, in his book *Danger and Survival* (1988), Bundy suggested that Kennedy employed "a certain excess of rhetoric," when Americans would have found more moderate language less alarming.

By far the most controversial aspect of Bundy's government service was his responsibility for the escalation of U.S. involvement in Vietnam. Despite some personal misgivings, Bundy acquiesced in the expansion of U.S. commitments to South Vietnam under both Kennedy and his successor, Lyndon B. Johnson. In 1966 Bundy left Johnson's administration to head the Ford Foundation, which he did until 1979. The issue of his responsibility for U.S. intervention in Vietnam perennially dogged Bundy, effectively destroying his chances of becoming secretary of state or president of a major university. Following the gentleman's code in which he was reared, Bundy refused either to defend his record or to criticize Johnson administration policies publicly, and for the rest of his life he rarely even discussed them. By late 1967 Bundy supported gradual troop withdrawals from Vietnam. After the massive early 1968 Tet offensive, Bundy and most of the other "Wise Men" the administration consulted told a shocked Johnson that victory was unattainable and recommended that the United States open peace negotiations with North Vietnam. For 10 years from 1979 Bundy taught at New York University, writing on nuclear policy and in 1982, together with George F. Kennan, Robert S. McNamara, and Gerard Smith, calling for no U.S. first use of nuclear weapons. On September 10, 1996, he died suddenly of heart failure in Boston.

Priscilla Roberts

See also: Bay of Pigs Invasion; Containment, Doctrine and Course of; Johnson, Lyndon Baines; Kennedy, John Fitzgerald; Khrushchev, Nikita Sergeyevich; McNamara, Robert Strange; Military Balance; Nuclear Arms Race; Rusk, Dean David; U-2 Overflights

References

Bird, Kai. *The Color of Truth: McGeorge Bundy and William Bundy, Brothers in Arms; A Biography.* New York: Simon and Schuster, 1998.

Bundy, McGeorge. *Danger and Survival: Choices about the Bomb in the First Fifty Years.* New York: Random House, 1988.

Goldstein, Gordon M. *Lessons in Disaster: McGeorge Bundy and the Path to War in Vietnam.* New York: Times Books, 2008.

Halberstam, David. *The Best and the Brightest.* New York: Random House, 1973.

Kabaservice, Geoffrey. *The Guardians: Kingman Brewster, His Circle, and the Rise of the Liberal Establishment.* New York: Henry Holt, 2004.

Nuenlist, Christian. *Kennedys rechte hand: McGeorge Bundys rolle als national sicherheitsberater, 1961–63* [Kennedy's Right Hand: McGeorge Bundy's Role as National Security Adviser, 1961–63]. Zurich: Center for Security Studies, 1999.

Preston, Andrew. *The War Council: McGeorge Bundy, the NSC, and Vietnam.* Cambridge, MA: Harvard University Press, 2006.

C

Castro, Fidel (1926–)

Cuban communist revolutionary guerrilla fighter and leader of Cuba, January 1959–July 2006. Fidel Alejandro Castro Ruz was born on August 13, 1926, in the municipality of Mayarí (Oriente Province). His father was a wealthy sugarcane planter of Spanish origin. Castro studied at the University of Havana. Here his political formation began in the action-oriented and often violent student politics of the period. As part of a movement by those disaffected with government corruption, he joined the new Ortodoxo (Orthodox) Party led by Eduardo Chibás and in 1947 participated in actions to overthrow Dominican Republic dictator Rafael Trujillo. In 1948 Castro attended a student congress in Bogotá, Colombia, where major disturbances erupted after the assassination of the popular radical politician Jorge Gaitán. In 1950 he earned his law degree.

After Gen. Fulgencio Batista's 1952 Cuban military coup, Castro and his Orthodox Party allies initiated a campaign of resistance against the newly installed dictatorship. On July 26, 1953, the youthful rebels attacked the Moncada military barracks in Santiago de Cuba, the country's second-largest city. The assault failed, and Castro was ultimately imprisoned on the island of Pines. His defense speech at his trial, titled "History Will Absolve Me," was a powerful denunciation of social and economic injustice that would subsequently become a rallying cry in his struggle against the Batista regime.

In 1955 Castro, released from prison as part of a general amnesty, took refuge in Mexico. There he and his comrades, who would eventually establish the July 26 Movement, connected with Argentinian physician and revolutionary Ernesto "Che" Guevara. In December 1956

Cuban president Fidel Castro, the epitome of a romantic revolutionary leader, eloquently criticizes the Eisenhower administration's economic policies toward Cuba during a televised address on July 19, 1960. His fear of the United States led Castro to turn to the Soviet Union for assistance. (AP/Wide World Photos)

Castro, Guevara, and their followers sailed from Mexico on board the yacht *Granma* and landed in southeastern Cuba, beginning a two-year military and political campaign to overthrow the U.S.-supported Batista regime. In the last days of 1958 Batista fled the island, and Castro entered Havana in triumph in January 1959.

From then onward, Castro steadily increased his influence. In February 1959 he made himself prime minister. In April 1959, Castro visited the United States, where his radical views and uncompromising behavior alarmed prominent U.S. officials, including Vice President Richard Nixon. Increasingly, Castro based his regime on anti-Americanism. During 1959–1962 he moved Cuba radically to the Left. His agrarian reforms and their consequences—confrontation with the United States over American investments in Cuba and U.S. support for counterrevolutionary movements culminating in the 1961 Bay of Pigs invasion—caused a break in diplomatic relations with the United States. In December 1961 Castro declared that he was a Marxist-Leninist. He strengthened Cuba's economic, political, and military ties with the Soviet Union steadily throughout the 1960s.

In summer 1962, Castro accepted a Soviet offer to install assorted short-, intermediate-, and medium-range nuclear-capable missiles in Cuba, as a deterrent against future U.S. invasions. In October 1962 U.S. overflights revealed the presence of missile installations to U.S. President John F. Kennedy, who publicly demanded that the Soviet Union withdraw these missiles. Castro urged Soviet leader Nikita Khrushchev to refuse these demands and if necessary to defend Cuba by initiating a nuclear first strike on the United States, counsel Khrushchev rejected. Indeed Castro was excluded from negotiations over the missiles, and the fact that he learned of the eventual settlement through the media deeply humiliated him, provoking Cuban anger over the perceived Soviet betrayal of Cuban interests.

As talks among Soviet, U.S., and UN representatives on the details of removing the missiles and other military hardware proceeded in November 1962, Castro turned recalcitrant. He issued his own proposals for a settlement, including the return to Cuba of the U.S. military base at Guantánamo Bay and the cessation of all U.S. sanctions against Cuba. He refused to allow on-site inspections of missile bases in Cuba, unsuccessfully attempted to retain tactical nuclear-capable missiles and several squadrons of Soviet Il-28 light bombers, and threatened to shoot down U.S. aircraft conducting reconnaissance overflights to ensure that the missiles had indeed departed. Seeking to mollify Castro, in April and May 1963 Khrushchev hosted him on a month-long visit during which he toured the Soviet Union, met top military and political leaders, and received substantial quantities of armaments, including tanks and antiaircraft equipment. Castro also persuaded Khrushchev to station a brigade of Soviet troops indefinitely on the island, forces that Khrushchev had originally hoped to remove.

The aftermath of the missile crisis initiated a complex period in Cuban-Soviet relations characterized by Castro's suspicion of the Soviet Union's motives tempered by a growing reliance on Soviet economic assistance. While Cuba became a member of Comecon and received important Soviet military aid in the 1960s, Castro's foreign policy, especially in Latin America, embraced the strategy of armed revolution conducted by guerrilla movements in Guatemala, Venezuela, Peru, and Bolivia. This challenged Soviet support for policies of peaceful coexistence with the West.

As the 1960s ended, the failure of the first wave of Castro-inspired guerrilla wars and the collapse of his ambitious plans to industrialize Cuba and produce a record 10 million–ton sugar crop in 1970 led to an accommodation with Soviet economic and strategic goals in the 1970s. Steady economic growth and institutionalization weakened Cuba's commitment to continental and even worldwide revolution. However, adjustment to Soviet economic orthodoxy did not completely erode Castro's commitment to socialist liberation movements.

As he had with Guevara's 1967–1968 revolutionary expedition in Bolivia, Castro assisted revolutionary movements and left-wing governments in the 1980s in Grenada, El Salvador, and Nicaragua. He began sending Cuban military forces to Angola in November 1975, which helped turn the tide there against South Africa's attempt to defeat the left-wing Movimento Popular da Libertação de Angola (MPLA) (Popular Movement for the

Liberation of Angola) in Angola. Some see the Cuban victory in the 1988 Battle of Cuito Carnavale as the beginning of the end of the apartheid regime.

The renewed Cold War of the 1980s ended with the defeat of the Cuban-supported Sandinista government in Nicaragua and a negotiated settlement ending the civil war in El Salvador, which pitted Cuban-supported Farabundo Martí National Liberation Front (FLMN) forces against a series of U.S.-backed governments. The collapse of communism in Eastern Europe and the dissolution of the Soviet Union itself in 1991 were serious setbacks for Castro both economically, with a sharp falloff in foreign aid, and diplomatically. In the 1990s Castro announced the launching of "The Special Period in Times of Peace," inaugurating a shift away from Soviet-style economic institutions toward limited tolerance of private economic enterprises. It also embraced tourism and encouraged investments from Europe, Asia, Canada, and Latin America.

The end of the Cold War did not, as most observers anticipated, precipitate the demise of Castro's regime. Notwithstanding his adoption of many Soviet models, the indigenous, nationalist roots of Cuba's noncapitalist path since 1959 continued to confound predictions. Suffering from health problems, on July 31, 2006, Castro transferred his responsibilities as president of Cuba, commander-in-chief, and Communist Party secretary to his younger brother Raúl on an acting basis. On Castro's initiative, in February 2008 Raúl formally succeeded to these positions in his own right. Although in his 80s, Fidel continued to write for the press and deliver occasional public speeches.

Priscilla Roberts

See also: Alekseev (Shitov), Aleksandr Ivanovich; ANADYR, Operation; Batista y Zaldívar, Fulgencio; Bay of Pigs Invasion; Castro, Raúl; Central Intelligence Agency; China, People's Republic of; Containment, Doctrine and Course of; Eisenhower, Dwight David; Guevara de la Serna, Ernesto "Che"; Kennedy, John Fitzgerald; Kennedy, Robert Francis; Khrushchev, Nikita Sergeyevich; Nuclear Arms Race; U-2 Overflights; United Nations

References

Balfour, Sebastian. *Castro.* 3rd ed. Harlow, England: Longmans, 2009.

Castro, Fidel, and Ignacio Ramonet. *My Life: A Spoken Autobiography.* Translated by Andrew Hurley. New York: Scribner, 2007.

Pérez, Louis A. *Cuba: Between Reform and Revolution.* 4th ed. New York: Oxford University Press, 2011.

Paterson, Thomas G. *Contesting Castro: The United States and the Triumph of the Cuban Revolution.* New York: Oxford University Press, 1994.

Szulc, Tad. *Fidel: A Critical Portrait.* New York: William Morrow, 1986.

Welch, Richard E., Jr. *Response to Revolution: The United States and the Cuban Revolution, 1959–1961.* Chapel Hill: University of North Carolina Press, 1985.

Castro, Raúl (1931–)

Gen. Raúl Castro, the younger brother of revolutionary and longtime Cuban leader Fidel Castro, became Cuba's second president and commander in chief in 2008. A longtime fixture in the government, he was the chosen successor to his elder brother, whose trusted confidant he had been since boyhood.

Raúl Castro Ruz was born on June 3, 1931, near the city of Biran in Oriente Province, the fifth of seven children of a Spanish immigrant father and a Cuban Creole mother. After attending Jesuit schools, he entered the University of Havana, where he became a passionate socialist, even traveling to Europe to attend communist youth rallies. After returning to Cuba, he joined his brother Fidel in an unsuccessful 1953 attempt to overthrow the government of Fulgencio Batista. For his efforts, Castro was sentenced to 15 years in prison. He received amnesty, was released from jail in 1954, and fled with Fidel to Mexico to organize a second coup against the Cuban government.

The Castro brothers, joined by other revolutionaries, trained in Mexico for 18 months and in November 1956 launched another attack, which was foiled by government soldiers. Thirty of the 82 rebels who had sailed in from Mexico escaped into the mountains of the Sierra Maestra. Assisted by Oriente peasants, Fidel and Raúl organized a new army, which succeeded in ousting Batista on January 1, 1959. When Fidel was sworn in as Cuba's prime minister on February 16, 1959, Raúl replaced him as commander of the armed forces. In October that year, his position became a cabinet-level ministership. His place in the government was secure from then onward, and he remained minister for the armed forces until 2008.

With fellow revolutionary Ernesto "Che" Guevara, like him already a committed communist, Raúl Castro was among the more radical members of the Cuban revolutionary government, which by 1961 was clearly orienting itself to the Soviet Union and adopting communist policies. The two men developed close ties with Aleksandr Alekseev, a KGB (Soviet espionage) agent who established himself in Cuba in October 1959 and became Soviet ambassador to Cuba in May 1962. In July 1960 Raúl Castro visited Moscow, meeting Soviet premier Nikita Khrushchev and other top leaders, and signing a joint communiqué whereby the Soviet Union affirmed its opposition to "an armed United States intervention against the Cuban republic." He also obtained promises of Soviet weaponry for Cuba. Raúl Castro was outspoken against the United States, which further disrupted Cuban-U.S. relations. His tirades grew in intensity after the April 1961 Bay of Pigs invasion attempt and the U.S. imposition of an even tighter economic embargo. As 1961 ended, he helped Fidel establish the single-party system of Marxist-Leninist ideology and what would eventually become the Cuban Communist Party.

Raúl Castro was elated when Soviet officials offered in June 1962 to base nuclear-capable missiles in Cuba. On a July 1962 visit to Moscow, he helped negotiate the draft Cuban-Soviet defense treaty detailing the terms governing the operations of the new Soviet forces in Cuba. Although he would have preferred an immediate public announcement of their deployment, as opposed to their surreptitious installation, the arrival of the missiles in September 1962 gave Raúl and other Cuban leaders a new sense of invulnerability to U.S. attack. In the aftermath of the crisis, he tried to repair Cuban-Soviet relations and defuse his brother Fidel's bitter resentment over Soviet concessions to the United States and the withdrawal of the missiles. In subsequent years, Raúl Castro often assumed the duties of foreign minister, traveling to the Soviet Union for meetings and to Africa to offer military support to emerging communist nations.

A government reorganization in 1972 made Castro—who served concurrently as minister for the armed forces from 1959 to 2008—first vice-premier; in 1976, he was appointed first vice president of both the Council of State and the Council of Ministers. He also served as deputy general secretary of the Communist Party. At the October 1997 party congress, Fidel made it clear that Raúl would succeed him as party leader. The first step toward this succession was taken in July 2006, when Raúl assumed de facto control of the presidency, the party, and the military as Fidel underwent surgery. As Fidel recovered over the next two years, Raúl quietly held power in Cuba, largely avoiding the limelight as Fidel's health remained a major story internationally and domestically. On February 18, 2008, Fidel publicly declared that, given his poor physical condition, he would resign the presidency. Six days later, the National Assembly of People's Power elected Raúl president by a unanimous show of hands, making him the second president of Cuba since the Cuban Revolution.

Raúl was regarded as more practical than Fidel on economic issues: in 1993 he helped push for economic reforms after the collapse of the Soviet Union. He was not, however, considered Fidel's equal in terms of charisma or diplomacy, which might handicap his effectiveness in a country where a cult of personality had been fostered since 1959.

Priscilla Roberts

See also: Alekseev (Shitov), Aleksandr Ivanovich; ANADYR, Operation; Bay of Pigs Invasion; Castro, Fidel; Guevara de la Serna, Ernesto "Che"; Khrushchev, Nikita Sergeyevich

References

Font, Mauricio A., with Scott Larson, eds. *Cuba: In Transition? Pathways to Renewal, Long-Term Development and Global Reintegration.* New York: The Bildner Center for Western Hemisphere Studies, City University of New York, 2006.

Fursenko, Aleksandr, and Timothy Naftali. *One Hell of a Gamble: Khrushchev, Castro, and Kennedy, 1958–1964.* New York: Norton, 1997.

Pérez, Louis A. *Cuba: Between Reform and Revolution.* 4th ed. New York: Oxford University Press, 2011.

Pérez-Stable, Marifeli. *The Cuban Revolution: Origins, Course, and Legacy.* New York: Oxford University Press, 1993.

Rosendahl, Mona. *Inside the Revolution: Everyday Life in Socialist Cuba.* Ithaca, NY: Cornell University Press, 1997.

Wright, Thomas C. *Latin America in the Era of the Cuban Revolution.* Rev. ed. Westport, CT: Praeger, 2001.

Central Intelligence Agency (CIA)

Principal intelligence and counterintelligence agency of the U.S. government, formally created in 1947. The Central Intelligence Agency's roots were in a World War II espionage organization, the Office of Strategic Services (OSS). The OSS was disbanded in October 1945, but the developing Cold War soon persuaded the administration of President Harry S. Truman that the United States' greatly expanded postwar international role demanded a much enhanced coordinated intelligence establishment as part of the growing defense bureaucracy.

A January 1946 presidential executive order created a Central Intelligence Group and National Intelligence Authority, whose personnel attempted to centralize postwar intelligence activities. These were disbanded when in 1947 Congress passed the National Security Act, which formally established the National Security Council (NSC) and, under it, the Central Intelligence Agency. According to this act, the CIA's mandate included

Aerial view of the San Cristobal medium range ballistic missile launch site number two, Cuba, November 1, 1962. In the immediate aftermath of the crisis, American overflights continued to monitor the presence on Cuba of Soviet missiles and their eventual removal. (U.S. Air Force)

advising the NSC on intelligence activities and making recommendations as to their coordination; the correlation, evaluation, and dissemination of intelligence; and the performance of such intelligence functions and other activities as the NSC might assign to it.

As the Cold War intensified, from December 1947 through 1948 the NSC promptly ordered an immediate and drastic expansion of the CIA's covert operations, and in September 1948 it established the agency's Office of Policy Coordination, to handle such activities with overall guidance from the State and Defense departments. The Central Intelligence Agency Act of 1949 exempted CIA activities from most accounting and procedural limitations on federal expenditures, enabling it to keep its budget secret.

The CIA's failure in June 1950 to predict North Korea's invasion of South Korea led its second director, Gen. Walter Bedell Smith, appointed the following October, to strengthen intelligence collection and analysis within the agency. He established the Office of National Estimates to provide coordinated intelligence analysis; the Office of Research and Reports to predict economic changes within the Soviet bloc; and the Directorate for Intelligence to furnish finished intelligence.

Allen Welsh Dulles, Smith's successor as director from 1953 to 1961 and the brother of Dwight D. Eisenhower's Secretary of State John Foster Dulles, was a lawyer and flamboyant former OSS operative who presided over what was perhaps the CIA's heyday. Apart from gathering and analyzing intelligence, the CIA launched a wide variety of sometimes spectacular clandestine operations, including the organization of successful pro-American coups in Iran and Costa Rica in 1953 and Guatemala in 1954 and less effective covert activities in Indonesia, Tibet, and Cuba. These culminated in the disastrous U.S.-backed Bay of Pigs invasion of Cuba in April 1961—a humiliating failure marked by inadequate planning and resources and wishful thinking, which brought about the resignation of Dulles and his deputy, Richard Bissell.

The CIA's new director, John A. McCone, put more emphasis on intelligence-gathering and analysis, though the agency still undertook a wide range of covert activities. Prominent among these was Operation MONGOOSE, a range of secret operations—some so far-fetched as to be comically fantastic—intended to destabilize and discredit Fidel Castro's government in Cuba and assassinate Castro himself. In summer 1962 a CIA group concluded that these ventures were unlikely to succeed, but sabotage and paramilitary operations continued, as the CIA infiltrated various anti-Castro guerrilla groups into Cuba.

During the Cuban Missile Crisis, U.S. intelligence was generally far more accurate than it had been during the Bay of Pigs invasion. Alerted by reports of growing deliveries of Soviet weaponry to Cuba, from August 1962 McCone suspected these might include nuclear armaments, and he pressed the White House to authorize surveillance overflights. On October 14 a high-flying U-2 reconnaissance plane produced photographic evidence of potential nuclear-capable missile sites on Cuba.

McCone was a frequent presence at the subsequent Executive Committee (ExComm) meetings of top U.S. officials convened to handle the situation. His preferred option was a full-scale U.S. invasion of Cuba, preceded by air strikes on the missile installations. Other CIA officials who attended in order to give briefings included Arthur C. Lundahl, head of the National Photographic Interpretation Center, who notified his superiors of the probable existence of missile sites on October 15. Ray Cline, CIA deputy director of intelligence, a strong advocate of a hard line against Cuba, also briefed ExComm members. As the crisis continued, the CIA flew additional U-2 missions over Cuba, which returned with evidence suggesting the presence of substantially more installations than those first detected. The only fatality of the Cuban Missile Crisis occurred on October 27, when Soviet surface-to-air missile batteries shot down the U-2 piloted by Maj. Rudolf Anderson.

Throughout the crisis, CIA officials continued to receive information from sources within Cuba. Unknown to ExComm members and without their authorization, during the crisis the CIA also sent several anti-Castro teams into Cuba, one of which was captured by Cuban forces on October 25. On November 8, with the process of dismantling the missile bases well under way, a CIA sabotage unit attacked and destroyed a Cuban industrial plant, adding a further level of tension to the last days of the crisis. Perhaps alarmed that the program was out of control and jeopardizing any potential rapprochement with Cuba, in spring 1963 the federal government closed down many training camps for Cuban exiles in the United States. Sabotage and assassination plots against Castro continued until April 1964, when the Johnson administration called a halt to them.

Throughout the 1960s the CIA mounted extensive covert operations in Southeast Asia in support of U.S. intervention in Vietnam. Growing opposition to the Vietnam War brought new congressional and public demands for CIA accountability. During the 1970s and 1980s books scathingly critical of CIA activities regularly appeared. In 1974 CIA director William E. Colby responded by providing Congress with a detailed list of all illegal domestic and overseas CIA covert operations. For decades, however, additional evidence and revelations of CIA involvement in a wide range of illicit or clandestine activities within and beyond the United States, of which Cuba-related operations were representative but by no means unique, continued to surface.

Priscilla Roberts

See also: Bay of Pigs Invasion; Bissell, Richard Mervin, Jr.; Castro, Fidel; Containment, Doctrine and Course of; Dulles, Allen Welsh; Dulles, John Foster; Eisenhower, Dwight David; Kennedy, John Fitzgerald; Kennedy, Robert Francis; Lansdale, Edward Geary; McCone, John Alex; MONGOOSE, Operation; U-2 Overflights

References

Brugioni, Dino. *Eyeball to Eyeball: The Inside Story of the Cuban Missile Crisis.* Edited by Robert F. McCort. New York: Random House, 1991.

Cline, Ray S. *Secrets, Spies and Scholars: Blueprint of the Essential CIA.* Washington, DC: Acropolis Books, 1976.

Dobbs, Michael. *One Minute to Midnight: Kennedy, Khrushchev, and Castro on the Brink of Nuclear War.* New York: Knopf, 2008.

Higgins, Trumbull. *The Perfect Failure: Kennedy, Eisenhower, and the CIA at the Bay of Pigs.* New York: Norton, 1987.

Jeffreys-Jones, Rhodri. *The CIA and American Democracy.* 2nd ed. New Haven, CT: Yale University Press, 1998.

Kornbluh, Peter, ed. *Bay of Pigs Declassified: The Secret CIA Report on the Invasion of Cuba.* New York: New Press, 1998.

McAuliffe, Mary S., ed. *CIA Documents on the Cuban Missile Crisis, 1962.* Washington, DC: Central Intelligence Agency, 1992.

Prados, John. *Presidents' Secret Wars: CIA and Pentagon Covert Operations from World War II through the Persian Gulf.* Rev. ed. Chicago: Ivan R. Dee, 1996.

Ranelagh, John. *The Agency: The Rise and Decline of the CIA.* London: Weidenfeld & Nicolson, 1986.

Weiner, Tim. *Legacy of Ashes: The History of the CIA.* New York: Doubleday, 2006.

China, People's Republic of (PRC)

The People's Republic of China was founded in 1949 when communists won control of the Chinese mainland in a civil war, restricting the former government to the island of Taiwan (Republic of China, or ROC). By 1959, when Fidel Castro established a leftist government in Cuba, Chinese Communist Party Chairman Mao Zedong was at odds with the Soviet Union. Disdaining Soviet premier Nikita Khrushchev's policies of peaceful coexistence with the West, Mao argued that armed struggle was the necessary precondition for the spread of communism. Mao advanced his own radical brand of communism as a rival to Soviet ideological theories. Mao's readiness to risk nuclear war with the United States by threatening Taiwan, a U.S. ally and client, also alarmed Khrushchev. In the late 1950s the Soviet Union ceased assisting China's nuclear program, and in 1960 Khrushchev recalled almost all Soviet technical advisers and experts from China. Both China and the Soviet Union publicly denounced each other's positions at a 1960 Romanian Communist Party Conference, and vitriolic mutual criticism continued throughout the 1960s.

The Sino-Soviet split intensified Khrushchev's eagerness to demonstrate his revolutionary bona fides by supporting Cuba. He also sought to keep Cuba in the Soviet rather than the Chinese camp, a concern Castro exploited to extract additional Soviet aid. From September 1960 onward, when

Cuba withdrew diplomatic recognition from Taiwan and opened diplomatic relations with the People's Republic, the first Latin American nation to do so, China sent substantial quantities of military technology to Cuba. In fall 1961, Castro asked the Soviet Union for much larger arms shipments than previously, especially of antiaircraft missiles. When Khrushchev proved slow to respond, Castro purged his government of several pro-Moscow communists and opened talks with China on possible economic assistance. He also began setting up partisan guerrilla groups to spread revolution throughout Latin America. When Soviet KGB officers cautiously declined to establish a training camp for this purpose in Cuba, Castro's representatives made unfavorable comparisons between Soviet and Chinese approaches to popular insurgencies. Khrushchev's desire to emphasize that he could champion international revolution more effectively than Mao was one factor impelling him to offer nuclear-capable missiles to Cuba in May 1962.

During the Cuban Missile Crisis, China enthusiastically supported the Soviets, publishing laudatory editorials in the state-controlled press, and Khrushchev responded by backing China in the concurrent Sino-Indian War. The U.S. military included the Chinese embassy in Havana, which had already featured as a possible target for clandestine U.S.-backed sabotage operations, among potential air strike objectives. The rapprochement was short-lived. Chinese leaders responded with disappointment to the peaceful resolution of the crisis. On October 29, 1962, the Chinese apparently sent a note to the Cubans "implying that the U.S.S.R. was an untrustworthy ally," one that had since 1959 refused to provide China with information on the production of nuclear arms. The Chinese privately urged Castro to withstand Soviet pressure for a swift settlement. At a World Peace Council meeting in Stockholm, Chinese delegates characterized the Soviet decision as "cowardly." Khrushchev, meanwhile, complained that the only Chinese assistance during the confrontation had been an offer by Chinese embassy staff in Cuba to donate blood to Cuba's hospitals.

As U.S.-Soviet negotiations on the details of removing missiles from Cuba proceeded, China vigorously supported demands by Castro for a complete U.S. withdrawal from Cuba, including the Guantánamo Bay military base, and the cessation of all U.S. measures against Cuba, including economic sanctions. Publicly, Chinese officials condemned the Soviet decision to withdraw the missiles as a Soviet Munich, criticizing Khrushchev's action in installing them as "adventurist" and their removal as "appeasement." In Beijing, Mao refused to meet the Soviet ambassador. With Cuban revolutionaries deeply divided and some siding openly with China, Castro proclaimed that Cuba would remain "neutral" toward the Sino-Soviet conflict.

In late 1962 and 1963 the war of words escalated. Khrushchev attacked the Chinese for tolerating the existence of colonial enclaves on their own territory, in Macau and Hong Kong. The Chinese responded by claiming that over 1 million square miles of Chinese territory in Siberia ceded to Russia in the 1860s likewise constituted a colonial enclave, implying they might no longer accept its loss. When Soviet officials embarked on "ideological consultations" with Chinese officials in July 1963 to repair the breach, the Chinese delegation, led by Deng Xiaoping, responded with further invective, again charging Khrushchev with rashness in deploying the missiles and "capitulationism" in ultimately withdrawing them. Chinese polemics also targeted the nuclear test ban treaty Khrushchev and U.S. president John F. Kennedy negotiated at that time, which the Chinese interpreted as directed at their own nuclear program. Kennedy and his advisers believed that the added strains the missile crisis and the treaty placed on Sino-Soviet relations did much to make the split permanent.

Priscilla Roberts

See also: Castro, Fidel; Guantánamo Bay Naval Base; Khrushchev, Nikita Sergeyevich; Partial Test Ban Treaty

References

Freedman, Lawrence. *Kennedy's Wars: Berlin, Cuba, Laos, and Vietnam.* New York: Oxford University Press, 2000.

Fursenko, Aleksandr, and Timothy Naftali. *Khrushchev's Cold War: The Inside Story of an American Adversary.* New York: Norton, 2006.

Fursenko, Aleksandr, and Timothy Naftali. *One Hell of a Gamble: Khrushchev, Castro, and Kennedy, 1958–1964.* New York: Norton, 1997.

Lüthi, Lorenz M. *The Sino-Soviet Split: Cold War in the Communist World.* Princeton, NJ: Princeton University Press, 2008.

Radchenko, Sergey. *Two Suns in the Heavens: The Sino-Soviet Struggle for Supremacy, 1962–1967.* Washington, DC, and Stanford, CA: Wilson Center Press and Stanford University Press, 2009.

Containment, Doctrine and Course of

Fundamental controlling U.S. Cold War strategy, designed to prevent further expansion of Soviet power.

As relations between the United States and the Soviet Union deteriorated in the months after World War II ended, in February 1946 the administration of President Harry S. Truman requested George F. Kennan, counselor in the U.S. embassy in Moscow and a Soviet expert, to explain the rationale behind Soviet policies. In perhaps the seminal document of the Cold War, Kennan replied with the 8,000-word "Long Telegram." He stated that, since Soviet antagonism toward the West arose from the need of Russian rulers to justify their oppressive domestic rule as essential to combat hostility from foreign powers, Western states could do little to alter Soviet policies. Instead, they must adopt policies of "long-term, patient but firm and vigilant containment," firmly resisting attempts to expand Soviet influence while awaiting internal changes to the nature of Soviet government. Kennan's telegram, circulated throughout the higher echelons of the U.S. government, and his subsequent article "The Sources of Soviet Conduct," published in the influential quarterly *Foreign Affairs,* quickly became definitive documents of U.S. Cold War strategy. From then until the early 1990s the word "containment" described the underlying U.S. policy toward the Soviet Union.

Kennan, who returned to Washington to head the newly created Policy Planning Staff, charged with the long-range planning of U.S. foreign policy, soon deprecated the increasingly military emphasis of containment, subsequently claiming he had envisaged that the United States would rely primarily upon peaceful economic and cultural counterpressure to check Soviet expansion. In a March 1947 address (the "Truman Doctrine" speech), President Harry S. Truman publicly pledged to assist any country where democracy was threatened either externally or internally by communism, simultaneously extending substantial economic and military aid to both Greece and Turkey, and some months later announcing the massive Marshall Plan or European Recovery Program to assist with Europe's economic rebuilding.

By 1950 prominent civilian and military officials sought to expand U.S. defense budgets substantially, considering this essential to enable the country to meet increasing international obligations, including membership in the 1949 North Atlantic Treaty Organization (NATO) West European security pact, it had assumed, and to counter the recent Soviet acquisition of atomic weapons and the establishment of a communist state in mainland China. Various State and Defense Department representatives, led by Paul H. Nitze, Kennan's successor on the Policy Planning Staff, argued that, should war break out, the United States lacked the military resources even to fulfill its existing commitments. Implicitly, they endorsed the 1947 Truman Doctrine. The planning paper NSC-68, which they drafted and delivered to Truman in April 1950, demanded massive enhancements in U.S. conventional and nuclear military capabilities, including substantially enhanced U.S. troop contributions to NATO forces in Europe, stating, "Without superior aggregate military strength, in being and readily mobilizable, a policy of 'containment' ... is no more than a policy of bluff." NSC-68 envisaged increasing the existing $13.5 billion U.S. defense budget to anywhere between $18 and $50 billion, recommendations the economy-conscious Truman initially rejected.

The outbreak of the Korean War in June 1950 proved crucial to both the implementation of NSC-68 and the effective globalization of the Cold War, broadening its initial primarily European focus. U.S. defense spending soared in Europe as well as Asia, reaching $48 billion in fiscal 1951 and $61 billion the following year, and after the armistice it still remained far higher than previously. In June 1950 the United States had 1,460,000 military personnel, of whom 280,000 were stationed abroad; four years later the totals were 3,555,000 and 963,000 respectively. The Mutual Security Program, instituted in 1951, furnished military assistance to a wide array of U.S. clients and allies. By the late 1950s the United States had established numerous additional security pacts, including the Rio Pact covering Latin America, the Central Treaty Organization (CENTO) in the Middle East, the Southeast Asian Treaty Organization, the ANZUS defense pact with Australia and New Zealand, and bilateral treaties with South Korea, Japan, and the Republic of China on Taiwan. Covert operations by the Central Intelligence Agency often ensured that any new overseas government unsympathetic to the United States proved short-lived, as in Iran, Guatemala, and later Chile.

Despite rhetorical pronouncements in the 1950s by the administration of President Dwight D. Eisenhower that the United States would "roll back" communism in Eastern Europe and elsewhere, in practice, after Communist Chinese intervention balked U.S. efforts to "liberate" North Korea in autumn 1950, U.S. strategy sought primarily to prevent further communist gains, particularly in countries undergoing decolonization, that were often perceived as subjects for U.S.-Soviet competition. In the late 1950s and early 1960s this outlook led successive U.S. presidents to increase incrementally aid to the southern portion of Vietnam, where communist takeover by the north threatened the existing regime. After 1975 the effective U.S. defeat in this costly conflict, the greatest military humiliation in U.S. history, led the United States to avoid further large-scale interventions, relying instead upon surrogates, such as anti-Soviet guerrilla forces in Afghanistan during the 1980s. Exploiting the Sino-Soviet split, from the early 1970s onward U.S. leaders differentiated between Chinese and Russian communism, using each socialist big power's distrust of the other to win concessions for the United States.

U.S. military strategy in the 1950s relied heavily on nuclear weapons—because they could inflict far greater casualties at much less cost than conventional forces—a policy termed the "New Look," whose potential to risk nuclear war over relatively minor issues aroused heavy criticism. In the 1960s U.S. strategic thinking emphasized flexible response, enhancing both conventional and counterinsurgency capabilities. The expansion of the United States' international commitments did not preclude efforts from the mid-1950s onward to reach an understanding with the Soviet Union that would prevent an accidental war and place ceilings on ever more expensive and destructive nuclear weapons. These attempts, culminating in the Strategic Arms Limitation Treaties of 1972 and 1979, demonstrated the fundamentally cautious nature of U.S. military strategy.

Alarmed by what he perceived as increasingly assertive Soviet foreign policies of the 1970s, during the 1980s President Ronald Reagan initially increased U.S. defense budgets dramatically, adopted a firmly anti-Soviet posture, and announced the development of a new antimissile shield that would render the United States invulnerable to Soviet attack. By the late 1980s, growing economic weakness led to the collapse of both the Soviet Union and the Soviet empire, which many Americans interpreted as validating the premises of the containment strategy adopted over 40 years earlier. As the 21st century began, no other strategic paradigm had yet attained similar intellectual dominance in the conceptualization of U.S. post–Cold War policy.

Priscilla Roberts

See also: Acheson, Dean Gooderham; Central Intelligence Agency; Dulles, John Foster; Eisenhower, Dwight David; Johnson, Lyndon Baines; Kennedy, John Fitzgerald; Military Balance; Nitze, Paul Henry; Nuclear Arms Race

References

Friedberg, Aaron L. *In the Shadow of the Garrison State: America's Anti-Statism and Its Cold War Grand Strategy.* Princeton, NJ: Princeton University Press, 2000.

Friedman, Norman. *The Fifty-Year War: Conflict and Strategy in the Cold War.* Annapolis, MD: Naval Institute Press, 2000.

Gaddis, John Lewis. *Strategies of Containment: A Critical Appraisal of Postwar American National Security Policy.* Oxford: Oxford University Press, 1982.

Hogan, Michael J. *A Cross of Iron: Harry S. Truman and the Origins of the National Security State, 1945–1954.* Cambridge: Cambridge University Press, 1998.

Kennan, George F. *Memoirs, 1925–1950.* Boston: Little, Brown, 1967.

May, Ernest R., ed. *American Cold War Strategy: Interpreting NSC 68.* Boston: Bedford Books, 1993.

Miscamble, Wilson D. *George F. Kennan and the Making of American Foreign Policy, 1947–1950.* Princeton, NJ: Princeton University Press, 1992.

Russell, Richard L. *George F. Kennan's Strategic Thought: The Making of an American Realist.* Westport, CT: Praeger, 1999.

Cordier, Andrew Wellington (1901–1975)

Andrew Wellington Cordier was born on March 3, 1901, near Canton, Ohio. After studying at Manchester College in Indiana and the University of Chicago, from 1927 to 1944 he chaired the Department of History and Political Science at Manchester College. In 1944 Cordier joined the U.S. State Department as adviser on international security, drafting early versions of the UN Charter. He also served on the U.S. delegation to the April 1945 San Francisco Conference and the Preparatory Commission for the UN, which met in London. In March 1946 Cordier became executive assistant to the first UN secretary general, Trygve Halvden Lie. Holding the rank of undersecretary, Cordier retained the position until 1962, serving under both Lie and his charismatic successor, Dag Hammarskjöld. In 1962 he left the UN to become dean of the School of International Affairs of Columbia University.

On the night of October 27, while awaiting Soviet premier Nikita Khrushchev's response to President John F. Kennedy's offer of a guarantee that the United States would not invade Cuba in exchange for the removal of the Soviet missiles there, Secretary of State Dean Rusk contacted Cordier, an old friend. He asked Cordier to prepare a proposal that the United States remove NATO Jupiter missiles from Turkey instead. Should Khrushchev reject Kennedy's offer, Rusk and Kennedy intended to ask Cordier to submit this proposal to acting UN secretary general U Thant, whom Cordier knew well. In those circumstances, they hoped that Thant would claim that this fallback suggestion was made on his own initiative. Cordier drafted such a document, but it was never used. That same evening, Attorney General Robert Kennedy, the president's brother, submitted secret proposals on similar lines to Anatoly Dobrynin, Soviet ambassador to the United States. Only in the late 1980s did U.S. officials reveal the existence of this backup plan, which would have represented a last-ditch attempt to avoid a full-scale invasion of Cuba. Cordier retired from Columbia in 1972. He died in Long Island, New York, on July 11, 1975.

Priscilla Roberts

See also: Dobrynin, Anatoly Fyodorovich; Jupiter Missiles (Turkey and Italy); Kennedy, John Fitzgerald; Kennedy, Robert Francis; Rusk, Dean David; U Thant; United Nations; U.S. Allies

References

Blight, James G., and David A. Welch. *On the Brink: Americans and Soviets Reexamine the Cuban Missile Crisis.* New York: Hill and Wang, 1989.

Firestone, Bernard J. *The United Nations under U Thant, 1961–1971.* Lanham, MD: Scarecrow Press, 2001.

Luard, Evan. *A History of the United Nations.* 2 vols. New York: St. Martin's Press, 1982–1989.

Meisler, Stanley. *The United Nations: The First Fifty Years.* New York: Atlantic Monthly Press, 1995.

Moore, John Alphin, Jr., and Jerry Pubantz. *To Create a New World?: American Presidents and the United Nations.* New York: Peter Lang, 1999.

Ostrower, Gary B. *The United Nations and the United States.* New York: Twayne, 1998.

White, Mark J. *The Cuban Missile Crisis.* London: Macmillan, 1996.

Cuba

Caribbean island nation comprising 42,803 square miles, about the size of the state of Ohio. The largest and western-most island of the West Indies chain, Cuba is in the Caribbean Sea, west of Hispaniola and 90 miles south of Key West, Florida. It had a 1945 population of approximately 5.68 million.

By the early 16th century, Spanish conquistadors and traders had already recognized Havana as an ideal port for trade with Spain. Beginning in the early 1800s, sugarcane production boomed, ensuring a huge influx of black slaves and the institution of a plantation economy. During the 1860s–1870s, a growing independence movement brought armed revolt against Spanish rule. Slavery was outlawed in 1886, and in 1895 Cuban nationalist and poet José Marti led the final struggle against the Spanish, which was fully realized thanks to U.S. involvement in the 1898 Spanish-American War.

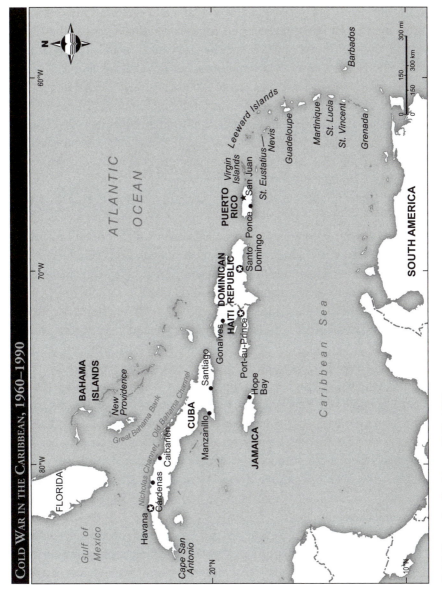

COLD WAR IN THE CARIBBEAN, 1960–1990

FLORIDA

Gulf of Mexico

BAHAMA ISLANDS

New Providence

ATLANTIC OCEAN

Cape San Antonio

Havana

Cárdenas

Caibarién

Nicholas Channel

Great Bahama Bank

Old Bahama Channel

CUBA

Manzanillo

Santiago

20°N

JAMAICA

Hope Bay

Gonaïves

Port-au-Prince

HAITI

DOMINICAN REPUBLIC

Santo Domingo

Caribbean Sea

Leeward Islands

Virgin Islands

PUERTO RICO

San Juan

Ponce

St. Eustatius

Nevis

Guadeloupe

Martinique

St. Lucia

St. Vincent

Grenada

Barbados

SOUTH AMERICA

80°W

70°W

60°W

10°N

N

0   150   300 mi

0   150   300 km

Cold War in the Caribbean, 1960–1990

The Spanish-Cuban-American War marked a watershed in Cuban-U.S. relations, as it greatly enhanced American influence on the island. However, the event was controversial because Cuban independence fighters saw the island's newfound freedom as an outcome of their 30-year struggle against Spain, whereas many Americans saw Cuban independence as a U.S. victory. The result was an uneasy compromise whereby Cuba became an independent republic with limitations to its sovereignty embodied in the 1901 Platt Amendment, an appendix to the Cuban constitution authorizing U.S. intervention in Cuban affairs at its own discretion. Cuba became a politically independent state on May 20, 1902.

The duality of opinions regarding Cuban sovereignty was central to the crisis that brought down the Cuban republic. For the first half of the 20th century, the United States set the standards to which the Cuban population aspired. In this context, the crisis of the Cuban economic model of dependence on the sugar industry was accompanied by a sympathetic attitude in Washington toward anticommunist dictators.

Gen. Fulgencio Batista's military coup on March 10, 1952, occurred only two months before an election in which nationalist forces were within reach of the presidency. In the context of McCarthyism in the United States, the destruction of the Cuban democracy by Batista's rightist junta generated no significant opposition in Washington. Indeed, the United States backed Batista as an ally in the Cold War. For its part, the Cuban authoritarian Right manipulated the West by presenting itself as a bulwark against communism. In practice, the Batista government actually undermined democracy through its repressive policies. Batista's regime did little, moreover, to improve living standards for poor Cubans, while the middle class and elites enjoyed close and lucrative relationships with American businesses.

A potent popular insurrection against Batista's regime had grown in the eastern and central parts of Cuba by 1958. The revolution's leaders, Fidel Castro and Ernesto "Che" Guevara, questioned both Cuban dependence on the United States and market economy principles. perceiving their movement as part of a developing-world rebellion against the West and as a natural ally of the communist bloc.

The United States was not prepared to deal with the charismatic and doctrinaire Castro. After his takeover, the United States underestimated the profound grievances provoked by U.S. support for the Batista regime. Some of Castro's early measures—such as land reform, the prosecution of Batista's cronies (with no guarantee of due process), and the nationalization of industries—were overwhelmingly popular, but they met stiff U.S. resistance.

Against this backdrop, Castro approached the Soviet Union for support, and in February 1960 a Soviet delegation led by Vice Premier Anastas Mikoyan visited Cuba and signed a trade agreement with Castro's government. The Soviet Union then began to replace the United States as Cuba's main trade and political partner. Soviet leader Nikita Khrushchev soon promised Cuba new machinery, oil, consumer goods, armaments, and a market for Cuban products now subject to U.S. sanctions.

In April 1961, Cuban-U.S. relations collapsed completely after the failed Bay of Pigs invasion by rebel Cuban exiles, sponsored by the U.S. Central Intelligence Agency (CIA). The invasion was doomed from the start, given Castro's popularity in Cuba and the lack of U.S. air support for the rebel force. The botched attack only encouraged closer relations between the Soviet Union and Cuba, especially when the CIA launched additional covert operations. The most important undertaking, Operation MONGOOSE, included 14 attempts to assassinate Castro. Khrushchev subsequently proposed installing nuclear-capable missiles in Cuba to gain a better bargaining position with the United States while offering protection to Cuba. Castro was elated. Khrushchev naively assumed that the missiles could be installed without U.S. detection. U.S. intelligence quickly discovered them, however, provoking the Cuban Missile Crisis, the most dangerous confrontation between the two Cold War superpowers. President John F. Kennedy declared a naval quarantine of the island in October 1962. For nearly two weeks the world stood at the edge of a nuclear abyss. Ultimately, Kennedy and Khrushchev worked out an agreement whereby the Soviets removed the missiles in return for U.S. promises not to invade Cuba and to withdraw Jupiter missiles from Turkey.

The end of Kennedy's quarantine did not conclude strife between Cuba and the United States, however. In addition to an embargo still in force in 2012, the United States mounted further covert operations against Castro's government. U.S. hostility was reinforced by the Cuban revolution's transformation from a nationalist rebellion against authoritarianism to a totalitarian state aligned with the Soviet Union, with serious shortcomings in civil and political liberties.

The resolution of the Cuban Missile Crisis also created serious strains between Havana and Moscow. Cuba's foreign policy was made in Havana, so Castro refused to accept Moscow's or Beijing's directives. In 1968, he cracked down on a group of Cuban communists, accusing them of working with Soviet agents in Havana. Eventually, he used the 1968 Soviet intervention in Czechoslovakia against the Prague Spring to broker a compromise by which Cuba preserved its autonomy but promised not to criticize the Soviet Union publicly. Cuba thus became a Comecon member, receiving significant additional economic aid from the communist bloc.

In Latin America, the Cuban government actively supported revolutionary movements with leftist or nationalist agendas, especially those that challenged U.S. hegemony in the region. But the 1960s witnessed successive failed Cuban attempts to export revolution. Guevara's 1967 murder in Bolivia concluded a series of subversive projects encouraged by Havana. Cuban revolutionary attempts were part of Cubans' core revolutionary beliefs and also a response to the rupture of diplomatic relations with Havana by all Latin American countries except Mexico.

From the 1970s to 1990, as part of the Cold War conflict, Cuba played a major international role. A high point of Castro's foreign policy came at the 1979 Sixth Summit of the Non-Aligned Movement in Havana. Cuba became a major conduit of alliance between the developing world and the communist bloc. Havana's diplomatic success and military involvement were accompanied by massive civilian involvement in health and education aid programs to African, Latin American, and Asian countries.

Cuba adopted a foreign policy suited to a medium-sized power. Castro sent 40,000 troops to Angola to support the pro-Soviet Popular Movement for the Liberation of Angola (MPLA) government in its struggle against the National Union for the Total Independence of Angola (UNITA) forces backed by South Africa and the United States. He also dispatched troops to aid the pro-Soviet government of Ethiopia. In all, Cuba deployed more than 300,000 troops or military advisers to Angola, Ethiopia, the Congo, Guinea-Bissau, Algeria, Mozambique, Syria, and South Yemen. The fight in southern Africa was ended through a skillfully designed tripartite agreement signed by Cuba, Angola, and South Africa and mediated by President Ronald Reagan's administration that led to Namibia's independence.

Paradoxically, due in part to these Cold War commitments, Cuba missed its best chance to solve its conflict with the United States. In the 1970s U.S. leaders sought serious negotiations with Cuba. Efforts at negotiation began during Richard Nixon's administration (1969–1974) and seemed most promising during Jimmy Carter's presidency (1977–1981). Carter demonstrated that he was serious in his desire to improve hemispheric relations and promote human rights. In 1977, Carter even stated that the United States did not consider a Cuban retreat from Angola a precondition for beginning negotiations. Castro, however, insisted on continuing what he defined as "revolutionary solidarity" and "proletarian internationalism."

The Cuban government was interested in negotiations with the United States but insisted on a radical leftist solution to problems. Castro took significant steps in releasing political prisoners and allowing Cuban exiles to visit the island as goodwill gestures toward the United States. In the international arena, in May 1978 Castro informed Lyle Lane, head of the State Department's U.S. Interest Section, that Cuba had no involvement in the Katangese invasion and rebellion in Zaire. Nevertheless, Castro gave priority to Cuban relations with other revolutionary movements, especially in Africa. In 1977, he sent 17,000 Cuban troops to Ethiopia to support the dictator Mengistu Haile Mariam in his territorial conflict with Somalia. This development, despite progress on several bilateral issues, represented a major blow to the prospect of improved Cuban-U.S. relations, as did Castro's support for the Sandinista government of Nicaragua in the 1980s.

A new development came in 1976 when Ricardo Boffill, Elizardo Sanchez, and Gustavo Arcos founded the first human rights group in Cuba since 1959. A new generation of opposition groups based on strategies of civil disobedience slowly emerged, gaining strength in the 1990s. Equally, during the 1970s Cuban civil society began to emerge from totalitarian ostracism that had reduced its religious communities to a minimum. This evolution continued, and by the late 1980s religious groups were growing rapidly.

The collapse of the communist bloc beginning in 1989 was a catastrophe for Castro's government, as Cuba lost its major benefactors. Simultaneously, the international community, particularly Latin America and the former communist countries, adopted general norms of democratic governance opposed to the Cuban leadership's goals and behavior. Without Soviet backing, Cuba adjusted its economy and foreign policy to survive in a world that was no longer safe for revolution. In 1988 Castro withdrew Cuban troops from Angola and reduced the Cuban military presence in the Horn of Africa.

Cuba's gross domestic product fell by almost one-third between 1989 and 1993. The collapse of the Cuban economy was particularly hard on imports, which fell from 8.6 billion pesos in 1989 to about 2 billion pesos in 1993. In response to the economic collapse, Castro permitted limited private enterprise, allowed Cubans to hold foreign currencies, and pushed for foreign investment, particularly in tourism. His reforms, however, did little to stem economic hemorrhaging. In addition, Cuban troops were withdrawn from wherever they were posted. In 2008, almost 20 years after the Cold War wound down, Castro, one of the last leaders of the old-style communist order, retired for reasons of ill health, handing his offices to his younger brother Raúl.

Arturo Lopez-Levy

References

Dominguez, Jorge I. *To Make a World Safe for Revolution: Cuba's Foreign Policy.* Cambridge, MA: Harvard University Press, 1989.

Font, Mauricio A., with Scott Larson, eds. *Cuba: In Transition? Pathways to Renewal, Long-Term Development and Global Reintegration.* New York: The Bildner Center for Western Hemisphere Studies, City University of New York, 2006.

Gleijeses, Piero. *Conflicting Missions: Havana, Washington, and Africa, 1959–1976.* Chapel Hill: University of North Carolina Press, 2002.

Morley, Morris H. *Imperial State and Revolution: The United States and Cuba, 1952–1986.* Cambridge: Cambridge University Press, 1987.

Morley, Morris, and Chris McGillion, eds. *Cuba, the United States, and the Post-Cold War World: The International Dimensions of the Washington-Havana Relationship.* Gainesville: University Press of Florida, 2005.

Morley, Morris, and Chris McGillion. *Unfinished Business: America and Cuba After the Cold War, 1989–2001.* Cambridge: Cambridge University Press, 2002.

Pastor, Robert. *The Carter Administration and Latin America.* Occasional Paper Series, Vol. 2, No. 3. Atlanta, GA: Carter Center of Emory University, 1992.

Pérez, Louis A., Jr. *Cuba and the United States: Ties of Singular Intimacy.* 2nd ed. Athens: University of Georgia Press, 1997.

Pérez, Louis A. *Cuba: Between Reform and Revolution.* 4th ed. New York: Oxford University Press, 2011.

Pérez-Stable, Marifeli. *The Cuban Revolution: Origins, Course, and Legacy.* New York: Oxford University Press, 1993.

Pérez-Stable, Marifeli. *The United States and Cuba: Intimate Enemies.* New York: Routledge, 2011.

Smith, Wayne. *The Closest of Enemies: A Personal and Diplomatic History of the Castro Years.* New York: Norton, 1987.

Staten, Clifford L. *The History of Cuba.* Westport, CT: Greenwood Press, 2003.

Wright, Thomas C. *Latin America in the Era of the Cuban Revolution.* Rev. ed. Westport, CT: Praeger, 2001.

D

Dillon, C(larence) Douglas (1909–2003)

U.S. secretary of the treasury, 1961–1965. C. Douglas Dillon was born on August 21, 1909, in Geneva, Switzerland, the only son of Clarence Douglas Dillon, self-made financier and founder of the prominent New York investment bank Dillon Read. After attending the elite Groton School, Massachusetts, and Harvard University, the younger Dillon became a stockbroker and investment banker, joining Dillon Read in 1938. He served in the U.S. Navy during World War II, then returned to Dillon Read as board chairman. Active in Republican politics, during 1951–1952 he campaigned actively for Dwight D. Eisenhower, the successful presidential candidate, who appointed Dillon ambassador to France in 1953. Joining the State Department in Washington as deputy undersecretary for economic affairs in January 1957, Dillon rose first to undersecretary for economic affairs and eventually, from April 1959 to January 1961, to undersecretary for political affairs, the department's second-highest position. Dillon, a dedicated internationalist, concentrated on promoting trade and economic development, coordinating mutual security assistance programs, and enhancing foreign aid's scope and effectiveness. His efforts contributed to founding the Inter-American Development Bank in 1959 and in 1960 to establishing the Act of Bogotá economic development program, a forerunner of the Alliance for Progress, and the European-backed Organization for Economic Cooperation and Development.

In December 1960 Democratic president-elect John F. Kennedy, seeking to reassure the financial community that he would not adopt "easy money" policies, named Dillon secretary of the treasury, a post he held until March 1965. Dillon also sat on the National Security Council. In

August 1961 he headed the U.S. delegation to the Punta del Este conference that created the Latin American Alliance for Progress program. Dillon served on the Executive Committee (ExComm) that decided policies during the Cuban Missile Crisis. He initially favored a quick air strike, without any warning, against Soviet missile facilities in Cuba. By October 20 Dillon had come around to favoring the announcement of a blockade, an ultimatum that might be followed by air strikes within three days if Soviet construction of missile bases continued. After Russian SA-2 surface-to-air missile batteries shot down a U-2 reconnaissance plane over Cuba on October 27, Dillon favored a quick, unannounced strike against them, one that would probably also target nearby missile sites. Although he considered the Jupiter nuclear missiles the United States had placed in Turkey strategically worthless, Dillon clearly found unpalatable the prospect of trading these publicly for Soviet missiles in Cuba.

Dillon returned to banking in March 1965. In March 1968, after the Tet Offensive, as one of President Lyndon B. Johnson's Senior Advisory Group on Vietnam he was among the "wise men" who urged Johnson to seek withdrawal from Vietnam. On January 10, 2003, following several weeks of illness, Dillon died at Presbyterian Hospital, New York.

Priscilla Roberts

See also: Alliance for Progress; Eisenhower, Dwight David; Jupiter Missiles (Turkey and Italy); Kennedy, John Fitzgerald; U-2 Overflights

References

Katz, Bernard S., and C. Daniel Vencill. *Biographical Dictionary of the United States Secretaries of the Treasury, 1789–1995.* Westport, CT: Greenwood Press, 1996.

May, Ernest R., and Philip D. Zelikow, eds. *The Kennedy Tapes: Inside the White House during the Cuban Missile Crisis.* Cambridge, MA: Harvard University Press, 1997.

Sobel, Robert. *The Life and Times of Dillon Read.* New York: Dutton, 1991.

Dobrynin, Anatoly Fyodorovich (1919–2010)

Soviet diplomat and ambassador to the United States. Born on November 16, 1919, in Krasnaya Gorka, Anatoly Dobrynin studied engineering at the Ordzhonikidze Moscow Aviation Institute and worked as a designer at

Experimental Aircraft Plant No. 115 in Moscow before being selected by the Personnel Department of the Communist Party of the Soviet Union (CPSU) Central Committee to attend the Higher Diplomatic School in 1944. He joined the CPSU the following year. In 1946 he graduated with a doctorate in history.

Dobrynin joined the Ministry of Foreign Affairs as assistant chief of the Education Department, serving simultaneously as an assistant professor of U.S. foreign policy at the Institute of International Relations. From 1947 to 1952 he worked on the staff of Deputy Foreign Minister Valerian Zorin, ultimately becoming his first assistant. Dobrynin was posted to Washington as counselor at the Soviet embassy in 1952, serving as minister-counselor from 1954 to 1955. Returning to Moscow in 1955, he was promoted to the rank of ambassador extraordinary and plenipotentiary in the Foreign Ministry before becoming an assistant to Foreign Minister Dmitri T. Shepilov. In 1957, Dobrynin was posted to the United Nations (UN) Secretariat as an undersecretary general, becoming director of the Department of Political and Security Council Affairs the next year.

In February 1960 Dobrynin was recalled to Moscow to head the Foreign Ministry's American Department, where he served until January 1962, returning briefly to the UN in summer 1960 to help Foreign Minister Andrey Gromyko lodge complaints regarding U.S. U-2 overflights of the Soviet Union. In January 1962 Dobrynin was appointed ambassador to the United States. Dobrynin served in this post until 1986, playing a critical role in almost every aspect of Soviet-U.S. relations. Kremlin officials did not inform Dobrynin of the Presidium's May 1962 decision to install nuclear-capable missiles on

Anatoly F. Dobrynin, appointed Soviet ambassador to the United States in April 1962, within months took part in secret behind-the-scenes negotiations during the Cuban Missile Crisis that were vitally important to its resolution. A highly effective diplomat, Dobrynin remained ambassador until 1986, becoming a fixture in Soviet-American relations. (Getty Images)

Cuba, leading him to misinform U.S. Attorney General Robert F. Kennedy on September 4 that only defensive weaponry was reaching the island and the Soviets would not introduce offensive weapons, including ballistic missiles. His private and secret discussions with Robert Kennedy on proposals to remove NATO Jupiter nuclear missiles from Turkey soon after Soviet nuclear-capable weapons left Cuba were instrumental to the peaceful resolution of the resulting Cuban Missile Crisis. During Richard Nixon's presidency, Dobrynin worked with National Security Adviser Henry Kissinger to resolve disputes in the SALT I negotiations and became an informal channel for U.S. communications with North Vietnam leading to the Paris Peace Talks. During the presidencies of Jimmy Carter and Ronald Reagan, Dobrynin provided a degree of stability in deteriorating Soviet-U.S. relations following the 1979 Soviet invasion of Afghanistan.

Dobrynin became a candidate member of the CPSU Central Committee in 1966 and a full member in 1977. In March 1986, new Soviet leader Mikhail Gorbachev recalled Dobrynin to join the CPSU Central Committee as secretary for foreign affairs and head of the International Department. He was also elected a deputy to the Supreme Soviet, serving until 1989. Dobrynin retired from the Central Committee in 1988 but continued to serve as a foreign policy adviser to Gorbachev until the collapse of the Soviet Union in late 1991. Beginning in 1995, Dobrynin became a consultant to the Russian Foreign Ministry. He died in Moscow on April 6, 2010.

Steven W. Guerrier

See also Gromyko, Andrey Andreyevich; Jupiter Missiles (Turkey and Italy); Kennedy, John Fitzgerald; Kennedy, Robert Francis; Khrushchev, Nikita Sergeyevich; Rusk, Dean David; United Nations; U-2 Overflights; Zorin, Valerian Aleksandrovich

References

Brugioni, Dino A. *Eyeball to Eyeball: Inside the Cuban Missile Crisis.* Edited by Robert F. McCort. New York: Random House, 1993.

Dobrynin, Anatoly. *In Confidence: Moscow's Ambassador to America's Six Cold War Presidents (1962–1986).* Rev ed. Seattle: University of Washington Press, 2001.

Friedman, Norman. *The Fifty-Year War: Conflict and Strategy in the Cold War.* Annapolis, MD: Naval Institute Press, 2000.

Gelman, Harry. *The Brezhnev Politburo and the Decline of Détente.* Ithaca, NY: Cornell University Press, 1984.

Dulles, Allen Welsh (1893–1969)

Director of the U.S. Central Intelligence Agency (CIA), 1953–1961. Born in Watertown, New York, on April 7, 1893, Allen Dulles obtained a BA and an MA in international law from Princeton University and in 1916 joined the U.S. Foreign Service. Assigned first to Vienna, by the time the United States entered World War I Dulles was in Bern, Switzerland, where he nurtured U.S. embassy contacts with Austro-Hungarian and Balkan exiles. He served on the U.S. delegation to the 1919 Paris Peace Conference and in various positions overseas, but in 1926 financial considerations caused him to join the prominent New York law firm of Sullivan and Cromwell, where his brother John Foster Dulles was a leading partner. Allen Dulles remained deeply interested in foreign affairs, focusing on international business and becoming active in the New York–based Council on Foreign Relations.

A strong supporter of U.S. intervention in World War II, in 1942 Dulles joined the newly created U.S. intelligence agency, the Office of Strategic Services (OSS), headed by Col. William J. Donovan, and spent most of the war based in Bern in neutral Switzerland, running a network of German intelligence agents. By 1944 the prospect of communist and Soviet expansion in Europe troubled Dulles.

In spring 1945 Dulles helped negotiate the surrender of Germany's remaining forces in northern Italy. In what some have perceived as the opening move of the Cold War, U.S. and British forces initiated the surrender talks without involving their ally the Soviet Union, leading Soviet leader Joseph Stalin to believe that they intended to negotiate a separate peace with Germany. In late 1945, President Harry S. Truman disbanded the OSS. Dulles remained a strong advocate of a permanent U.S. foreign intelligence service and helped to draft the 1947 National Security Act, which created the CIA. In 1950 Dulles became CIA deputy director, and from 1953 to 1961 he served as the agency's third director. He deliberately publicized his agency's existence and accomplishments and was responsible for building its permanent headquarters in Langley, Virginia. President Dwight D. Eisenhower's 1953 appointment of John Foster Dulles as secretary of state, a post he held until his death in 1959, further enhanced the CIA director's official influence.

Besides analyzing intelligence, under Dulles the CIA mounted extensive covert operations, among them successful antileftist coups against the governments of Mohammed Mossadegh in Iran in 1953 and Jacobo Arbenz in Guatemala in 1954. Dulles later authorized a comparable effort to overthrow the radical new regime headed by Fidel Castro in Cuba. In March 1961 a poorly planned and botched U.S.-backed invasion attempt by Cuban exiles landing at the Bay of Pigs ended in highly publicized failure, a major international humiliation for the United States. President John F. Kennedy publicly accepted full responsibility but privately blamed Dulles, who resigned a few months later. In the early 1970s congressional investigations uncovered evidence on some of the CIA's past excesses overseas during the Dulles years that severely damaged the organization's reputation.

Dulles subsequently served on the Warren Commission that investigated Kennedy's assassination, undercutting its credibility when he admitted that to safeguard what they considered to be national security, CIA operatives might well lie even when giving evidence before the commission. In retirement Dulles wrote several books on intelligence. He died in Washington, D.C., on April 7, 1969.

Priscilla Roberts

See also: Bay of Pigs Invasion; Bissell, Richard Mervin, Jr.; Castro, Fidel; Central Intelligence Agency; Containment, Doctrine and Course of; Dulles, John Foster; Eisenhower, Dwight David; Kennedy, John Fitzgerald

References

Grose, Peter. *Gentleman Spy: The Life of Allen Dulles.* Boston: Houghton Mifflin, 1994.

Lucas, Scott. *Freedom's War: The American Crusade against the Soviet Union.* New York: New York University Press, 1999.

Ranelagh, John. *The Agency: The Rise and Decline of the CIA.* New York: Simon and Schuster, 1986.

Srodes, James. *Allen Dulles: Master of Spies.* Washington, DC: Regnery, 1999.

Zegart, Amy B. *Flawed by Design: The Evolution of the CIA, JCS, and NSC.* Stanford, CA: Stanford University Press, 1999.

Dulles, John Foster (1888–1959)

U.S. secretary of state (1953–1959). Born in Washington, D.C., on February 25, 1888, John Foster Dulles studied under Woodrow Wilson at Princeton University and at the Sorbonne, earned a law degree from George

Washington University, and in 1911 joined the prestigious Wall Street law firm of Sullivan and Cromwell. Appointed to the U.S. delegation at the 1919 Paris Peace Conference, Dulles unsuccessfully sought to restrain Allied reparations demands on Germany.

Active between the wars in internationalist organizations, during World War II Dulles focused intensely on postwar planning and became prominent in Republican politics. Seeking to secure bipartisan political support on foreign policy, President Harry S. Truman included Dulles in virtually all major international meetings, beginning with the 1945 San Francisco Conference that drafted the final United Nations Charter. Briefly appointed Republican senator for New York in 1948–1949, Dulles strongly supported creation of the North Atlantic Treaty Organization (NATO). He also favored European integration as a means of strengthening the continent's economies and militaries. By the late 1940s Dulles had become a dedicated anticommunist.

As a foreign affairs adviser to the Republican presidential campaign in 1952, Dulles argued that the Truman administration had been timorous in merely containing Soviet communism when it should have moved to roll back Soviet influence in Eastern Europe.

Named secretary of state by President Dwight D. Eisenhower in 1953, Dulles deferred to the president's leadership, although the two men were very different in style. A supporter of Eisenhower's New Look defense policy of heavy reliance on nuclear weapons, in tactics that came to be known as "brinkmanship" Dulles rhetorically threatened "massive retaliation" against the United States' enemies. In practice, he was often more cautious and followed pragmatic policies, effectively respecting established Soviet interests in Europe. When discontented East Berlin workers triggered an uprising in the German Democratic Republic (GDR) (East Germany) in 1953 and again when Hungarians rebelled against Soviet rule in 1956, Dulles and Eisenhower welcomed refugees but offered no further support.

Dulles and Eisenhower ended the Korean War in 1953, pressuring both sides to accept an armistice, and established a series of alliances around Asia and the Middle East. When possible, Eisenhower avoided direct major military interventions, preferring to rely on covert operations orchestrated by the Central Intelligence Agency (CIA), headed by Dulles's younger brother Allen. The CIA played key roles in coups that overthrew Left-leaning governments in Iran in 1953 and Guatemala in 1954. These were precursors of subsequent CIA-orchestrated efforts to overthrow the radical government Fidel Castro established in Cuba in 1959.

The emergence of Nikita Khrushchev as top Soviet leader in the mid-1950s seemed to promise relaxation of U.S.-Soviet tensions, as Khrushchev openly repudiated Stalinist tactics and called for peaceful coexistence between communist and noncommunist nations. Eisenhower hoped to conclude substantive disarmament agreements with Khrushchev. In practice, however, Khrushchev was often far from accommodating. The Soviet Union's success in launching the first space satellite (*Sputnik*) in 1957, Soviet possession of nuclear and thermonuclear weapons, and Khrushchev's seeming readiness from late 1958 onward to provoke an international crisis over Berlin all alarmed U.S. leaders, including the ailing Dulles, diagnosed in 1957 with cancer. When his health deteriorated, he resigned as secretary on April 15, 1959. Dulles died in Washington, D.C., on May 24, 1959.

Priscilla Roberts

See also: Berlin Crises; Central Intelligence Agency; Containment, Doctrine and Course of; Dulles, Allen Welsh; Eisenhower, Dwight David; Khrushchev, Nikita Sergeyevich; Military Balance; Nuclear Arms Race

References

Hoopes, Townsend. *The Devil and John Foster Dulles.* Boston: Little, Brown, 1973.

Immerman, Richard H. *John Foster Dulles: Piety, Pragmatism, and Power in U.S. Foreign Policy.* Wilmington, DE: Scholarly Resources, 1999.

Marks, Frederick W., III. *Power and Peace: The Diplomacy of John Foster Dulles.* Westport, CT: Praeger, 1993.

Toulouse, Mark G. *The Transformation of John Foster Dulles: From Prophet of Realism to Priest of Nationalism.* Macon, GA: Mercer University Press, 1985.

Tudda, Chris. *The Truth is Our Weapon: The Rhetorical Diplomacy of Dwight D. Eisenhower and John Foster Dulles.* Baton Rouge: Louisiana State University Press, 2006.

E

Eisenhower, Dwight David (1890–1969)

U.S. Army general, president of the United States (1953–1961). Born in Denison, Texas, on October 14, 1890, Dwight Eisenhower grew up in Abilene, Kansas, and graduated from the U.S. Military Academy, West Point, in 1915. In December 1943 he was named to command the Allied forces scheduled to invade Western Europe in 1944, and in spring 1945 he was promoted to general of the army. Military success translated into political viability. In 1952 the Republican Party, desperate to choose a candidate assured of victory, turned to Eisenhower, who won the subsequent election.

As president, Eisenhower largely endorsed existing Cold War policies, staunchly opposing global communism. He solidified U.S. defense commitments around the world into a network of bilateral and multilateral alliances. A fiscal conservative uneasy with high defense budgets, Eisenhower introduced the New Look strategy of relying heavily on nuclear weapons rather than on conventional forces. Alarmed by the increasing destructiveness of nuclear armaments, however, Eisenhower was the first president to attempt, albeit rather unsuccessfully, to reach arms-control agreements with the Soviet Union.

As the Bandung Non-Aligned Movement gained strength around the developing world—especially in decolonizing Asia, Africa, and the Middle East, where nationalist sentiments frequently ran high—Eisenhower sought to entice Third World nations into the U.S. camp. As president, Eisenhower was generally cautious in risking American troops in overseas interventions. Instead, he relied heavily on covert activities, authorizing the Central Intelligence Agency (CIA) to back coups in both Iran

As president, Dwight D. Eisenhower imposed sanctions on Fidel Castro's revolutionary regime and set in motion plans to overthrow Castro. Eisenhower's actions did much to set Cuba and the United States on a collision course and impelled Castro to turn to the Soviet Union for assistance. (Library of Congress)

and Guatemala in 1953 and 1954 and encouraging it to undertake numerous other secret operations.

After leftist insurgents led by Fidel Castro overthrew the government of Fulgencia Batista in Cuba in January 1959, there followed policies of radical land reform and nationalization that often expropriated American businesses in Cuba. The Eisenhower administration quickly turned against the new regime, with assorted economic sanctions. From spring 1959 Castro, despite public declarations that he was not a communist, therefore covertly sought Soviet aid and military protection, and U.S. economic pressure and commercial boycotts soon impelled him to move openly into the Soviet camp. In response, in March 1960 Eisenhower authorized the CIA to devise a scheme to train Cuban exiles based in Guatemala to invade the island and overthrow Castro. Eisenhower had no schedule for such an invasion, but he did want a plan to be in place and ready to execute at his decision. In early January 1961, shortly before leaving office, Eisenhower took the measure of ending U.S. recognition of Castro's government.

After the failure of the April 1961 Bay of Pigs invasion attempt, President John F. Kennedy consulted Eisenhower, who criticized his successor's non-authorization of air cover for the invading force and his reluctance to reveal the extent of U.S. backing for the exiles. While promising to support Kennedy's efforts to exclude communism from the Western Hemisphere, Eisenhower also warned that the American people would support intervention by U.S. military forces only when clear and serious provocation existed.

On October 17, 1962, CIA director John McCone briefed Eisenhower on the presence of Soviet nuclear-capable missiles in Cuba. The former president characterized the situation as "intolerable," pledged his support to Kennedy, and recommended prompt and decisive military action. On October 20, McCone again briefed Eisenhower on potential options: air strikes alone, air strikes plus invasion, and a naval blockade against Cuba. Consulted by Kennedy in person two days later, Eisenhower advised against air strikes alone but refused to choose between the other alternatives. Informed by Kennedy of his intention to impose a naval blockade, Eisenhower offered his support. A week later, Kennedy spoke to him again, outlining Soviet premier Nikita Khrushchev's agreement to withdraw the missiles in return for a U.S. commitment not to invade Cuba. Eisenhower warned Kennedy to exercise caution over the precise wording of the non-invasion pledge. In November 1962 he also urged McCone to insist that U.S. inspection teams enter Cuba to ensure all missiles had been removed, something Castro adamantly refused to sanction and on which Kennedy, to Eisenhower's private annoyance, was unwilling to insist. Eisenhower died in Washington, D.C., on March 28, 1969.

Priscilla Roberts

See also: Batista y Zaldívar, Fulgencio; Bay of Pigs Invasion; Berlin Crises; Castro, Fidel; Central Intelligence Agency; Containment, Doctrine and Course of; Dulles, Allen Welsh; Dulles, John Foster; Kennedy, John Fitzgerald; Khrushchev, Nikita Sergeyevich; McCone, John Alex; Missile Gap; Military Balance; Nuclear Arms Race; U-2 Overflights

References

Ambrose, Stephen E. *Eisenhower: The President.* 2 vols. New York: Simon and Schuster, 1984.

Ambrose, Stephen E., and Richard H. Immerman. *Ike's Spies: Eisenhower and the Espionage Establishment.* Garden City, NY: Doubleday, 1981.

Bowie, Robert R., and Richard H. Immerman. *Waging Peace: How Eisenhower Shaped an Enduring Cold War Strategy.* New York: Oxford University Press, 1998.

Dockrill, Saki. *Eisenhower's New Look: National Security Policy, 1953–1961.* New York: St. Martin's Press, 1996.

Korda, Michael. *Ike: An American Hero.* New York: HarperCollins, 2007.

Newton, Jim. *Eisenhower: The White House Years.* New York: Doubleday, 2011.

Perret, Geoffrey. *Eisenhower.* New York: Random House, 1999.

Rabe, Stephen G. *Eisenhower and Latin America: The Foreign Policy of Anticommunism.* Chapel Hill: University of North Carolina Press, 1988.

Smith, Jean Edward. *Eisenhower in War and Peace.* New York: Random House, 2012.

Welch, Richard E., Jr. *Response to Revolution: The United States and the Cuban Revolution, 1959–1961.* Chapel Hill: University of North Carolina Press, 1985.

F

Feklisov (Fomin), Aleksandr (1914–2007)

KGB officer, head of Soviet intelligence, Washington, D.C., 1960–1963. Aleksandr Feklisov was born in Moscow on March 9, 1914, the son of a railway signalman. In 1939 he joined the NKVD—the Soviet intelligence service, predecessor of the KGB—taking the cover name "Fomin" and specializing in gathering foreign scientific and technological information. Based in New York from 1941 to 1947 and then in London, he helped recruit and run highly effective espionage networks of scientists working on nuclear technology, electronic devices, radio equipment, and jet aircraft, including the now infamous spies Klaus Fuchs and Julius and Ethel Rosenberg. On Fuchs's arrest in 1950, Feklisov returned to Moscow, served in Czechoslovakia, and from 1955 to 1960 headed the KGB First Chief Directorate, responsible for overseas espionage.

From 1960 to 1964 Feklisov, officially counselor at the Soviet embassy in Washington, D.C., headed its KGB operations. In March 1962 he reported that an outright U.S. invasion of Cuba was unlikely unless the Cubans attacked the U.S. naval base at Guantánamo Bay or the Soviets installed nuclear-capable missiles on the island. Once the Cuban Missile Crisis became public, gossip circulated by American journalists convinced Feklisov that a U.S. invasion of Cuba was imminent. Acting apparently on his own volition, without KGB or Politburo authorization, on October 26, 1962, he contacted John Scali, an ABC News State Department correspondent with good contacts in the Kennedy administration, to discuss a potential settlement. During their lunchtime conversation, Feklisov reportedly warned Scali that, should the United States invade Cuba, Soviet forces would attack West Berlin, and suggested a settlement whereby the

Soviet Union would remove its missiles from Cuba, whose leader, Fidel Castro, would agree not to accept any further offensive weaponry, in exchange for a U.S. pledge not to invade Cuba. Later that day Scali reported this conversation to the State Department, where Secretary of State Dean Rusk interpreted it, however unauthorized, as a positive indication of Soviet willingness to compromise. Scali and Feklisov met again that evening, when Scali confirmed these terms might represent an acceptable basis for a settlement. U.S. officials believed that Feklisov's initiative marked a shift in the original intransigent Soviet position, and a letter Premier Nikita Khrushchev dispatched on October 26, conveying similar proposals, seemed to confirm this. Although Feklisov was effectively freelancing, his report to Moscow helped convince top Soviet officials that an arrangement along these lines might prove feasible.

In further conversations with Scali on October 29 and November 3, Feklisov warned that Soviet officials found it very hard to control Castro, who deeply resented that they had conducted settlement negotiations with the United States without consulting him and was proving intransigent over accepting the terms agreed. Scali assured Feklisov that Kennedy did not seek to humiliate Khrushchev, and then relayed Feklisov's information to ExComm.

Reassigned to Moscow in 1964, Feklisov trained spies at the KGB's Red Banner Institute until his retirement 10 years later. In later life he earned a doctorate in history, wrote several volumes of memoirs—which critics alleged exaggerated his significance in the Cuban Missile Crisis and other events—and hinted at his involvement in other secret operations "too recent to be told." He died in Moscow on October 26, 2007.

Priscilla Roberts

See also: Castro, Fidel; Guantánamo Bay Naval Base; Kennedy, John Fitzgerald; Khrushchev, Nikita Sergeyevich; Rusk, Dean David

References

Andrew, Christopher, and Oleg Gordievsky. *The KGB: The Inside Story of Its Foreign Operations from Lenin to Gorbachev.* London: Hodder and Stoughton, 1990.

Feklisov, Alexander. *The Man behind the Rosenbergs.* Translated by Catherine Dop. New York: Enigma Books, 2001.

Fursenko, Aleksandr, and Timothy Naftali. *One Hell of a Gamble: Khrushchev, Castro, and Kennedy, 1958–1964.* New York: Norton, 1997.

Salinger, Pierre. *With Kennedy.* New York: Avon Books, 1966.

G

Gilpatric, Roswell Leavitt (1906–1996)

Roswell Gilpatric was born in Brooklyn on November 4, 1906. In 1931 he joined the premier New York law firm Cravath, Swaine & Moore (then Cravath, de Gersdorff, Swaine & Wood). As legal representative for the Finnish government and large industrial clients, during World War II Gilpatric acquired a lifelong interest in defense policy and government service. In May 1951, during the Korean War, Gilpatric became assistant secretary of the Air Force for matériel, directing aircraft procurement and production; in October 1951 he was promoted to undersecretary, a position he held until January 1953. Gilpatric served on the 1956–1957 Rockefeller Brothers Fund panel on defense, which produced the Gaither report, recommending major increases in weapons research and spending.

In January 1961 President John F. Kennedy appointed Gilpatric, who had advised him on national security issues during his campaign, deputy secretary of defense. Serving under Robert McNamara, Gilpatric supervised procurement and overseas weapons sales, successfully persuading European allies to strengthen their defenses and narrow the dollar gap through massive purchases of U.S. military supplies.

As one of the Executive Committee (ExComm) of top-level advisers Kennedy created to handle the Cuban Missile Crisis, Gilpatric usually accompanied McNamara to meetings. Although he habitually said little, he made one important intervention on October 20, when ExComm debated whether to launch direct air strikes on Cuban missile sites or merely impose a naval blockade on Cuba. McNamara and Gilpatric consistently favored the second, less risky option. Gilpatric finally summed up: "Essentially, Mr. President, this is a choice between limited action and unlimited action; and most of us think that it's better to start with limited action." Kennedy followed his advice. Once the crisis was resolved, Gilpatric took part in lengthy negotiations with Soviet deputy prime minister Vasily V. Kuznetsov on the settlement's detailed implementation.

After leaving office in late 1963, Gilpatric wrote extensively on disarmament, military policy, and international affairs, consistently endorsing successive disarmament treaties and urging rationalization of the defense establishment. On March 15, 1996, he died of prostate cancer in Manhattan.

Priscilla Roberts

See also: Kennedy, John Fitzgerald; Kuznetsov, Vasili Vasilyevich; McNamara, Robert Strange; Nuclear Arms Race; U.S. Allies

References

Borklund, Carl W. *The Department of Defense.* New York: Praeger, 1968.

Borklund, Carl W. *Men of the Pentagon: From Forrestal to McNamara.* New York: Praeger, 1966.

Nalty, Bernard C., ed. *Winged Shield, Winged Sword: A History of the USAF.* 2 vols. Washington, DC: Air Force History and Museums Program, United States Air Force, 1997.

Shapley, Deborah, *Promise and Power: The Life and Times of Robert McNamara.* Boston: Little, Brown, 1993.

Gribkov, Anatoli Ivanovich (1919–2008)

Soviet major general, deputy head of the Main Operations Directorate, Soviet General Staff. Anatoli Gribkov was born on March 23, 1919, in Dukhovoye, in the Liskinsky District of Voronezh Province in Russia, one of ten children of a peasant family. He served as a tank officer in the Russo-Finnish War and then in Latvia. When German forces invaded Russia in June 1941, Gribkov fought in Belarus, Smolensk, and the defense of Moscow, and then spent five months studying at the J. V. Stalin Armored Troops School. He saw combat service on the Kalinin front, took part in the Battle of Kursk, and fought on the southern front in the Ukraine, winning numerous decorations. After the war Gribkov studied at the General Staff Academy, receiving high honors, and served in the Leningrad and

Kiev military districts, winning promotion to major general in 1958. In early 1961 Gribkov became chief of operations in the Main Operations Directorate of the Soviet General Staff.

In May 1962 Col. Gen. Semyon Pavlovich Ivanov, head of the Main Operations Directorate, instructed Gribkov to prepare detailed plans for Operation ANADYR, the deployment to Cuba of over 50,000 Soviet combat troops, equipped with conventional and nuclear-capable weapons, together with a substantial naval force of cruisers, destroyers, and submarines, some of which would likewise carry nuclear armaments. Under considerable pressure, between May and October 1962 Gribkov and his subordinates planned and implemented this operation, observing great secrecy. In September 1962, after U.S. President John F. Kennedy warned publicly against any Soviet installation of nuclear-capable weapons on Cuba, Soviet leaders reduced the naval component to four nuclear-armed submarines but supplemented the nuclear-capable weaponry with a squadron of Il-28 light bombers, equipped with six atomic bombs, and three detachments of Luna short-range missiles, with a total of 12 two-kiloton warheads.

In October 1962, growing Soviet fears that the U.S. government was likely to discover and react strongly to the presence of these forces in Cuba impelled Soviet defense minister Rodion Malinovsky to dispatch Gribkov to Cuba, heading a military mission whose purpose was to accelerate the construction of military installations and the deployment of Soviet weapons. A second objective of Gribkov's presence was to underline the Kremlin's insistence that Gen. Issa Alexandrovich Pliyev, who commanded Soviet forces in Cuba, refrain from any use of R-12 medium-range or R-14 intermediate-range nuclear-armed ballistic missiles against U.S. targets without specific Kremlin authorization and employ only tactical Luna and FKR short-range tactical nuclear-armed weapons in actual battlefield situations if he lost contact with superiors in Moscow. On October 22, Gribkov later recalled, as Kennedy publicly demanded the withdrawal of Soviet nuclear-capable missiles from Cuba, Malinovsky tightened Kremlin control when he cabled further instructions to Pliyev that no nuclear-armed weapons whatever should be used even in combat situations. How effective these constraints would have been in battlefield conditions, especially since subsequent instructions from Moscow on the subject over the next week were somewhat ambivalent, has never been entirely clear. When the crisis was resolved, Gribkov remained in Cuba until late November, supervising the removal of the R-12 and R-14 missiles and warheads, the Il-28s, and one batch of short-range missiles before returning to Moscow.

Gribkov was luckier than Colonel General Ivanov, who took the blame for the abortive Cuban venture and was dismissed as head of the General Staff's Operations Directorate. Gribkov, by contrast, flourished, receiving the Order of Lenin in 1963 and promotion to lieutenant general for his accomplishments, and became deputy chief of the Operations Directorate. He later commanded the Seventh Guards Army, stationed in Armenia, and the Leningrad Military District, rising to colonel general in 1973 and general of the army in 1976. From then until 1989 he served simultaneously as chief of staff of the Warsaw Pact armed forces and first deputy chief of the Soviet Armed Forces General Staff. For three additional years he served as inspector general of the Soviet armed forces, retiring in 1992.

Gribkov's revelations, at a 1992 conference of former Soviet, American, and Cuban officials held at Havana, that at the height of the crisis in October 1962 there were almost 42,000 Soviet military personnel on Cuba, together with 36 nuclear warheads for 24 medium-range ballistic missile sites, many of them operational, 80 nuclear warheads for FKR short-range cruise missiles, 12 nuclear warheads for short-range Luna rockets, and six atomic bombs suitable for delivery by specially adapted Il-28s, created a sensation. So, too, did his statement that for substantial periods during the crisis Pliyev had discretionary authority from the Kremlin to use the short-range tactical weapons in battlefield combat against any U.S. attackers. In retirement Gribkov wrote his memoirs, published in German in 1992, and numerous other works. He died in Moscow on February 12, 2008.

Priscilla Roberts

See also: ANADYR, Operation; Castro, Fidel; Kennedy, John Fitzgerald; Khrushchev, Nikita Sergeyevich; Malinovsky, Rodion Yakovlevich; Pliyev, Issa Alexandrovich

References

Blight, James G., Bruce J. Allyn, and David A. Welch. *Cuba on the Brink: Castro, the Missile Crisis, and the Soviet Collapse.* New York: Pantheon Books, 1993.

Fursenko, Aleksandr, and Timothy Naftali. *One Hell of a Gamble: Khrushchev, Castro, and Kennedy, 1958–1964.* New York: Norton, 1997.

Gribkov, Anatoli I. *Im Dienste der Sowjet-Union: Erinnerungen eines Armeegenerals* [In the Service of the Soviet Union: Memoirs of a General of the Army]. Berlin: edition q, 1992.

Gribkov, Anatoli I., and William Y. Smith. *Operation ANADYR: U.S. and Soviet Generals Recount the Cuban Missile Crisis.* Edited by Alfred Friendly, Jr. Chicago, Berlin, Tokyo, and Moscow: edition q, 1994.

Gromyko, Andrey Andreyevich (1909–1989)

Soviet diplomat, foreign minister (1957–1985), and president (1985–1988). Born on July 18, 1909, to a peasant family in Starye Gromyki, Belorussia, Andrey Gromyko studied agricultural economics at the Minsk School of Agricultural Technology, earning a degree in 1936. After working as a research associate and economist at the Soviet Academy of Sciences in Moscow, he entered the Foreign Affairs Ministry, where he was named chief of the U.S. division of the People's Commissariat of Foreign Affairs in 1939. That same year he began working at the Soviet embassy in Washington, D.C. In 1943 Soviet leader Josef Stalin appointed Gromyko as Moscow's youngest-ever ambassador to the United States.

Gromyko played an important role in coordinating the wartime alliance between the United States and the Soviet Union, attending the February 1945 Yalta Conference, the July–August 1945 Potsdam Conference, and the October 1945 conference establishing the United Nations (UN). He became Moscow's UN representative in 1946. Gromyko served briefly as ambassador to the United Kingdom during 1952–1953 and then returned to the Soviet Union. In 1956 Gromyko attained full membership on the Central Committee of the Communist Party of the Soviet Union (CPSU). In 1957 he began his 28-year tenure as foreign minister. In 1973 he ascended to the Politburo. During his long career, Gromyko became known as an expert and cunning negotiator. In the West he was dubbed "Mr. Nyet" (Mr. No) because of his hard bargaining and staunch communist views. At home, he exhibited a great talent for adjusting to ruling leaders, failing to develop his own characteristic political line.

From 1958 to 1964 Gromyko readily adapted to Premier Nikita Khrushchev's erratic whims, playing a key role in the Berlin Crises and the Cuban Missile Crisis. Reportedly, Gromyko originally opposed Khrushchev's plan to install nuclear-capable missiles secretly on Cuba, though he later acquiesced in the proposal. Visiting the United States, on October 18, 1962, Gromyko met with U.S. President John F. Kennedy and Secretary of State Dean Rusk, who unbeknown to him were already aware of the presence of Soviet missiles on Cuba. Gromyko's assurances that Cuba possessed no offensive weapons annoyed both men, but neither betrayed this. Gromyko sent reassuring but inaccurate messages back to Moscow that the Kennedy administration had not discovered the real situation in Cuba.

Soviet leader Leonid Brezhnev, who dominated Soviet politics from Khrushchev's ouster in 1964 to his own death in 1982, gave Gromyko virtual free rein in setting Soviet foreign policy. Under Brezhnev, Gromyko reached the apogee of his powers. During 1973–1975 Gromyko negotiated on behalf of the Soviet Union during the Conference on Security and Co-operation in Europe, which led to the landmark 1975 Helsinki Final Act. This act recognized Europe's postwar borders and set a political template for further negotiations concerning human rights, science, economics, and cultural exchanges. The Helsinki Final Act marked the full flowering of East-West détente, but because it did not match expectations about liber-alization in the Soviet Union and Eastern Europe, it precipitated mounting dissent at home and protest abroad.

In 1985 Soviet leader Mikhail Gorbachev appointed his own protégé, Eduard Shevardnadze, as foreign minister and named Gromyko president of the Presidium of the Supreme Soviet of the USSR, by then a purely symbolic position. He remained in this post until 1988. Gromyko died on July 2, 1989, in Moscow.

Beatrice de Graaf

See also: Dobrynin, Anatoly Fyodorovich; Kennedy, John Fitzgerald; Khrushchev, Nikita Sergeyevich; Rusk, Dean David; United Nations

References

Gromyko, Anatoli. *Andrey Gromyko: In the Kremlin's Labyrinth.* Moscow: Avtor, 1997.

Gromyko, Andrei. *Memories.* New York: Arrow Books, 1989.

Guantánamo Bay Naval Base

The only U.S. military base on communist-held territory and the site of much East-West discord during the Cold War. Located on both sides of an impressive harbor on the southwestern coast of Cuba, the Guantánamo Bay naval base (officially termed Naval Station Guantánamo Bay) has been occupied by the United States since the early 20th century.

U.S. troops first landed at Guantánamo Bay in June 1898, during the Spanish-American War. In a 1903 agreement, the United States leased 28,817 acres, or about 45 square miles of land and water, around Guan-tánamo Bay from the new Republic of Cuba. A 1934 treaty modified the original lease, stipulating that the base would revert to Cuban sovereignty only if both nations agreed to the change.

Cuba's post-1959 government, led by communist dictator Fidel Castro, steadfastly refused to accept the legality of the base or the payments stipulated in the lease. Cubans argued that the original lease was forced on a weak, newly independent Cuba as part of the 1902 Platt Amendment, which gave the United States the right to intervene in Cuban affairs indefinitely.

U.S. strategic justifications for retaining the base have undergone various permutations. Guantánamo was initially built as a coaling station to resupply the U.S. fleet. As coal-fueled ships became obsolete, the United States sought other pretexts to keep the base. Guantánamo, it was subsequently argued, gave the United States control over Atlantic entry to the Caribbean as well as sea routes between its Atlantic coast ports and the Panama Canal. When changes in military technology and the end of the Cold War inspired a debate over the base's future in the 1990s, Washington argued that the base was vital to U.S. efforts to interdict drug smugglers from Central and South America.

Cuban critics have condemned the U.S. government's use of the base to interfere in the economic and political affairs of Cuba. Indeed, Guantánamo was used to stage U.S. interventions in Cuba in 1906 and 1912 and during 1917–1919, ostensibly to stabilize political disturbances and to protect U.S.-owned sugar properties in the region.

Following the 1959 Cuban Revolution, Guantánamo was at the center of the Cold War conflict between the United States and communist Cuba, supported by the Soviet Union. During John F. Kennedy's presidency, his brother, Attorney General Robert F. Kennedy, intermittently contemplated faking an attack on the base by Cuban revolutionary forces to provide a pretext for a U.S. invasion of the island. During the Cuban Missile Crisis, U.S. officials anticipated that one response to any U.S. moves against the island would be Soviet and Cuban attacks on Guantánamo. They therefore ordered the evacuation from the base of U.S. dependants and nonessential personnel, while airlifting an additional 3,600 Marine troops and 3,200 tons of military equipment into the base to reinforce its defenses. On October 26 and 27, with the crisis still unresolved, several hundred Soviet troops moved nuclear-capable cruise missiles to advance positions from which they could launch an attack on Guantánamo. One truck bearing a missile overturned, crushing two soldiers and a Cuban bystander to death. In the immediate aftermath of the crisis, as Soviet and U.S. representatives negotiated details of the removal of Soviet missiles in November and December 1962, Castro unavailingly sought to include the return of Guantánamo as part of the crisis settlement.

In subsequent years the base remained a U.S.-Cuban flashpoint. Defecting Cubans entering Guantánamo, a 1964 attempt by the Cuban government to cut water supplies to the base, and clashes between U.S. and Cuban troops along the fence surrounding the base all created tension. The Cubans also interpreted naval maneuvers conducted from Guantánamo during the Jimmy Carter, Ronald Reagan, and George H. W. Bush administrations as assaults on Cuban sovereignty.

In 1992, Camp X-Ray was built at the base to house Haitian refugees seeking entrance to the United States. In 1994, Guantánamo received thousands of Cubans who wished to leave the island. Eight years later, prisoners captured in the U.S. invasion of Afghanistan began to be ferried to the base for indefinite detention. Evidence of ill treatment of prisoners at the base provoked a wide-ranging debate within the United States and abroad during 2002–2007.

Priscilla Roberts

See also: ANADYR, Operation; Castro, Fidel; Kennedy, John Fitzgerald; Kennedy, Robert Francis

References

Dobbs, Michael. *One Minute to Midnight: Kennedy, Khrushchev, and Castro on the Brink of Nuclear War.* New York: Knopf, 2008.

Hansen, Jonathan M. *Guantánamo: An American History.* New York: Hill and Wang, 2011.

Lipman, Jana K. *Guantánamo: A Working-Class History between Empire and Revolution.* Berkeley: University of California Press, 2008.

Mason, Theodore. *Across the Cactus Curtain: The Story of Guantánamo Bay.* New York: Dodd, Mead, 1984.

Ricardo, Roger. *Guantánamo: The Bay of Discord.* Melbourne, Australia: Ocean Press, 1994.

Schwab, Stephen Irving Max. *Guantánamo, USA: The Untold History of America's Cuban Outpost.* Lawrence: University Press of Kansas, 2009.

Strauss, Michael J. *The Leasing of Guantanamo Bay.* Westport, CT: Praeger Security International, 2009.

Guevara de la Serna, Ernesto "Che" (1928–1967)

Argentine Marxist revolutionary and contributor to the doctrine of revolutionary warfare, Cuban minister of the interior, 1959–1965. Born on

June 14, 1928, to a middle-class family in Rosario, Argentina, Ernesto "Che" Guevara de la Serna trained as a medical doctor at the University of Buenos Aires, graduating in 1953. That same year he traveled throughout Latin America, witnessing the early months of the Bolivian National Revolution and the last months of the October Revolution in Guatemala during the presidency of Jacobo Arbenz. America's covert 1954 operation that ousted the leftist Arbenz from power radicalized Guevara, as did his later encounter in Mexico with several Cuban revolutionaries, including Fidel Castro. Guevara subsequently joined Castro's expedition to Cuba in December 1956 and fought with his July 26 Movement until it triumphed in January 1959.

Guevara became Cuba's first president of the National Bank and then minister of industry in Cuba's early postrevolutionary government. With Fidel Castro's brother Raúl, he was among the strongest proponents of communism within the Cuban government. He developed close ties with Aleksandr Alekseev, a Soviet KGB espionage agent who first came to Havana in October 1959 and was appointed Soviet ambassador in May 1962. Guevara and Raúl Castro both believed that a July 1960 Soviet declaration warning the United States against attacking Cuba had deterred an anticipated U.S.-backed invasion attempt in October 1960. In November 1960, Guevara visited Moscow, Prague, and Beijing, celebrating the November 7 anniversary of the Russian Revolution with Soviet leaders. At this time, he reportedly broached the idea of basing Soviet nuclear-capable missiles in Cuba with Party Secretary Nikita Khrushchev, a suggestion that may have sown the seeds of the Cuban Missile Crisis. Visiting Moscow in August 1962, Guevara initialed the secret Cuban-Soviet defense agreement governing the installation and operation of nuclear-capable missiles and other Soviet forces in Cuba.

Guevara, like Fidel Castro, deplored Khrushchev's decision to make concessions to the United States in October 1962 and remove Soviet missiles from Cuba. He warned Soviet officials that their actions during the crisis had weakened the Soviet Union's credibility around the world as a leader of international revolutionary movements. After the crisis had been resolved, Guevara told Anastas Mikoyan, a senior member of the Soviet Presidium, who visited Cuba in November 1962 to supervise the removal of the missiles, of his deep skepticism that the United States would honor its pledge not to invade Cuba in the future. In the economic sphere, he subsequently rejected the counsel of more orthodox Marxist and Soviet advisers and followed Chinese Communist developmental teachings as propounded by Chairman Mao Zedong, which proved largely unsuccessful in Cuba as in China.

Guevara left Cuba in 1965, possibly motivated by disagreement with its political leadership and certainly because of a long-standing commitment to promoting worldwide revolution. Guevara traveled to the Congo in 1965 and then to Bolivia in 1966, in the hope of initiating an insurrection that would become a focus for the transformation of neighboring countries. Guevara's overwhelming goal was to provide a diversion that would weaken U.S. resolve and resources then dedicated to waging war in Vietnam.

A Bolivian Army unit captured Guevara in the Yuro ravine on October 8, 1967, and summarily executed him the next day at La Higuera, Villagrande. One of his hands was removed to facilitate identification by U.S. intelligence. Guevara's body was uncovered in an unmarked site in Bolivia in 1997 and, together with the remains of a number of other Cuban revolutionaries who died in Bolivia, repatriated to Cuba for interment in a monument in Santa Clara City.

Priscilla Roberts

See also: Alekseev (Shitov), Aleksandr Ivanovich; Castro, Fidel; Castro, Raúl; China, People's Republic of; Khrushchev, Nikita Sergeyevich; Mikoyan, Anastas Ivanovich

References

Anderson, Jon Lee. *Che Guevara: A Revolutionary Life*. Rev. ed. New York: Grove Press, 2010.

Castañeda, Jorge. *Companero: The Life and Death of Che*. New York: Vintage, 1998.

Fursenko, Aleksandr, and Timothy Naftali. *One Hell of a Gamble: Khrushchev, Castro, and Kennedy, 1958–1964*. New York: Norton, 1997.

Guevara, Ernest Che. *Che: The Diaries of Ernesto Che Guevara*. New York: Ocean Press, 2009.

Löwy, Michael. *The Marxism of Che Guevara: Philosophy, Economics and Revolutionary Warfare*. New York: Monthly Review Press, 1974.

Reid-Henry, Simon. *Fidel* and *Che: A Revolutionary Friendship*. London: Sceptre, 2008.

H

Harriman, William Averell (1891–1986)

Ambassador-at-large, 1961; assistant secretary of state for Far Eastern affairs, 1962–1963; undersecretary of state for political affairs, 1963–1964. William Averell Harriman was born in New York City on November 15, 1891. He inherited the massive fortune of his father, the railroad tycoon E. H. Harriman. During World War II Harriman served as President Franklin D. Roosevelt's special envoy to British prime minister Winston Churchill and Soviet leader Joseph Stalin (1941–1943), and then as U.S. ambassador to the Soviet Union (1943–1946). Under President Harry S. Truman, he was ambassador to Great Britain (1946), secretary of commerce (1946–1948), special representative in Europe for the Economic Cooperation Administration (1948–1950), special assistant to the president (1950–1951), and head of the Mutual Security Administration (1951–1953). In 1954 he was elected governor of New York, serving one four-year term.

Harriman considered himself a Russian expert. In 1959 he toured the Soviet Union, where he had lengthy interviews with Soviet premier Nikita Khrushchev. When Khrushchev visited the United States later that year, Harriman reciprocated his hospitality. The two men fundamentally agreed on the need for arms-control agreements. Although not initially close to John F. Kennedy, in 1960 the office-hungry Harriman made strenuous efforts to win a foreign policy post. Beginning as ambassador-at-large, he became assistant secretary of state for Far Eastern affairs in 1962 and in March 1963 worked his way up to undersecretary of state for political affairs, third in seniority in the Department of State. In these years he developed a warm relationship with both the president and his brother Robert, the attorney general.

W. Averell Harriman, former U.S. ambassador to the Soviet Union and a close friend of Attorney General Robert F. Kennedy, was not formally a member of the Executive Committee (ExComm) of the National Security Council. During the Cuban Missile Crisis he made his views known and was a voice for moderation. (National Archives)

Initially, Kennedy largely ignored the advice Harriman was eager to offer him: to remain cool, calm, and relaxed when Khrushchev blustered and threatened and maintain a firm line on such issues as the status of Berlin, but do so through negotiations rather than military demonstrations. During the Cuban Missile Crisis, Harriman was not one of the Executive Committee (ExComm) inner circle of presidential advisers who deliberated over the U.S. response. As matters hung in the balance after Kennedy's public announcement on October 22 of the U.S. naval blockade of Cuba, Harriman worried that the United States might be forcing the beleaguered Khrushchev into a confrontation he wished to avoid. He shared these concerns with Arthur Schlesinger, Jr., Kennedy's special assistant, in the hope that they would reach the president. He also wrote to Robert Kennedy on October 22, warning that Khrushchev found particularly galling the presence of NATO Jupiter missiles in Turkey. In July 1963, Khrushchev agreed to resume negotiations for a nuclear test ban treaty, as Kennedy requested in his final public exchange of letters during the crisis. Harriman headed the delegation that negotiated an agreement whereby both powers as well as Britain agreed to halt atmospheric nuclear tests.

Harriman viewed with apprehension growing U.S. involvement in Indochina. In 1961–1962 he brokered a settlement between warring factions in Laos that sought to neutralize that country's participation in the burgeoning insurgency in South Vietnam. Harriman believed internal reforms and a negotiated settlement with the Viet Cong represented the best solution to South Vietnam's problems. Demoted by Lyndon B. Johnson, Kennedy's successor, to ambassador-at-large, and excluded from Johnson's inner circle of advisers, Harriman consistently advocated a bombing halt and the opening of negotiations with North Vietnam. In 1968 he represented the United States when such talks began in Paris, resigning when Richard M. Nixon took office in January 1969. Well into his 80s, Harriman remained active in Democratic Party politics. He died in Yorktown Heights, New York, on July 26, 1986.

Priscilla Roberts

See also: Berlin Crises; Containment, Doctrine and Course of; Jupiter Missiles (Turkey and Italy); Kennedy, John Fitzgerald; Kennedy, Robert Francis; Khrushchev, Nikita Sergeyevich; Johnson, Lyndon Baines; Nuclear Arms Race; Partial Test Ban Treaty; Schlesinger, Arthur Meier, Jr.

References

Abramson, Rudy. *Spanning the Century: The Life of W. Averell Harriman 1891–1986.* New York: Morrow, 1992.

Costigliola, Frank. *Roosevelt's Lost Alliances: How Personal Politics Helped Start the Cold War.* Princeton, NJ: Princeton University Press.

Halberstam, David. *The Best and the Brightest.* New York: Random House, 1973.

Harriman, W. Averell, and Eli Abel. *Special Envoy to Churchill and Stalin, 1941–1946.* New York: Random House, 1975.

Isaacson, Walter, and Evan Thomas. *The Wise Men: Six Friends and the World They Made.* New York: Simon and Schuster, 1986.

Mayers, David. *The Ambassadors and America's Soviet Policy.* New York: Oxford University Press, 1995.

Olson, Lynne. *Citizens of London: The Americans Who Stood with Britain in its Darkest, Finest Hour.* New York: Random House, 2010.

J

Johnson, Lyndon Baines (1908–1973)

Prominent Texas politician who served as 36th president of the United States from 1963 to 1969, succeeding the charismatic John F. Kennedy after his assassination in November 1963. Lyndon Johnson was born in Stonewall in the Texas Hills near Austin, Texas, on August 27, 1908. As a Democratic congressman from 1937 to 1948, senator for Texas from 1949 to 1960, and Senate majority leader from 1955 to 1960, Johnson won a towering political reputation, based on his ability to persuade often balky senators and congressmen to reach consensus on sometimes controversial legislation. During his political career Johnson acquired a respectable understanding of U.S. foreign policies, a perspective informed by the orthodox bipartisan Cold War internationalist consensus on the need to resist the expansion of Soviet communism that most leading American politicians of his time shared. He supported the economic embargo the United States imposed on Cuba in October 1960.

Selected in 1960 as Kennedy's running mate, as vice president Johnson had little input into policy and was excluded from Kennedy's inner circle of advisers. He was left ignorant of planning for the failed April 1961 Bay of Pigs invasion of Cuba. Johnson was, however, a member of the Executive Committee (ExComm) Kennedy established on October 16 to decide how the U.S. government should react to the discovery of Soviet nuclear-capable missile sites in Cuba. Although absent from October 17 to 20, he participated in the final week's deliberations, taking charge when Kennedy was not present.

Johnson initially favored surprise U.S. air strikes to destroy the missile installations and only reluctantly came round to supporting a blockade.

He adamantly opposed suggestions that the United States might consider resolving the Cuban impasse by allowing East Germany to take over West Berlin, a repeated demand of Soviet and East German officials since the late 1950s. He was, however, a strong advocate of removing NATO Jupiter missiles in Turkey in exchange for the dismantling of Soviet missile bases in Cuba, an arrangement that Attorney General Robert F. Kennedy, the president's brother, eventually negotiated as a secret U.S.-Soviet understanding. Johnson also unsuccessfully advised Kennedy against consulting congressional leaders on the crisis, warning that the president would not "get much help out of them." Johnson regarded the outcome of the Cuban Missile Crisis as a U.S. victory. The narrow escape from nuclear war apparently impelled not only President Kennedy but also Johnson actively to seek U.S.-Soviet détente, a policy Johnson supported after becoming president in November 1963.

While still vice president, Johnson concluded that the threat that communist Cuba under Fidel Castro represented to the United States had been "grossly exaggerated." He believed that encouraging Latin American economic development through the Alliance for Progress, a Kennedy administration initiative he strongly supported, was the most productive means of combating radical leftism.

As president, Johnson feared that secret Central Intelligence Agency (CIA) Operation MONGOOSE plots to destabilize Cuba and kill Castro might have impelled Lee Harvey Oswald, a leftist American who belonged to the Free Cuba committee, and Cuban radicals to retaliate by assassinating Kennedy. In late 1963 Johnson ordered the cessation of such operations. Although Johnson initially broke off secret negotiations between Kennedy and Castro, using U.S. and Cuban UN delegates as intermediaries, in early 1964 he began to explore the possibility of normalizing U.S. relations with Cuba, extending highly unofficial secret feelers to Castro while maintaining the economic blockade and continuing to sanction some covert intelligence efforts to sabotage the existing regime. In spring 1964 minor crises—later peacefully resolved—occurred when the U.S. coast guard seized Cuban fishing boats in U.S. waters and Castro retaliated by cutting off the water supply to the U.S. military base at Guantánamo Bay. Johnson's growing preoccupation with the escalating war in Vietnam may have prevented him devoting adequate attention to potential rapprochement with Cuba and also undermined his efforts to improve U.S.-Soviet relations. Ultimately, Johnson's failure to attain victory in Vietnam and growing popular disillusionment with the war destroyed his presidency, and in March 1968 he declared that he would not seek another presidential term. Johnson died at his Texas ranch on January 22, 1973, four years after leaving office.

Priscilla Roberts

See also: Bay of Pigs Invasion; Castro, Fidel; Central Intelligence Agency; Containment, Doctrine and Course of; Guantánamo Bay Naval Base; Jupiter Missiles; Kennedy, John Fitzgerald; Kennedy, Robert Francis; MONGOOSE, Operation; United Nations; U.S. Allies; U.S. Congress

References

Dallek, Robert. *Flawed Giant: Lyndon Johnson and His Times, 1961–1973.* New York: Oxford University Press, 1998.

Dumbrell, John. *President Lyndon Johnson and Soviet Communism.* Manchester: Manchester University Press, 2004.

Schwartz, Thomas A. *Lyndon Johnson and Europe: In the Shadow of Vietnam.* Cambridge, MA: Harvard University Press, 2003.

Woods, Randall B. *LBJ: Architect of American Ambition.* New York: Free Press, 2006.

Joint Chiefs of Staff

The U.S. Joint Chiefs of Staff (JCS) is a military committee consisting of the chiefs of staff of the U.S. Army and Air Force, the chief of naval operations, and the commandant of the Marine Corps. Its chairman, a separate officer drawn from one of the services, is a U.S. National Security Council member. Originating during World War II, the committee was formalized and codified under the 1947 National Security Act that created a Department of Defense incorporating the former War and Navy departments. The JCS advise the president, the secretary of defense, and the National Security Council and provide guidance to commanders in the field.

President John F. Kennedy's relationship with the JCS was difficult. One of the first decisions he faced when he took office was whether to endorse the plan formulated under his predecessor, President Dwight D. Eisenhower, for a CIA-sponsored invasion of Cuba by refugee Cuban exiles. Kennedy accepted the scheme in principle but insisted that the United States should not provide overt military support for the exiles and moved the projected landing site. He also severely limited the number and nature of U.S. air strikes and air cover during the operation. In the aftermath of the botched April 1961 Bay of Pigs invasion, which became a humiliating and embarrassing fiasco for the United States, Kennedy and his top civilian aides blamed the JCS for endorsing the plan, albeit with some qualifications, and not pointing out its weaknesses sufficiently forcefully. In his view, the JCS had expected that, should the invasion force encounter problems, Kennedy would drop the pretense of noninvolvement and intervene overtly to assist the rebels, something he was not prepared to sanction. On their side, the JCS considered Kennedy's refusal to give the rebels greater support evidence of weak and irresolute leadership. Adm. Arleigh Burke, chief of naval operations, had since early 1960 supported the overthrow of the Castro government and publicly cast doubt on Soviet premier Nikita Khrushchev's July 1960 pledge that the Soviet Union would if necessary use nuclear weapons to defend Cuba against U.S. attack. As the invading forces encountered greater resistance than anticipated, Burke begged Kennedy to allow him to send naval or air support, but after some wavering Kennedy refused.

One major casualty of the Bay of Pigs was Kennedy's relationship with the JCS. The JCS despised him for failing to escalate U.S. intervention, while Kennedy distrusted them. His relationship with Gen. Lyman Lemnitzer, chairman of the JCS, was particularly bad; the two men could scarcely bear to be in the same room. Burke, who soon leaked to the press information on the Bay of Pigs detrimental to Kennedy, had nothing but contempt for both the president and his secretary of defense, Robert S. McNamara. He retired as chief of naval operations on August 1, 1961, replaced by Adm. George Whelan Anderson, Jr. On June 30, 1961, the forceful Gen. Curtis LeMay also replaced Thomas D. White as chief of staff of the U.S. Air Force. In late April 1961, Kennedy brought in Maxwell D. Taylor, former chief of staff of the U.S. Army under Eisenhower, who had retired four years earlier, to investigate the Bay of Pigs. He soon appointed Taylor his principal military adviser, to serve as liaison with the JCS and as chairman of the Special Group (Augmented) on Cuba. On October 1, 1962, Kennedy appointed Taylor chairman of the Joint Chiefs of Staff, a post he held until mid-1964. Simultaneously, Earle G. Wheeler replaced George Decker as army chief of staff.

During the Cuban Missile Crisis, Taylor generally represented the JCS in the Executive Committee (ExComm) of the president's advisers. Initially he recommended a surgical strike against the missile bases, followed by a naval blockade to prevent the arrival of further weapons. Later that day, after consulting the JCS, he recommended massive air strikes on Cuban military facilities over several days but hoped to avoid outright U.S. invasion. The JCS met as a group with Kennedy on October 19, recommending massive air strikes against Cuban targets without advance warning, preferably on October 23. With the exception of Taylor, they also favored following this with a full-scale U.S. invasion of the island, measures they further assumed would mean war with the Soviet Union. By October 20 ExComm leaned toward favoring a naval blockade (or "quarantine") of Cuba. Taylor expressed disagreement on behalf of the JCS but pledged their complete backing for the president's decision. After Kennedy's public announcement of the quarantine on October 22, Taylor continued to support massive air strikes targeting all identified nuclear-capable and surface-to-air missile sites, plus all Soviet and Cuban airplanes and airfields. Anderson planned, implemented, and enforced the naval quarantine. On October 27, with negotiations with Khrushchev at a critical stage, the JCS once again recommended launching massive air strikes against Cuba on October 29, followed by an invasion one week later.

The JCS reacted with dismay when Khrushchev and Kennedy reached agreement on October 28, drafting a message to Kennedy characterizing the Soviet response as "an insincere proposal to gain time" that would leave missiles in Cuba and warning against any "relaxation of alert procedures." Anderson told Kennedy, "We have been had." LeMay described the understanding as "the greatest defeat in our history" and continued to urge an invasion. JCS invasion preparations continued into the first week of November. As lengthy negotiations over the removal of the weapons ensued, the JCS deplored Cuba's refusal to allow on-site inspections of missile sites in Cuba. LeMay unavailingly suggested that U.S. naval squadrons and bombers be positioned around Cuba and that, should Castro reject U.S. demands for access, they bomb the Cuban military command center. Castro also sought to retain Soviet Il-28 light bombers in Cuba. Informed of this in mid-November, the Joint Chiefs unanimously recommended that unless these left Cuba, the United States should either bomb them or land military personnel on Cuba to remove them. The dispute was resolved peacefully when Soviet officials agreed to send the Il-28s back to Russia. For the rest of his life Kennedy believed that, had he followed the advice of the JCS, full-scale nuclear war and global devastation would have resulted.

Priscilla Roberts

See also: Bay of Pigs Invasion; Castro, Fidel; Central Intelligence Agency; Eisenhower, Dwight David; Kennedy, John Fitzgerald; McNamara, Robert Strange; Taylor, Maxwell Davenport

References

Brugioni, Dino. *Eyeball to Eyeball: The Inside Story of the Cuban Missile Crisis.* Ed. Robert F. McCort. New York: Random House, 1991.

Dobbs, Michael. *One Minute to Midnight: Kennedy, Khrushchev, and Castro on the Brink of Nuclear War.* New York: Knopf, 2008.

Freedman, Lawrence. *Kennedy's Wars: Berlin, Cuba, Laos, and Vietnam.* New York: Oxford University Press, 2000.

Goduti, Philip A., Jr. *Kennedy's Kitchen Cabinet and the Pursuit of Peace: The Shaping of American Foreign Policy, 1961–1963.* Jefferson, NC: McFarland Press, 2009.

Gribkov, Anatoli I., and Smith, William Y. *Operation ANADYR: U.S. and Soviet Generals Recount the Cuban Missile Crisis.* Edited by Alfred Friendly, Jr. Chicago, Berlin, Tokyo, and Moscow: edition q, 1994.

McMaster, H. R. *Dereliction of Duty: Lyndon Johnson, Robert McNamara, the Joint Chiefs of Staff, and the Lies That Led to Vietnam.* New York: HarperCollins, 1997.

Polmar, Norman, and John D. Gresham. *DEFCON-2: Standing on the Brink of Nuclear War during the Cuban Missile Crisis.* New York: John Wiley, 2006.

Jupiter Missiles (Turkey and Italy)

In the late 1950s the United States developed virtually identical Jupiter and Thor intermediate-range ballistic missiles (IRBMs). Seeking to repair relations with Britain after the previous year's divisive Suez crisis, in March 1957 U.S. President Dwight D. Eisenhower offered such weapons to British prime minister Harold Macmillan, who agreed that 60 Thor missiles should be deployed on British territory, under joint U.S. and British control. They arrived in batches in 1959. In late 1957, in the aftermath of the Soviet launching of *Sputnik,* the first space satellite, the United States decided to offer Jupiter missiles to other U.S. North Atlantic Treaty Organization (NATO) allies in Europe. Following lengthy negotiations, France, West Germany, and Greece declined them, but in 1959 Italy agreed to accept 30 Jupiter missiles and Turkey 15. The warheads were to remain under U.S. control, with launching requiring approval from both U.S. and host governments. Soviet premier Nikita Khrushchev objected particularly strongly to Jupiter deployments in Turkey, because their 1,700-mile range meant these could reach numerous targets in western Soviet territory within a few minutes. Installation of missile bases in Italy was completed during 1961.

By 1961, the liquid-fueled, immobile Jupiters and Thors, highly vulnerable to a Soviet first strike, were already obsolete, as solid-fueled mobile missiles, often based on Polaris submarines, became available. Between February and April 1961, many U.S. officials recommended against installing Jupiters in Turkey, but Turkish leaders resisted cancellation and construction of the installations went ahead, with deployments completed between November 1961 and March 1962. Khrushchev repeatedly assailed the presence of missiles in Turkey, uncomfortably close to his Black Sea dacha. By summer 1962 the United States and Britain had agreed to remove increasingly obsolete Thor missiles within a year. U.S. officials sought similar arrangements with Turkey, but Turkish leaders protested strongly and the missiles remained undisturbed.

When U.S. reconnaissance planes discovered Soviet missile emplacements in Cuba in October 1962, sparking the Cuban Missile Crisis, from the outset President John F. Kennedy and his advisers recognized the possibility that Khrushchev would demand removal of NATO missiles in Turkey as a quid pro quo for dismantling Soviet nuclear-capable missile bases in Cuba. During the crisis, newspaper pundits, including the influential columnist Walter Lippmann and Max Frankel of the *New York Times,* openly suggested such a trade, as did Bruno Kreisky, Austria's foreign minister. Kennedy was reluctant to make a public bargain along these lines but allowed his brother, U.S. Attorney General Robert Kennedy, to explore the possibility with Anatoly Dobrynin, the Soviet ambassador in Washington, and Georgi Bolshakov, a Soviet military intelligence operative. Soviet and U.S. officials informally agreed that the United States would implement the withdrawal of Jupiter missiles in Turkey and Italy within a few months. Had these negotiations failed, Kennedy was ready to encourage U Thant, acting secretary general of the United Nations, to propose a similar arrangement. To sweeten the deal, if necessary Macmillan was also prepared to offer the (already settled) removal of Thor missiles from the United Kingdom, though as events transpired this inducement was not required. There are also some indications that, had the United States launched air strikes against Soviet bases in Cuba, U.S. officials considered not retaliating further should Khrushchev in response order attacks on Turkish Jupiter bases.

Fearful of repercussions, President Kennedy restricted knowledge of the U.S.-Soviet understanding to a very small circle—his brother Robert, Secretary of State Dean Rusk, National Security Adviser McGeorge Bundy, Defense Secretary Robert McNamara, and Ambassador Llewellyn Thompson—that excluded even most ExComm members. Most Soviet officials likewise remained ignorant of the agreement, since Khrushchev kept his word and maintained great secrecy regarding it. On October 29, 1962, McNamara established an interdepartmental task force to supervise removal of the missiles by April 1, 1963. Turkish officials, who had welcomed the Jupiter missiles enthusiastically, were reluctant to sanction their removal; Italian leaders were readier to relinquish their missiles in return for alternative security arrangements. To encourage Turkish and Italian compliance, the United States offered additional conventional and dual-purpose weapons, including F-104G fighter jets. In February 1963 the Kennedy administration announced the withdrawal of the Jupiters before consulting NATO's governing body, the North Atlantic Council, that supposedly controlled their deployment. By the end of April all Italian and Turkish Jupiter missiles had been dismantled. In their place, nuclear-armed U.S. Polaris submarines patrolled the Mediterranean.

Priscilla Roberts

See also: Bolshakov, Georgi Nikitovich; Bundy, McGeorge; Dobrynin, Anatoly Fyodorovich; Eisenhower, Dwight David; Kennedy, John Fitzgerald; Kennedy, Robert Francis; Khrushchev, Nikita Sergeyevich; McNamara, Robert Strange; Military Balance; Missile Gap; Nuclear Arms Race; Rusk, Dean David; Thompson, Llewellyn Edward, Jr.; U Thant; United Nations; U.S. Allies

References

Frankel, Max. *High Noon in the Cold War: Kennedy, Khrushchev, and the Cuban Missile Crisis.* New York: Ballantine Books, 2004.

Fursenko, Aleksandr, and Timothy Naftali. *One Hell of a Gamble: Khrushchev, Castro, and Kennedy, 1958–1964.* New York: Norton, 1997.

Nash, Philip. *The Other Missiles of October: Eisenhower, Kennedy, and the Jupiters, 1957–1963.* Chapel Hill: University of North Carolina Press, 1997.

K

Kennedy, John Fitzgerald (1917–1963)

U.S. congressman (1946–1952), senator (1953–1961), and president of the United States (1961–1963). John F. Kennedy was born in Brookline, Massachusetts, on May 29, 1917, into a large and wealthy Irish Catholic family. His father, Joseph P. Kennedy, was a multimillionaire with presidential aspirations, and his mother, Rose Fitzgerald, came from a prominent and politically active Boston family. After attending the elite Choate Preparatory School in Wallingford, Connecticut, Kennedy earned his bachelor's degree from Harvard University in 1940. During World War II Kennedy served four years in the U.S. Navy, winning the Navy and Marine Corps Medals and the Purple Heart for action as commander of PT-109, which was rammed and sunk by a Japanese destroyer in the South Pacific.

After the war, Kennedy worked briefly as a newspaper correspondent before entering national politics at the age of 29, winning election as a Democratic congressman from Massachusetts in 1946. Kennedy was elected to the U.S. Senate in 1952. His career there was relatively undistinguished, due in part to several serious health problems, including chronic back problems and Addison's disease. In 1960, he nonetheless won the Democratic nomination for president on the first ballot. As a candidate, Kennedy promised more aggressive defense policies, health care reform, and housing and civil rights programs. He also proposed his New Frontier agenda, designed to revitalize the flagging U.S. economy and to bring young people into government and humanitarian service. Winning by the narrowest of margins, he became the nation's first Roman Catholic president. Only 43 years old, he was also the youngest man ever elected to that office.

Democrat John F. Kennedy, elected president in November 1960, liked to project an image of Cold War toughness. In practice, during the Cuban Missile Crisis, he nonetheless proved flexible and sought to avoid a nuclear conflagration. (John F. Kennedy Presidential Library)

In his inaugural address, Kennedy urged Americans to be active citizens and to sacrifice for the common good. His address, in some respects a rather bellicose call to arms, ended with the now-famous exhortation "ask not what your country can do for you—ask what you can do for your country." As president, Kennedy set out to fulfill his campaign pledges. Once in office, he was forced to respond to the ever-more-urgent demands of civil rights advocates, although he did so rather reluctantly and tardily. By establishing both the Alliance for Progress and the Peace Corps, Kennedy delivered American idealism and goodwill to aid developing countries.

Despite Kennedy's idealism, his presidency witnessed growing tensions in U.S.-Soviet Cold War rivalry. Privately, in 1959 he had suggested that President Dwight Eisenhower's failure to welcome Cuba's revolutionary leader Fidel Castro when he visited the United Nations that year had been a mistake. During the 1960 presidential campaign Kennedy nonetheless excoriated the Eisenhower administration for its failure to eradicate Cuba's communist government. One of his first attempts to address the perceived communist threat was to authorize a band of U.S.-supported Cuban exiles to invade the island in an attempt to overthrow Castro's government. The April 1961 Bay of Pigs invasion, which turned into an embarrassing debacle for the president, had been planned by the Central Intelligence Agency (CIA) during Eisenhower's administration. Although Kennedy harbored reservations about the operation, he nonetheless approved it. Its failure heightened existing Cold War tensions with the Soviet Union and ultimately set the stage for the Cuban Missile Crisis. Kennedy and Castro to some degree became global competitors for the allegiance of idealistic young people around the world.

Cold War confrontation was not limited to Cuba. In spring 1961, the Soviet Union renewed its campaign to control West Berlin. Kennedy spent two days in Vienna in June 1961 discussing the hot-button issue with Soviet premier Nikita Khrushchev. In the months that followed, the construction of the Berlin Wall, which prevented East Berliners from escaping to the West, further intensified the Berlin crisis. Kennedy responded to the provocation by reinforcing troops in the Federal Republic of Germany (FRG) (West Germany) and increasing the nation's military strength. The Berlin Wall, albeit perhaps unintentionally, eased tensions in Central Europe that had nearly resulted in a superpower conflagration. Meanwhile, Kennedy began deploying what would become some 16,000 U.S. military "advisers" to prop up Ngo Dinh Diem's regime in the Republic of Vietnam (RVN) (South Vietnam), a commitment that set the United States on the slippery slope toward full-scale military intervention in Vietnam.

After the Bay of Pigs, Kennedy authorized various CIA and other covert initiatives intended, in tandem with economic sanctions, to sabotage, undermine, and destroy Castro's government. Fearing a second U.S. invasion attempt, and seeking to redress the nuclear strategic balance in their own favor, in May 1962 Soviet leaders decided to clandestinely install nuclear-capable missiles in Cuba. On October 14, 1962, U.S. reconnaissance planes photographed the construction of missile-launching sites in Cuba. The placement of nuclear-capable missiles only 90 miles from U.S. shores threatened to destabilize the Western Hemisphere and undermine the uneasy Cold War nuclear deterrent. Kennedy imposed a naval quarantine on Cuba, designed to interdict any offensive weapons bound for the island. On October 22 U.S. armed forces moved to DEFCON-3, a heightened state of alert, upgraded to DEFCON-2, only one level short of war, on October 25. For several days the outcome hung in the balance, as the two Cold War superpowers appeared close to thermonuclear war, but ultimately Soviet leaders agreed to remove the missiles. In return, the United States pledged not to preemptively invade Cuba and privately agreed to remove obsolete NATO nuclear missiles from Turkey. During the crisis, Kennedy secretly taped the discussions of his Executive Committee (ExComm) of senior advisers. When released in the 1990s, the transcripts revealed a man who, despite his initial belief that U.S. air strikes against the installations on Cuba were almost inevitable, soon leaned to the less confrontational option of a naval quarantine or blockade and was prepared to make substantial concessions in order to avoid escalation into a full-scale nuclear war.

These events sobered both Kennedy and Khrushchev. Following the nerve-wracking crisis, Kennedy took up the causes of civil rights and disarmament. Cold War tensions diminished when the Soviet, British, and

U.S. leaders signed the Partial Test Ban Treaty on August 5, 1963, forbidding atmospheric testing of nuclear weapons and also their testing under water or in outer space. In October 1963, the same three nations agreed to refrain from placing nuclear weapons in orbit. To avoid potential misunderstandings and miscalculations in a future crisis, a hotline was installed that directly linked the Oval Office with the Kremlin.

In July 1963 the U.S. Treasury Department imposed regulations forbidding all U.S. citizens to have any commercial or financial relations with Cuba. Despite his noninvasion pledge, in June 1963 Kennedy endorsed further CIA covert sabotage operations intended to destabilize Castro's government. Paradoxically, working through William Attwood, an adviser to Adlai Stevenson, the U.S. representative at the United Nations (UN), and Carlos Lechuga, Cuba's ambassador to the UN, Kennedy also responded favorably to exploratory feelers from Castro on the possibility of normalizing U.S.-Cuban relations. He suggested that the United States might lift its sanctions on Cuba if Castro dropped his support for revolutionary movements elsewhere in Latin America. On November 22, 1963, Kennedy's assassination in Dallas, Texas, during a political campaign trip cut short these overtures. Kennedy's successor, Lyndon B. Johnson, when informed of the Attwood-Lechuga channel in December 1963, ended the talks, considering them too politically compromising, liable to expose him to Republican charges that he was soft on communism. Lee Harvey Oswald, arrested for murdering the president, held leftist political views that had impelled him to join a Fair Play for Cuba Committee. Oswald, himself shot two days later by a nightclub owner, never stood trial, and it remained unclear how far sympathy for Cuba motivated him to gun down Kennedy. In a great national outpouring of grief, Kennedy was laid to rest in Arlington National Cemetery on November 25, 1963.

Lacie A. Ballinger

See also: Alliance for Progress; Bay of Pigs Invasion; Berlin Crises; Castro, Fidel; Central Intelligence Agency; Containment, Doctrine and Course of; Eisenhower, Dwight David; Johnson, Lyndon Baines; Kennedy, Robert Francis; Khrushchev, Nikita Sergeyevich; Military Balance; Missile Gap; Nuclear Arms Race; Partial Test Ban Treaty; Stevenson, Adlai Ewing II; United Nations; Vienna Conference

References

Beschloss, Michael R. *The Crisis Years: Kennedy and Khrushchev, 1960–1963.* New York: HarperCollins, 1991.

Bradlee, Benjamin C. *Conversations with Kennedy.* New York: Norton, 1975.

Dallek, Robert. *An Unfinished Life: John F. Kennedy, 1917–1963.* Boston: Little, Brown, 2003.

Freedman, Lawrence. *Kennedy's Wars: Berlin, Cuba, Laos, and Vietnam.* New York: Oxford University Press, 2000.

Kennedy, Robert F. *Thirteen Days: A Memoir of the Cuban Missile Crisis.* New York: Norton, 1999.

Lechuga, Carlos M. *In the Eye of the Storm: Castro, Kennedy, Khrushchev, and the Missile Crisis.* Translated by Mary Todd. Melbourne, Victoria, Australia: Ocean Press, 1995.

Rabe, Stephen G. *The Most Dangerous Area in the World: John F. Kennedy Confronts Communist Revolution in Latin America.* Chapel Hill: University of North Carolina Press, 1999.

Schlesinger, Arthur M., Jr. *A Thousand Days: John F. Kennedy in the White House.* New York: Houghton Mifflin, 1965.

White, Mark J. *The Kennedys and Cuba: The Declassified Documentary Record.* Chicago: Ivan R. Dee, 1999.

Kennedy, Robert Francis (1925–1968)

U.S. attorney general (1961–1964), U.S. senator (1965–1968), and chief adviser to his brother, President John F. Kennedy (1961–1963). Born in Boston on November 20, 1925, Robert F. Kennedy was the seventh child of Joseph P. Kennedy, multimillionaire business tycoon and U.S. ambassador to Great Britain. Robert Kennedy served in the U.S. Navy Reserve during 1944–1946 before graduating from Harvard University in 1948. In 1951 he earned a law degree from the University of Virginia. He began his legal career as an attorney in the Criminal Division of the U.S. Department of Justice in 1951 and later served as chief counsel to the Senate Select Committee on Improper Activities in the Labor and Management Field. Robert managed his brother John's successful U.S. senatorial campaign in 1952 and his 1960 presidential campaign.

Following the 1960 election, President-elect Kennedy appointed his younger brother to his cabinet as U.S. attorney general. Robert Kennedy was also President Kennedy's closest adviser on both foreign and domestic policy. Once the president approved the proposed April 1961 Bay of Pigs invasion attempt by U.S.-trained Cuban exiles, his brother enthusiastically endorsed this decision and squelched potential critics. Robert was one

Robert F. Kennedy, attorney general of the United States, was the closest adviser of his brother President John F. Kennedy. During the Cuban Missile Crisis, he and Soviet ambassador Anatoly Dobrynin conducted crucial backstage negotiations over the removal of Jupiter missiles from Turkey that helped to resolve the crisis peacefully. (Lyndon B. Johnson Presidential Library)

of a panel that investigated the reasons for the invasion's failure. He also aggressively backed new measures aimed at Castro's overthrow, including economic sanctions and a wide range of covert sabotage operations within Cuba initiated by both the Central Intelligence Agency (CIA), known as Operation MONGOOSE, and the Special Group (Augmented) on Cuba, of which he was an influential member and eventually chair. CIA efforts involved cooperation with leading American Mafia figures and repeated attempts to assassinate Castro. It remains unclear exactly how much the attorney general, who was undoubtedly almost obsessively determined to remove Castro, knew of these matters.

From April 1961 onward Robert Kennedy opened an unofficial diplomatic back channel with Georgi Bolshakov, a military intelligence agent based at the Soviet embassy in Washington whose reports went to Soviet premier Nikita Khrushchev. In over 40 meetings and communications, for 18 months he represented the president in efforts to defuse U.S.-Soviet tensions over Berlin, Laos, and Cuba and promote disarmament and superpower cooperation. Ironically, in summer 1962 Khrushchev used Bolshakov to request a cessation of U.S. aerial surveillance of Soviet shipping, facilitating the clandestine installation of nuclear-capable missiles on Cuba.

When the Kennedy administration discovered these missiles in October 1962, Robert Kennedy was a crucial figure in the deliberations of the Executive Committee (ExComm) of senior presidential advisers. Initially, on October 16, he favored immediate air strikes to destroy the missile bases, but within three days he had become the most influential proponent of a naval quarantine or blockade, the least aggressive course considered and the one that President Kennedy chose. In confidential talks with Anatoly Dobrynin, Soviet ambassador to the United States, Robert Kennedy also negotiated a secret understanding whereby the United States agreed to remove obsolete NATO Jupiter nuclear missiles from Turkey in exchange for Soviet withdrawal of those on Cuba. His posthumously published account of the Cuban missile crisis, *Thirteen Days* (1969), became a bestseller but was by no means entirely accurate in depicting his stance.

Once the missile crisis was resolved, in December 1962 Robert Kennedy concluded an agreement whereby Castro released the Cuban exiles captured at the Bay of Pigs in exchange for $53 million in American medicines, food, and machinery. His hostility to Cuba was still strong, however, and throughout 1963 both Kennedy brothers continued to endorse proposed covert operations intended to facilitate Castro's overthrow and military contingency plans to invade Cuba. The Kennedy administration's dedication to attacking Castro may have been one reason Lee Harvey Oswald, a leftist American who supported Cuba, assassinated the president in November 1963. Some historians have speculated that guilt over the possibility that his near-obsessive crusade against Cuba provoked Oswald's action may have intensified Robert Kennedy's devastating grief over his brother's death. After President Kennedy's assassination, Robert Kennedy resigned his cabinet post in the autumn of 1964 to run for a seat in the U.S. Senate, representing New York. Sworn into the Senate in January 1965, he became a vigorous advocate of social reform and minority rights. Although he had initially supported his brother's increasing military and economic aid to South Vietnam, he became sharply critical of President Lyndon B. Johnson's steep escalation of the war. When Johnson declined to seek renomination for the presidency in March 1968, Kennedy became a candidate for the Democratic presidential nomination, campaigning across the country in the Democratic primaries. On June 4, 1968, just after he had won the California primary, Sirhan B. Sirhan, a Jordanian American, shot Kennedy in the head; he died two days later and was buried in Arlington National Cemetery.

Lacie A. Ballinger

See also: Bay of Pigs Invasion; Bolshakov, Georgi Nikitovich; Castro, Fidel; Central Intelligence Agency; Dobrynin, Anatoly Fyodorovich; Johnson, Lyndon Baines; Jupiter Missiles (Turkey and Italy); Kennedy, Robert Francis; MONGOOSE, Operation; Taylor, Maxwell Davenport

References

Hilty, James W. *Robert Kennedy: Brother Protector.* Philadelphia: Temple University Press, 1997.

Kennedy, Robert F. *Robert Kennedy in His Own Words: The Unpublished Recollections of the Kennedy Years.* New York: Bantam, 1988.

Schlesinger, Arthur M., Jr. *Robert Kennedy and His Times.* 2 vols. Boston: Houghton Mifflin, 1978.

Thomas, Evan. *Robert Kennedy: His Life.* New York: Simon and Schuster, 2000.

Khrushchev, Nikita Sergeyevich (1894–1971)

Soviet politician, first secretary of the Communist Party of the Soviet Union (CPSU), 1953–1964, and premier of the Soviet Union, 1958–1964. Born on April 17, 1894, in Kalinovka, Kursk Province, to a peasant family, Nikita Sergeyevich Khrushchev worked beginning at age 15 as a pipe fitter in various mines near his home. In 1918 he joined the Russian Communist Party, and in 1919 he became a political commissar in the Red Army. Early

Soviet premier Nikita Khrushchev's love of diplomatic braggadocio and brinkmanship did much to precipitate the Cuban Missile Crisis. Fear of nuclear devastation nonetheless ultimately made him willing to concede the withdrawal of Soviet missiles from Cuba. (AP/Wide World Photos)

recognizing the importance of Communist Party Secretary Joseph Stalin, Khrushchev nurtured a friendship with Stalin's associate and party secretary in Ukraine, Lars Kaganovich, who helped him secure a full-time party post in the Moscow city party apparatus in 1931.

By 1935 Khrushchev was secretary general of the Moscow Communist Party, in effect mayor of the capital. In 1938 he became a candidate (nonvoting member) of the Politburo, and in 1939, a full member. He was one of few senior party officials to survive Stalin's Great Purges. After the German invasion of the Soviet Union in June 1941, Khrushchev was made a lieutenant general and placed in charge of resistance in Ukraine and relocating heavy industry eastward.

In 1949, Khrushchev returned to his previous post as head of the Communist Party machinery in Moscow. In 1952, at the 19th Party Congress, Khrushchev received the assignment of drawing up a new party structure, which led to the replacement of the old Politburo by the Presidium of the Central Committee. As one of the powerful committee secretaries, Khrushchev benefited from this change.

Following Stalin's death on March 5, 1953, a brief power struggle ensued, with no one individual on the 10-member Presidium dominating. Khrushchev, chosen as party secretary in 1953, emerged as supreme leader over the next two years, becoming premier in 1958. Khrushchev's greatest—and perhaps most risky—achievement as Soviet leader was to repudiate Stalin and attempt to de-Stalinize Soviet society. The most powerful blow to the Stalinists came during his famous speech at a closed session of the 20th Party Congress on February 25, 1956, in which Khrushchev documented some of the crimes and purges of the Stalinist period. Under Khrushchev, the Soviet Union gradually became more liberal, and oppressive domestic repression relaxed considerably. Soviet success during the 1950s in economic policy, industrial production, and the space program, in which he took special interest, compelled Khrushchev to proclaim that by 1970, the Soviet Union would surpass the United States in per capita production. In 1980, he grandiosely predicted, the United States would embrace communism.

Khrushchev's foreign policies within and beyond the communist bloc tended to be ambivalent. He restored Soviet relations with Yugoslavia in 1955, repairing the Tito-Stalin break of 1948. He promoted de-Stalinization programs in Eastern bloc states and allowed overseas communist parties a certain limited autonomy but was prepared to suppress dissent if he thought this in Soviet best interests. When his secret 1956 speech on Stalin and the ensuing de-Stalinization campaign led to revolts in Poland

and Hungary, he intervened in both cases, ordering the 1956 Hungarian Revolution crushed by brute force. When Albanian and Chinese officials criticized his de-Stalinization policies and rapprochement with the West, this led to crises and permanent schisms in Soviet relations with both countries. Particularly serious was the Sino-Soviet split, which became highly and publicly acrimonious.

Khrushchev generally attempted to ease tensions with the West, particularly with the United States. He rejected Stalin's thesis that wars between capitalist and socialist countries were inevitable and instead sought peaceful coexistence. On the whole, until 1960, Soviet-U.S. relations improved. Khrushchev's 1959 visit to the United States was a remarkable success. His talks with President Dwight D. Eisenhower produced, at least briefly, a warming termed the Spirit of Camp David. But Khrushchev also engaged in some rather dubious and dangerous foreign policy initiatives. He initiated the 1958–1961 Berlin Crises, authorized the construction of the Berlin Wall in 1961, and used the U-2 Affair in 1960 to provoke a showdown and derail the May 1960 Paris summit meeting with Eisenhower.

In 1959, Khrushchev welcomed the emergence of a radical revolutionary regime in Cuba, one whose leader, Fidel Castro, soon sought Soviet economic and military assistance. Fears that U.S. President John F. Kennedy intended forcibly to overthrow Castro's government, and a desire to redress the massive advantage the United States possessed over the Soviet Union in strategic nuclear missiles, impelled Khrushchev in May 1962 to offer to station Soviet military units equipped with short-, medium-, and intermediate-range nuclear-capable ballistic missiles and other conventional weapons on Cuba. The plan was very much Khrushchev's own initiative. He intended to install both men and missiles on the island in great secrecy before publicly announcing their presence there and, he hoped, using them to pressure U.S. officials on Berlin, Cuba, and other issues. In October 1962, when the missile bases were still under construction, the Kennedy administration discovered their existence, and a brief but extremely tense confrontation ensued, as Kennedy demanded the removal of all nuclear warheads and nuclear-capable delivery vehicles from Cuba. For some days, thermonuclear war between the superpowers seemed a distinct possibility. Khrushchev eventually decided to dismantle the missiles and ship them back to Russia, winning in return a public pledge by the United States not to invade Cuba. Secretly, Kennedy also agreed to withdraw NATO Jupiter intermediate-range missiles recently installed in Turkey and Italy, within easy reach of the Soviet Union, a concession that Khrushchev never revealed publicly. The narrow escape from nuclear war sobered leaders on both sides. Nine months later, on July 25, 1963, the United States, Britain, and the Soviet Union signed a Partial Nuclear Test Ban Treaty.

The debacle in Cuba contributed to the decision of the Soviet Communist Party's Central Committee to oust Khrushchev from power on October 14, 1964, as did his increasingly unpredictable and unstable behavior and his failed agricultural policies. Living quietly in semi-disgrace, he then wrote his memoirs, which were published in the West beginning in 1970. Khrushchev died in Moscow on September 11, 1971, following a massive heart attack.

Magarditsch Hatschikjan

See also: ANADYR, Operation; Bay of Pigs Invasion; Berlin Crises; Castro, Fidel; Eisenhower, Dwight David; Jupiter Missiles (Turkey and Italy); Military Balance; Missile Gap; Nuclear Arms Race; Partial Test Ban Treaty; Vienna Conference

References

Beschloss, Michael R. *The Crisis Years: Kennedy and Khrushchev, 1960–1963.* New York: HarperCollins, 1991.

Fursenko, Aleksandr, and Timothy Naftali. *Khrushchev's Cold War: The Inside Story of an American Adversary.* New York: Norton, 2006.

Haslam, Jonathan. *Russia's Cold War: From the October Revolution to the Fall of the Wall.* New Haven, CT: Yale University Press, 2011.

Khrushchev, Nikita S. *Khrushchev Remembers.* Introduction and commentary by Edward Crankshaw. Translated by Strobe Talbott. Boston: Little, Brown, 1970.

Khrushchev, Nikita S. *Khrushchev Remembers: The Glasnost Tapes.* Translated and edited by Jerrold L. Schecter with Vyacheslav V. Luchkov. Boston: Little, Brown, 1990.

Khrushchev, Nikita S. *Khrushchev Remembers: The Last Testament.* Translated and edited by Strobe Talbott. Boston: Little, Brown, 1974.

Khrushchev, Nikita S. *Memoirs of Nikita Khrushchev.* Edited by Sergei Khrushchev and translated by George Shriver. University Park: Pennsylvania State University Press, 2004.

Medvedev, Roi A. *Khrushchev.* Translated by Brian Pearce. Oxford, UK: Blackwell, 1982.

Taubman, William. *Khrushchev: The Man and His Era.* New York: Norton, 2003.

Zubok, Vladislav M. *A Failed Empire: The Soviet Union in the Cold War from Stalin to Gorbachev.* Chapel Hill: University of North Carolina Press, 2007.

Zubok, Vladislav, and Constantine Pleshakov. *Inside the Kremlin's Cold War: From Stalin to Khrushchev.* Cambridge, MA: Harvard University Press, 1996.

Kohler, Foy David (1908–1990)

U.S. diplomat, ambassador to the Soviet Union, 1962–1966. Foy Kohler was born in Oakwood, Ohio, on February 15, 1908. He attended Toledo University and the University of Ohio before joining the Foreign Service in 1931, undertaking a variety of foreign postings. From 1947 to 1949 he served in the U.S. embassy in Moscow, and from 1949 to 1952 was director of the Voice of America radio broadcasting network. During the 1950s he spent stints with the Policy Planning Staff and the Bureau of Near Eastern Affairs and as counselor in the U.S. embassy in Turkey and was detailed to the International Cooperation Agency. From December 1959 to August 1962, Kohler was assistant secretary of state for European Affairs.

Appointed U.S. ambassador to the Soviet Union in September 1962, Kohler arrived in Moscow only weeks before the Cuban Missile Crisis began. On October 16 Kohler, just arrived in Moscow, reported a conversation with Soviet premier Nikita Khrushchev, in which the latter promised to do nothing to complicate relations with the United States before the approaching early November congressional midterm elections. Kohler was not close to President John F. Kennedy, and during the Cuban Missile Crisis the U.S. embassy in Moscow functioned largely as a conduit and translation bureau for urgent messages between Khrushchev and U.S. officials in Washington. This system proved so slow and clumsy that in June 1963 the Soviet Union and the United States established a dedicated transatlantic telephone "hotline" to enable leaders in both countries to communicate directly with each other. Kohler was present at the August 1963 negotiations in Moscow that resulted in the Partial Nuclear Test Ban Treaty. Retiring from the Foreign Service in 1967 as deputy undersecretary for political affairs, Kohler became a professor of international relations at the University of Miami, Coral Gables, Florida. He died in Jupiter, Florida, on December 23, 1990.

Priscilla Roberts

See also: Kennedy, John Fitzgerald; Khrushchev, Nikita Sergeyevich; Partial Test Ban Treaty

Reference

Fursenko, Aleksandr, and Timothy Naftali. *One Hell of a Gamble: Khrushchev, Castro, and Kennedy, 1958–1964.* New York: Norton, 1997.

Kohler, Foy D. *Understanding the Russians: A Citizen's Primer.* New York: Harper and Row, 1970.

Mayers, David. *The Ambassadors and America's Soviet Policy*. New York: Oxford University Press, 1995.

Kozlov, Frol Romanovich (1908–1965)

Soviet communist leader. Born in Loshchinino, Ryazan, in central Russia on August 18, 1908, Frol Kozlov joined the Communist Party of the Soviet Union (CPSU) and rose steadily in that organization. In 1947 he became second secretary of the Kuybyshev provincial party committee. In 1949 he was assigned to Leningrad, and in 1953 he became first secretary of the CPSU in that city.

Closely allied with Nikita Khrushchev, Kozlov became a full member of the Presidium in 1957. He was briefly premier of the Russian Soviet Federated Socialist Republic (RSFSR) during 1957–1958 but resigned this post to become the deputy chairman of the Council of Ministers of the Soviet Union, or deputy premier. In 1960 he assumed the powerful post of secretary of the CPSU Central Committee.

Kozlov was among Soviet hard-liners who favored an uncompromising stance toward the West. He was a key player in enforcing an uncompromising approach against the June 2, 1962, workers' strike in Novocherkassk that resulted in several deaths when Red Army soldiers fired on demonstrators, an event kept secret for almost 30 years. Kozlov, the Presidium member who followed intelligence activities most closely, likewise endorsed an assertive policy on Cuba. In March 1961 he assured Raúl Castro, younger brother of Cuban leader Fidel Castro, that the Soviet Union was "prepared to give Cuba whatever she needed" militarily, provided "Soviet specialists were sent to Cuba" to supervise the use of such weaponry. In May 1962 Politburo meetings he spoke in favor of Khrushchev's decision to deploy nuclear-capable weapons in Cuba. At the end of October, however, he endorsed the removal of such missiles, acquiescing in Khrushchev's pragmatic recognition that nuclear war over these with the United States was unacceptable.

Kozlov was considered the heir apparent to Khrushchev, whose position with his colleagues in the party hierarchy was weakened following the 1960 U-2 Affair and especially after the Cuban Missile Crisis. This all became moot when Kozlov suffered a stroke in April 1963. Without this health setback, Kozlov and not Leonid Brezhnev might have become the next Soviet leader. Despite his near-complete incapacitation, Kozlov retained his posts until he was forced to resign in November 1964 after Khrushchev's removal from power. Kozlov died in Moscow on January 30, 1965.

Spencer C. Tucker

See also: Castro, Raúl; Khrushchev, Nikita Sergeyevich

References

Fursenko, Aleksandr, and Timothy Naftali. *Khrushchev's Cold War: The Inside Story of an American Adversary.* New York: Norton, 2006.

Fursenko, Aleksandr, and Timothy Naftali. *One Hell of a Gamble: Khrushchev, Castro, and Kennedy, 1958–1964.* New York: Norton, 1997.

Linden, Carl. *Khrushchev and the Soviet Leadership, 1957–1964.* Baltimore, MD: Johns Hopkins University Press, 1966.

Medvedev, Roi A. *Khrushchev.* Translated by Brian Pearce. Oxford, UK: Blackwell, 1982.

Taubman, William. *Khrushchev: The Man and His Era.* New York: Norton, 2003.

Kuznetsov, Vasili Vasilyevich (1901–1990)

Soviet politician, first deputy foreign minister, 1955–1977. Vasili Kuznetsov was born on February 13, 1901, in Sofilovka, Kostroma Province, Russia. He studied engineering and metal processing, the latter in the United States from 1931 to 1933 at the Carnegie Institute of Technology in Pennsylvania. He joined the Soviet Communist Party in 1927. Rising through various government and party positions, he was chairman of the All-Union Central Council of Trade Unions from 1944 to 1953, and from 1946 to 1950 he also chaired the Soviet of Nationalities. After the death of Soviet leader Joseph Stalin, in 1953 Kuznetsov switched to the foreign ministry, serving briefly as Soviet ambassador to China. He attended the 1954 Geneva conference on Indochina as a Soviet representative. In 1955 Kuznetsov became first deputy foreign minister, a post he held until 1977, working closely with Foreign Minister Andrey Gromyko.

At the end of October 1962, Khrushchev dispatched Kuznetsov to the United Nations (UN) to negotiate the details of the removal of Soviet missiles from Cuba. He worked intensely with UN acting secretary general U Thant and the American John J. McCloy, hammering out bargains whereby the U.S. government accepted that Cuban premier Fidel Castro would not permit on-site inspections in Cuba and thus it would rely on aerial surveillance and sea inspections of departing freighters to confirm the removal of Soviet weapons. Despite last-ditch efforts by Castro and Soviet defense minister Rodion Malinovsky to leave these in place, at U.S. insistence Soviet Il-28 light bombers and tactical nuclear-capable missiles were also withdrawn from Cuba. The United States did not, as Kuznetsov requested, pledge unequivocally not to invade Cuba, nor did Kuznetsov promise that all Soviet troops would leave the island. In late December 1962, as their negotiations came to an end, Kuznetsov warned McCloy, "we will honor this agreement. But I will tell you something. The Soviet Union is not going to find itself in a position like this ever again." His words signaled Soviet leaders' determination to build up their nuclear forces to something approaching parity with the United States. In May 1963 Kuznetsov nonetheless unsuccessfully opposed Khrushchev's public statement, in a Cuban-Soviet communiqué issued at the end of a visit by Castro, that the Soviet Union would if necessary use nuclear weapons to defend Cuba's independence. In 1977 Kuznetsov became first deputy chairman of the Soviet Presidium, a post he held until he retired in 1986, serving as the Soviet Union's acting head of state after the deaths of Soviet leaders Leonid Brezhnev, Yuri Andropov, and Konstantin Chernenko. He died in Moscow on June 5, 1990.

Priscilla Roberts

See also: Castro, Fidel; Gromyko, Andrey Andreyevich; Khrushchev, Nikita Sergeyevich; Malinovsky, Rodion Yakovlevich; McCloy, John Jay; U Thant; United Nations

References

Bird, Kai. *The Chairman: John J. McCloy and the Making of the American Establishment.* New York: Simon and Schuster, 1992.

Fursenko, Aleksandr, and Timothy Naftali. *One Hell of a Gamble: Khrushchev, Castro, and Kennedy, 1958–1964.* New York: Norton, 1997.

L

Lansdale, Edward Geary (1908–1987)

U.S. Air Force officer, intelligence operative, purportedly the model for the leading characters in two novels—*The Quiet American* by Graham Greene and *The Ugly American* by Eugene Burdick and William Lederer. Born in Detroit, Michigan, on February 6, 1908, Edward Lansdale graduated from the University of California at Los Angeles in 1931 and was commissioned in the army through ROTC. During the Great Depression, he sold advertising in California. He went on active duty during World War II in the U.S. Army, serving with the Office of Strategic Services (OSS) and finishing his wartime service as a major with the U.S. Army Air Forces as chief of the Intelligence Division in the western Pacific. In 1950, at the request of Filipino president Elpidio Quirino, Lansdale became a member of the U.S. Military Assistance Group, undertaking operations to suppress the communist Hukbalahap rebellion. In 1953 Washington dispatched Lansdale to join the U.S. mission in Vietnam as adviser on counter-guerrilla operations. After a brief tour in the Philippines, he returned to Vietnam in 1954 to serve with the U.S. Military Advisory Group there.

After helping solidify South Vietnamese prime minister Ngo Dinh Diem's rule, Lansdale returned to Washington in 1957 and held assorted military and Defense Department positions. He was promoted to brigadier general in 1960 and major general upon his retirement in 1963. From 1959 to 1961, as deputy assistant secretary of defense for special operations he played a prominent role in training Cuban exiles for the disastrous April 1961 Bay of Pigs invasion. Until his retirement in November 1963, he also worked with the Central Intelligence Agency (CIA) and Attorney General

Robert F. Kennedy on various unsuccessful attempts to foment rebellion in Cuba and assassinate Cuban leader Fidel Castro.

Lansdale's convoluted career included two years of service as a consultant to the Food for Peace Program. He returned to South Vietnam in 1965 as senior liaison officer of the U.S. Mission to the Republic of Vietnam and then became assistant to U.S. ambassador Ellsworth Bunker in 1967. Lansdale retired for good in 1968, wrote his memoirs, and died in McLean, Virginia, on February 23, 1987.

Daniel E. Spector

See also: Bay of Pigs Invasion; Castro, Fidel; Central Intelligence Agency; Kennedy, Robert Francis; MONGOOSE, Operation

References

Bohning, Don. *The Castro Obsession: U.S. Covert Operations against Cuba, 1959–1965.* Washington, DC: Potomac Books, 2005.

Currey, Cecil B. *Edward Lansdale: The Unquiet American.* Washington, DC: Brassey's, 1998.

Lansdale, Edward G. *In the Midst of Wars: An American's Mission to Southeast Asia.* New York: Harper and Row, 1972.

Nashel, Jonathan. *Edward Lansdale's Cold War: A Cultural Biography of a Legendary Cold War Figure.* Amherst: University of Massachusetts Press, 2004.

Lovett, Robert Abercrombie (1895–1986)

U.S. secretary of defense (1951–1953), presidential adviser. Born in Huntsville, Texas, on September 14, 1895, Robert Lovett moved in 1909 with his family to New York. He attended Yale University, temporarily dropping out to serve as a naval aviator after the United States entered World War I. In the early 1920s he joined and soon became a partner in the venerable investment bank Brown Brothers, later Brown Brothers Harriman. In 1940 Lovett's continuing interest in aviation and his concern to build up U.S. aerial production capacities led Secretary of War Henry L. Stimson to appoint him assistant secretary of war for air, a post he held for almost five years.

In 1947 Lovett's former superior George C. Marshall, whom President Harry S. Truman had just appointed secretary of state, persuaded Lovett to become undersecretary of state. He remained in office until late 1948, overseeing the development of the Marshall Plan and the North Atlantic Treaty Organization (NATO). In September 1950, when Marshall became secretary of defense during the Korean War, Lovett once again served as his deputy, supervising a major military buildup and succeeding Marshall when the latter retired in late 1951.

Lovett left office when the Truman administration ended, but successive presidents repeatedly sought his views on assorted foreign policy issues, regarding him as a key member of the "Wise Men," the establishment figures who presided over the mid-20th-century expansion of U.S. international power. In the mid-1950s Lovett presciently warned that the Central Intelligence Agency (CIA) had become overly enamored of covert operations. In 1960 he

Former secretary of defense Robert A. Lovett held no official position in John F. Kennedy's administration but was one of the trusted "Wise Men" of the American foreign policy establishment whose advice Kennedy sought from time to time. By the mid-1950s, Lovett had come to deplore the Central Intelligence Agency's intrusive covert operations in other countries. The CIA's efforts to overthrow Castro's government in Cuba were a prime example of such operations. (Library of Congress)

forcefully attacked CIA plans to invade Cuba and unsuccessfully demanded a complete reassessment of overall covert policies, advice the Eisenhower administration resisted. Afterward Lovett publicly stated, "What right do we have barging into other people's countries, buying newspapers and handing out money to opposition parties or supporting a candidate for this or that office?"

During the Cuban Missile Crisis President John F. Kennedy consulted Lovett, who counseled moderation, favoring the imposition of a naval blockade on Cuba, with gradual increases of pressure if appropriate. He stressed the "desirability of taking a mild and not very bloodthirsty step first," to give the Soviets an opportunity to retreat. Lovett believed that air strikes would not necessarily succeed in destroying all the missiles. On October 20 he helped Kennedy draft the announcement of a naval quarantine. Lovett died in Locust Valley, Long Island, New York, on September 14, 1986.

Priscilla Roberts

See also: Bay of Pigs Invasion; Central Intelligence Agency; Kennedy, John Fitzgerald

Reference

Isaacson, Walter, and Evan Thomas. *The Wise Men: Six Friends and the World They Made.* New York: Simon and Schuster, 1986.

M

Malinovsky, Rodion Yakovlevich (1898–1967)

Marshal of the Soviet Union, minister of defense, 1957–1967. Born to a poor peasant family near Odessa on November 23, 1898, Rodion Malinovsky enlisted in the Russian Army at the outbreak of World War I, fighting in France and North Africa. Malinovsky returned to Russia via Vladivostok in August 1919, joined the Red Army and fought against the White forces. In 1926 he joined the Communist Party and a year later entered the Frunze Military Academy for a three-year officers' training program. He was a military adviser to the Republican forces during 1937–1938 in the Spanish Civil War. During World War II Malinovsky saw service in the Ukraine, took part in the ill-fated June 1942 Kharkov Offensive, and played a key role in the Battle of Stalingrad, in December defeating Army Group Don, the German relief force under Field Marshal Erich von Manstein.

He also began a long association with Nikita Khrushchev, then a political officer reportedly assigned by Soviet leader Joseph Stalin to watch Malinovsky. He played a major role in the Battle of Kursk in July 1943 and then spearheaded the drive across the Ukraine, taking Odessa in April 1944. From the Ukraine, he led Soviet forces into Romania, Hungary, Austria, and Czechoslovakia. In September 1944 he was promoted to marshal of the Soviet Union. When the war in Europe ended, Malinovsky took command of the Transbaikal Front in the Far East, pushing into Japanese-held Manchuria. A prominent member of the Soviet military hierarchy after the war, he headed the Far East Command during 1947–1953 and the Far East Military District during 1953–1956.

Malinovsky served as deputy minister of defense during 1956–1957, then succeeded Marshal Georgi Zhukov as minister of defense. In this post Malinovsky introduced strategic missiles into the Soviet arsenal and oversaw Soviet military modernization.

From mid-1960 onward, Malinovsky approved the dispatch of increasingly substantial quantities of military assistance to Cuba, including tanks, rifles, pistols, machine guns, field artillery and antitank guns, and antiaircraft guns, plus ammunition. In May 1961, additional supplies earmarked for Cuba included 41 fighter jets and reconnaissance aircraft, 80 additional tanks, 54 antiaircraft guns, and 128 field artillery pieces. By spring 1962, the Soviet Union had sent over $250 million worth of weaponry to Cuba and had promised five rocket batteries and three surface-to-air missile (SAM) batteries, with 196 missiles.

By May 1962, Malinovsky was an enthusiastic advocate of Khrushchev's plan to base nuclear-capable missiles on Cuba, overriding opponents who queried it in meetings. He apparently considered this an excellent opportunity to project Soviet military power into the Western Hemisphere and thereby redress the nuclear balance in the Soviets' favor, deterring U.S. leaders from ever considering a first strike against the Soviet Union. Malinovsky was responsible for implementing the decision, supervising preparations to move and install the missiles and the Soviet military personnel operating them quickly and in great secrecy. He actively discouraged subordinates from suggesting that U-2 surveillance overflights would probably detect the missile bases before they became operational. In August 1962 Malinovsky initialed the secret Soviet-Cuban defense treaty governing the installation and operation of the missiles and other Soviet military facilities and forces on Cuba. After President John F. Kennedy publicly warned the Soviet Union in September 1962 against installing offensive weapons on Cuba, Khrushchev and Malinovsky expanded the program of deliveries to include shipments of short-range Luna missiles and R-11m cruise missiles, plus a squadron of Il-28 light bombers with nuclear bombs. Malinovsky argued that the United States would not react to the missiles when discovered, but he anticipated that, if necessary, a show of Soviet naval power in the Caribbean would suffice to quell U.S. objections; indeed, he hoped to increase permanently the Soviet submarine and surface naval presence there.

On October 22, as apprehensive Kremlin officials waited for Kennedy to make a public statement, Malinovsky urged that the Soviet commander in Cuba, Gen. Issa Pliyev, be instructed to use only conventional weapons in response to any U.S. military action. An authorization to employ nuclear-capable missiles was held in reserve but never sent. On October 25, Malinovsky remained silent as Khrushchev and the Politburo made the decision to remove the missiles. On October 27, anticipating potential U.S. air strikes, Khrushchev and Malinovsky signed an order authorizing Pliyev to use "all available means of air defense." No such air strikes occurred, however. On October 28, Khrushchev decided to accept Kennedy's proposals, and Malinovsky instructed Pliyev to begin dismantling the missile sites. In the aftermath of the crisis, Malinovsky initially tried to retain 100 short-range tactical nuclear warheads in Cuba, together with several squadrons of Il-28s, and begin training Cubans to use these, but Khrushchev overruled him. Despite the immediate post-crisis acrimony Cuban officials displayed toward the Soviet Union, Malinovsky felt it important to maintain cooperative military relations with Cuba, and he still considered the island an important strategic asset to the Soviet Union. Malinovsky died in office of cancer in Moscow on March 31, 1967.

Michael Share and Spencer C. Tucker

See also: ANADYR, Operation; Castro, Fidel; Gribkov, Anatoli Ivanovich; Kennedy, John Fitzgerald; Khrushchev, Nikita Sergeyevich; Military Balance; Missile Gap; Nuclear Arms Race; Pliyev, Issa Alexandrovich; U-2 Overflights

References

Erickson, John. "Rodion Yakovlevich Malinovsky." Pp. 117–124 in *Stalin's Generals,* edited by Harold Shukman. New York: Grove, 1993.

Fursenko, Aleksandr, and Timothy Naftali. *One Hell of a Gamble: Khrushchev, Castro, and Kennedy, 1958–1964.* New York: Norton, 1997.

Gribkov, Anatoli I., and William Y. Smith. *Operation ANADYR: U.S. and Soviet Generals Recount the Cuban Missile Crisis.* Edited by Alfred Friendly, Jr. Chicago, Berlin, Tokyo, and Moscow: edition q, 1994.

Mann, Thomas C. (1912–1999)

U.S. State Department official and Latin American specialist. Born on November 11, 1912, in Laredo, Texas, Thomas Mann graduated from Baylor University in 1934 with BA and LLB degrees and then practiced law. He began working for the Department of State in 1942 as a special assistant to the U.S. ambassador to Uruguay.

In 1952 as deputy assistant secretary of state for Inter-American Affairs, Mann argued that disparities in wealth between the United States and Latin America would spur anti-Americanism and economic nationalism and that communists would exploit these circumstances. Willing to jettison the U.S. nonintervention pledge, he concluded that Washington must intervene in Latin America if communism threatened to gain a foothold there.

Although he was among the creators of the multilateral Inter-American Development Bank, in 1959 Mann articulated fears that plans for a large U.S. aid program for Latin America would raise unreasonably high expectations that could not be met, resulting in disillusionment and increased anti-Americanism in the region. His misgivings were largely borne out in the Alliance for Progress, launched by President John F. Kennedy in 1961, that disproportionately benefited the wealthy.

Before the April 1961 Bay of Pigs invasion attempt, Mann produced a devastating assessment. Believing that landing Cuban exile paramilitary units on the island was unlikely to trigger a popular uprising against Cuban leader Fidel Castro, he warned that the United States would then face the unpalatable alternatives of abandoning these men or overt military intervention to rescue them and overthrow Castro. Mann also pointed out that the operation violated international law and would damage U.S. credibility. Presented to Kennedy in February 1961, together with a memorandum by CIA deputy director Richard Bissell favoring the invasion, Mann's warnings failed to dissuade Kennedy from sanctioning the operation.

From December 1963, under President Lyndon B. Johnson, Mann was both assistant secretary for Inter-American Affairs and head of the Agency for International Development, which ran the Alliance for Progress. Concurrently, he was made a special assistant to the president. He essentially directed U.S. policy in Latin America. Following Johnson's cue, the so-called Mann Doctrine shifted the emphasis of the Alliance for Progress toward anticommunism and the protection of U.S. investments, promoting cooperation with military or nondemocratic regimes provided they sanctioned U.S. investment on nondiscriminatory terms and adopted anti-Soviet policies. In March 1965 Johnson appointed Mann undersecretary of state for economic affairs.

That same year, however, key congressmen asserted that the administration's April 1965 intervention in the Dominican Republic, which Mann strongly supported, had greatly overstated the communist threat. With the 1966 appointment of Lincoln Gordon as assistant secretary of state for Inter-American Affairs, Mann's influence over Latin American policy effectively ended. He resigned from the Department of State in May 1966, yet future administrations would adopt many of his policies.

From 1967 to 1971 Mann served as president of the Automobile Manufacturers Association. He died on January 23, 1999, in Austin, Texas.

James F. Siekmeier

See also: Alliance for Progress; Bay of Pigs Invasion; Bissell, Richard Mervin, Jr.; Central Intelligence Agency; Johnson, Lyndon Baines; Kennedy, Robert Fitzgerald

References

Lafeber, Walter. "Thomas C. Mann and the Devolution of Latin America Policy: From the Good Neighbor to Military Intervention." Pp. 166–203 in *Behind the Throne: Servants of Power to Imperial Presidents, 1898–1968,* edited by Thomas McCormick and Walter Lafeber. Madison: University of Wisconsin Press, 1993.

Siekmeier, James F. *Aid, Nationalism, and Inter-American Relations: Guatemala, Bolivia, and the United States, 1945–1961.* Lewiston, NY: Edwin Mellen, 1999.

Walker, William O. "The Struggle for the Americas: The Johnson Administration and Cuba." Pp. 97–144 in *The Foreign Policies of Lyndon Johnson: Beyond Vietnam,* edited by H. W. Brands. College Station: Texas A&M University Press, 1999.

McCloy, John Jay (1895–1989)

Presidential arms control adviser, 1961–1974. Born in Philadelphia on March 31, 1895, John J. McCloy attended Amherst College and Harvard Law School. During World War I he interrupted his studies to serve in the U.S. Army, becoming a captain of artillery and acquiring an internationalist outlook. In 1924 McCloy joined the prestigious New York corporate law firm of Cravath, de Gersdorff, Swaine, and Moore, rising to partner in 1929.

In 1940 McCloy joined the War Department as a consultant to Secretary Henry Lewis Stimson, a lifelong hero and role model of McCloy's. Appointed assistant secretary the following year, McCloy was involved in virtually every major political and military wartime decision until he left that position in November 1945. From 1949 to 1952 McCloy was U.S. high commissioner in the Federal Republic of Germany, responsible for implementing that country's return to independent statehood. McCloy was president of the Chase Manhattan Bank from 1953 to 1960, after which he returned to law. He was one of the "Wise Men," recognized foreign policy experts whom successive presidents consulted on a wide range of international issues. The journalist Richard H. Rovere even termed him the "chairman" of the American Establishment.

In 1961 President John F. Kennedy appointed McCloy director of the new Arms Control and Disarmament Agency, entrusted with formulating broad disarmament policies and revitalizing stalled U.S.-Soviet negotiations for a treaty to ban atmospheric nuclear arms tests. Whether McCloy learned in advance of the Bay of Pigs invasion plan remains unclear. In its aftermath, he criticized the operation for frivolously diverting resources from more serious problems, including Berlin, NATO defense, and disarmament negotiations. Considering Cuba strategically insignificant to the United States, McCloy warned that, by arming Cuban anti-Castro rebels, the U.S. government undermined the legal basis of its protests against Soviet backing of Laotian and South Vietnamese insurgents.

On October 16, when Kennedy learned of the presence of Soviet missile installations in Cuba, McCloy was in Europe. Even before meeting with his Executive Committee (ExComm) of senior officials, Kennedy consulted him by telephone. McCloy recommended an air strike to destroy the missile sites, if necessary followed by a full-scale U.S. invasion of Cuba. While believing the missiles made little practical difference to the U.S.-Soviet nuclear balance, McCloy viewed their presence in Cuba as a test of U.S. international credibility, fearing that if they remained his country's NATO partners would lose all faith in U.S. commitments to Western Europe.

Recalled home on October 21, McCloy briefed United Nations (UN) delegates on the crisis. He remained at the UN for most of the crisis, in part because many ExComm members feared that Adlai Stevenson, U.S. ambassador to the UN, might be too conciliatory when responding to UN initiatives on the crisis. After Kennedy publicly imposed a naval blockade of Cuba on October 22, McCloy resisted suggestions by UN officials that Kennedy agree to temporarily lift the quarantine if Soviet premier Nikita Khrushchev suspended further weapons shipments to Cuba, a position he reiterated at an ExComm meeting on October 26. Returning to the UN, he responded favorably to suggestions from acting secretary general U Thant that the United States might pledge not to invade Cuba in exchange for the removal of Soviet missiles, and he endorsed the president's decision to withdraw NATO missiles from Turkey.

After Khrushchev agreed to dismantle the missiles, throughout November and December 1962 McCloy chaired a three-man UN Special

Coordinating Committee of U.S. officials that handled detailed negotiations with Soviet deputy foreign minister Vasili Kuznetsov and Soviet UN delegate Valerian A. Zorin to facilitate the departure of Soviet weaponry from Cuba. McCloy hoped these talks would give added momentum to subsequent U.S.-Soviet arms-control efforts. McCloy also pragmatically suggested that the United States should respond favorably to any overtures from Cuban leader Fidel Castro to normalize U.S.-Cuban diplomatic relations. McCloy was aware that a small combat brigade of Soviet troops would remain in Cuba. In 1979, when press revelations of the continuing presence of Soviet military personnel in Cuba embarrassed President Jimmy Carter's administration, McCloy defused the crisis when he publicly stated that their deployment on the island did not breach the understandings U.S. and Soviet representatives had reached in late 1962. McCloy continued as a presidential arms control adviser until 1974, welcoming progress on U.S.-Soviet détente and helping negotiate various disarmament agreements. He died in Stamford, Connecticut, on March 11, 1989.

Priscilla Roberts

See also: Bay of Pigs Invasion; Castro, Fidel; Jupiter Missiles (Turkey and Italy); Kennedy, John Fitzgerald; Kuznetsov, Vasili Vasilyevich; Nuclear Arms Race; Stevenson, Adlai Ewing II; U Thant; United Nations; U.S. Allies; Zorin, Valerian Aleksandrovich

References

Bird, Kai. *The Chairman: John J. McCloy and the Making of the American Establishment.* New York: Simon and Schuster, 1992.

Isaacson, Walter, and Evan Thomas. *The Wise Men: Six Friends and the World They Made.* New York: Simon and Schuster, 1986.

McCone, John Alex (1902–1991)

Industrialist and director of the Central Intelligence Agency (CIA), 1961–1965. Born in San Francisco, California, on January 4, 1902, John Alex McCone graduated from the University of California at Berkeley in 1922. A successful businessman who advanced from riveter to vice president of the Consolidated Steel Corporation in the 1920s, McCone made a fortune in the steel and shipbuilding industries during World War II under the banner of the Bechtel-McCone engineering firm.

In 1950, he became undersecretary of the Air Force, in which position he urged President Harry Truman to begin a program of building guided missiles, which was not immediately done. In 1951, he returned to private business but continued to serve Washington in special missions. In 1958, President Dwight D. Eisenhower appointed him head of the Atomic Energy Commission.

On September 27, 1961, several months after the abortive Bay of Pigs invasion of Cuba, President John F. Kennedy appointed McCone, a conservative Republican with virtually no intelligence experience, to head the CIA, succeeding Allen Dulles. He inherited an agency in considerable turmoil.

McCone proceeded to restore CIA credibility. He immediately convened a study group to identify the duties of the director and submit suggestions on agency reorganization. This substantially improved scientific and technological research and development capabilities, added a cost-analysis system, and created a position of comptroller. In addition, Kennedy publicly strengthened the agency by announcing that the director would be charged with developing policies and coordinating procedures at all levels across the intelligence community. The announcement came less than a month after the president's Foreign Intelligence Advisory Board recommended dismantling the CIA.

Alerted by reports of growing deliveries of Soviet weaponry to Cuba, from August 1962 McCone suspected these might include nuclear armaments and he pressed the White House to authorize surveillance overflights. On October 14 a high-flying U-2 reconnaissance plane produced photographic evidence of potential nuclear-capable missile sites on Cuba. McCone, a longtime advocate of overthrowing Fidel Castro's government in Cuba, an objective he believed would require direct U.S. military intervention, attended many of the subsequent Executive Committee (ExComm) meetings of top U.S. officials convened to handle the situation. His preferred option was a full-scale U.S. invasion of Cuba, preceded by air strikes on the missile installations. Subsequently, his access to the president waned after he bragged too loudly for too long how accurate his predictions of Soviet missiles in Cuba had been.

McCone remained CIA director after Kennedy's November 1963 assassination. His criticism of President Lyndon B. Johnson's escalation of the war in Vietnam as unlikely to prove effective may have hastened his departure from the CIA in 1965. McCone later served on the boards of

several major corporations, including ITT. He died on February 14, 1991, in Pebble Beach, California.

Paul R. Camacho

See also: Bay of Pigs Invasion; Castro, Fidel; Central Intelligence Agency; Dulles, Allen Welsh; Eisenhower, Dwight David; Kennedy, John Fitzgerald; U-2 Overflights

References

Brugioni, Dino. *Eyeball to Eyeball: The Inside Story of the Cuban Missile Crisis.* Edited by Robert F. McCort. New York: Random House, 1991.

Fursenko, Aleksandr, and Timothy Naftali. *One Hell of a Gamble: Khrushchev, Castro, and Kennedy, 1958–1964.* New York: Norton, 1997.

Hersh, Burton. *The Old Boys: The American Elite and the Origins of the CIA.* New York: Charles Scribner's Sons, 1992.

McNamara, Robert Strange (1916–2009)

U.S. secretary of defense, 1961–1968. Born in San Francisco on June 9, 1916, McNamara was an Army Air Corps officer in World War II, when he used statistical techniques acquired at the Harvard Business School to improve the logistics, planning, and analysis of strategic bombing raids over Europe and Japan. Joining the Ford Motor Company after the war, in November 1960 he was appointed president but left almost immediately when President John F. Kennedy recruited him as secretary of defense.

McNamara moved immediately to enlarge his personal staff and centralize decision making in the secretary's office, developing and employing a planning-programming-budgeting system (PPBS) in efforts to enhance cost-effectiveness by eliminating duplication, waste, and overlapping programs among the three services and subjecting proposed weapons systems to close cost-benefit analysis. These and other efficiency measures, including proposals to close unneeded military bases and consolidate the National Guard and Army Reserves into one system, provoked fierce opposition from many military men and from powerful congressional and civilian lobbies.

McNamara made an early mistake in endorsing the disastrous April 1961 Bay of Pigs invasion of Cuba. During the Cuban Missile Crisis,

Secretary of Defense Robert McNamara was one of the key members of the Executive Committee of the National Security Council. As the crisis developed, he oversaw the mobilization of U.S. forces for potential military action against Cuba. In retirement, he participated in several enlightening gatherings of Soviet, Cuban, and American officials involved in the Cuban Missile Crisis. (Yoichi R. Okamoto/Lyndon B. Johnson Presidential Library)

however, he was generally credited with devising the relatively moderate naval quarantine response strategy that Kennedy decided to follow. Determined to avoid nuclear war, McNamara repeatedly stated that the presence of medium- and intermediate-range Soviet nuclear-capable missiles on Cuba made little if any difference to the strategic balance. By October 27, however, the Soviet failure to halt the construction of missile sites and the shooting down of a U-2 reconnaissance plane over Cuba had brought McNamara to endorse massive U.S. air strikes followed by an invasion of the island, a move averted only by Kennedy's determination to allow the Soviet Union additional time before launching such drastic measures.

McNamara supported the 1963 Partial Nuclear Test Ban Treaty, which he hoped would facilitate U.S.-Soviet arms-limitation talks, even as he supported developing a U.S. second-strike capability, the ability to retaliate ferociously even after absorbing a massive nuclear attack. He also broke with President Dwight D. Eisenhower's emphasis on threatening massive retaliation in all crises to support expanding the military by 300,000 personnel to develop flexible-response capabilities, a mobile striking force prepared for conventional or guerrilla warfare. Defense Department budgets rose from $45.9 billion in 1960 to $53.6 billion in 1964. Another reason for this surge was McNamara's early decision to increase land-based U.S. intercontinental ballistic missiles (ICBMs) to 1,000, a move that may have triggered a similar Soviet buildup and arms race. He publicly defended the

nuclear strategy of mutually assured destruction (MAD), arguing that it served as a deterrent to nuclear war.

During the Kennedy presidency McNamara's reputation soared, only to fall dramatically and permanently under Kennedy's successor, Lyndon B. Johnson. Growing U.S. involvement in the Republic of Vietnam (RVN) (South Vietnam), which McNamara endorsed, undercut his efforts at rationalization. Military intellectuals later criticized McNamara's decision to permit the demands of the Vietnam War to denude U.S. North Atlantic Treaty Organization (NATO) forces. By 1966 McNamara had become increasingly pessimistic over the war's outcome, especially when antiwar protests intensified and he became a prime target for ferocious criticism, although as late as mid-1967 he seemed on occasion to believe that the war could be won. In late 1967 Johnson rejected his recommendations to freeze U.S. troop levels, cease bombing North Vietnam, and transfer ground combat duties largely to the South Vietnamese Army. McNamara announced his impending resignation in November 1967, leaving three months later to become president of the World Bank.

McNamara remained at the World Bank until 1982, dramatically expanding its lending and development programs. During Ronald Reagan's presidency, McNamara was one of several leading U.S. diplomats who openly sought a pledge by the United States that it would never be the first state to use nuclear weapons. In 1986 he published proposals designed to reduce the risk of conflict. In 1995 he finally published his memoirs and concurrently became heavily involved in continuing efforts by Vietnamese and Western scholars and officials to attain greater understanding of each other's position in the Vietnam conflict. He also participated in several conferences that brought together Soviet, American, and Cuban participants from the 1962 missile crisis. In 2003 he cooperated in producing a documentary, *The Fog of War,* on his experiences from World War II onward, including the Cuban Missile Crisis. He publicly criticized the 2003 U.S. invasion of Iraq.

McNamara remained perennially controversial. His persistent refusal to characterize the U.S. decision to intervene in Vietnam as inherently immoral and unjustified, as opposed to mistaken and unwise, generated passionate and often highly personal criticism from American former opponents of the war. He died peacefully in Washington, D.C., on July 6, 2009.

Priscilla Roberts

See also: Bay of Pigs Invasion; Eisenhower, Dwight David; Johnson, Lyndon Baines; Kennedy, John Fitzgerald; Military Balance; Missile Gap; Nuclear Arms Race; Partial Test Ban Treaty; U-2 Overflights

References

Blight, James G., and Janet M. Lang. *The Fog of War: Lessons from the Life of Robert S. McNamara.* Lanham, MD: Rowman and Littlefield, 2005.

Halberstam, David. *The Best and the Brightest.* New York: Random House, 1972.

McNamara, Robert S., with Brian VanDeMark. *In Retrospect: The Tragedy and Lessons of Vietnam.* New York: Times Books, 1995.

Shapley, Deborah. *Promise and Power: The Life and Times of Robert McNamara.* Boston: Little, Brown, 1993.

Mikoyan, Anastas Ivanovich (1895–1978)

Soviet politician, Politburo member (1926–1966), and chairman of the Presidium of the Supreme Soviet (1964–1965). Born the son of a carpenter in Sanain, Armenia, on November 25, 1895, Anastas Mikoyan joined the revolutionary Bolshevik Party in 1915. He fought in the Russian Civil War. In 1922 Mikoyan was elected to the Soviet Communist Party's Central Committee. A supporter of Joseph Stalin, in 1926 Mikoyan became a candidate member of the Politburo and was appointed commissar for foreign trade. He became a full member of the Politburo in 1935 and was deputy prime minister from 1937 to 1955. There are indications that Stalin, believing that Mikoyan was plotting to unseat him, was planning Mikoyan's death when he himself died in 1953. In the post-Stalin succession struggle in 1953, Mikoyan salvaged his political career by supporting Nikita Khrushchev. Even before Khrushchev's denunciation of Stalin in 1956, Mikoyan often referred to the "evils" of Stalin's dictatorship. He soon became one of Khrushchev's closest advisers.

Mikoyan, who in November 1959 received in person the first reports on Cuba delivered by KGB intelligence agent Aleksandr Alekseev, became an early Kremlin supporter of aid to the Cuban revolution. That same month he recommended that Moscow barter Soviet goods for Cuban sugar. In February 1960 he visited Cuba, the first top Soviet official to do so, had lengthy talks with Fidel Castro and other Cuban leaders, and negotiated a package of trade credits for Cuba. In response to growing U.S. hostility to Cuba, in July 1960, during a visit to Moscow by Castro's brother Raúl, Mikoyan offered the Cubans substantial armaments, including 100,000 automatic rifles and 30 tanks, without expecting payment in return.

Mikoyan nonetheless remained wary of moves the United States might find unduly provocative. In May 1962, Mikoyan was the only Politburo

member who initially opposed Khrushchev's decision to send troops and nuclear-capable missiles secretly to Cuba, warning that U.S. surveillance aircraft would easily detect these. After President John F. Kennedy publicly demanded that the Soviet Union withdraw the missiles, in a Presidium meeting on October 25 Mikoyan endorsed Khrushchev's decision to do so, provided the United States would agree not to invade Cuba.

In November 1962 Khrushchev dispatched Mikoyan to Cuba, where he spent a month on the unenviable task of persuading Castro to accept the terms on which the Cuban Missile Crisis was settled while defusing his anger. Mikoyan—whose wife died just as he arrived in Cuba—bore the brunt of Castro's resentment and was forced to endure repeated lengthy tirades condemning Soviet behavior during the crisis as pusillanimous and a betrayal of Cuba. Castro also attempted to sabotage the settlement by refusing to allow on-site inspections and seeking to shoot down overflying U.S. reconnaissance aircraft verifying the dismantling of the missile sites. Mikoyan bluntly informed Castro that Soviet antiaircraft batteries and personnel would not attack U.S. airplanes. Soviet leaders also refused to allow Il-28 light bombers to remain in Cuba, as Castro demanded. On his own initiative, Mikoyan refused a further request from Castro to allow tactical nuclear-capable cruise missiles to remain in Cuba.

On leaving Cuba, Mikoyan met with United Nations secretary general U Thant, who had brokered many of the arrangements for removing the missiles, and with Kennedy. Kennedy and Mikoyan clashed over the missiles, which Mikoyan claimed had been purely defensive in nature, while Kennedy assailed Soviet behavior in installing the missiles as deliberate deception but assured Mikoyan that his country "would not attack Cuba" though Americans "still consider Castro our adversary."

In July 1964 Mikoyan was elected chair of the Presidium of the Supreme Soviet, making him titular head of state. He timidly supported Khrushchev's ouster from power in October 1964. With new leadership headed by Leonid Brezhnev, Mikoyan found himself increasingly isolated, and he relinquished his chairmanship in December 1965. He retired from the Politburo in April 1966, although he remained a member of the Communist Party Central Committee until 1976. Mikoyan died in Moscow on October 21, 1978.

Paul Wingrove

See also: Alekseev (Shitov), Aleksandr Ivanovich; Castro, Fidel; Castro, Raúl; Kennedy, John Fitzgerald; Khrushchev, Nikita Sergeyevich; U Thant; U-2 Overflights; United Nations

References

Fursenko, Aleksandr, and Timothy Naftali. *One Hell of a Gamble: Khrushchev, Castro, and Kennedy, 1958–1964.* New York: Norton, 1997.

Medvedev, Roy A. *All Stalin's Men.* New York: Doubleday, 1984.

Mikoyan, Anastas. *The Memoirs of Anastas Mikoyan.* Madison, WI: Sphinx, 1988.

Military Balance (1945–1990)

The Cold War military balance was not merely a comparison of U.S. and Soviet military capabilities but just as much a reflection of perceptions, ideas, and assumptions, fueled by the necessity of protecting not just the physical security of a nation but also its core values and way of life. This balance, moreover, was an evolutionary process driven by how leaders on both sides of the Iron Curtain perceived and responded to events on the world stage. While much is known about decision-making dynamics within the U.S. national security establishment during the Cold War, the same cannot be said for the Soviet Union, even after some Soviet archives were opened after the Cold War ended.

The Cold War military balance was defined by three phases. The first phase, marked by the U.S. nuclear monopoly, was ushered in when atomic weapons were used in August 1945 to persuade Japan to surrender. Because the beginning of the Cold War coincided with the dawn of the nuclear age, the history of the two would become inextricably intertwined.

As the postwar period progressed, relations between the United States and the Soviet Union rapidly deteriorated. From the Soviet perspective, U.S. insistence upon free elections in what it considered its sphere of influence in Central and Eastern Europe, the threat of capitalist encirclement by the North Atlantic Treaty Organization (NATO) in 1949, and the U.S. nuclear monopoly combined to convey a hostile picture of the West. In much the same way, Western democracies perceived a growing Soviet threat to liberal capitalist democracies around the globe. Communist threats to both Greece and Turkey in 1947, the communist coup in Czechoslovakia in 1948, and the Berlin Blockade (1948–1949) all seemed to confirm that the Soviets were intent upon world domination.

Yet despite this growing hostility, U.S. officials were reasonably confident that as long as the United States held the nuclear monopoly, the threat of Soviet military aggression against core interests was minimal. In the immediate postwar period, this monopoly proved vital in counterbalancing the Soviet Union's massive conventional military advantage, itself a by-product of the war against Germany on the Eastern Front. This correlation of forces ensured that relations between the two Cold War powers remained relatively stable.

August 29, 1949, however—when the Soviet Union detonated its first atomic weapon, years ahead of most predictions—marked a crucial shift in the Cold War military balance. U.S. national security planners came to believe, moreover, that by 1954 the Soviets would possess sufficient nuclear capacity to launch a devastating strike against the United States, meaning that the Soviet Union could initiate a conventional assault on Western Europe and rest relatively secure in the knowledge that the threat of a nuclear counter-response from the Kremlin would thwart any U.S. nuclear response. If the United States and NATO chose not to increase their conventional forces, Soviet aggression after 1954 would force either free world appeasement or nuclear devastation. This urgency, combined with the outbreak of the Korean War in June 1950, underpinned President Harry Truman's response to the National Security Council's NSC-68 report, which called for a massive conventional and nuclear military buildup. This policy, driven by the shattering of the U.S. nuclear monopoly and the Korean War, ushered in the second phase of the Cold War military balance: U.S. nuclear superiority.

The underlying fear of the consequences that accompanied Soviet nuclear capabilities in the absence of an adequate conventional deterrent defined the Truman administration's new post-1950 defense posture, which redressed the military balance through a vast conventional rearmament program both at home and in Western Europe. Because conventional forces were generally more expensive than nuclear weapons, the Korean War stalemate and the U.S. preoccupation with rearmament led to budget deficits, inflation, rigid governmental controls on prices and wages, materials shortages, and what many considered to be the beginnings of a U.S. garrison state. Capitalizing on these difficulties, Republican presidential candidate Dwight D. Eisenhower based his 1952 election platform on a more cost-effective national security posture. The Korean War seemed to provide ample evidence that the Truman administration's approach was based too heavily on reaction rather than prevention, allowed the Soviet Union too much initiative, and in the long run would be economically unsustainable. Eisenhower therefore adopted the so-called New Look defense strategy, predicated on massive retaliation.

Eisenhower administration officials believed that the only way to deter the Soviet Union was to create the perception that the United States would initiate a nuclear response to any level of Soviet aggression, ranging from a limited conventional incursion against a peripheral interest to a full-scale nuclear strike against the United States. To further heighten its perceived credibility, massive retaliation was deliberately cloaked in ambiguity. It was believed that Soviet leaders would refrain from aggression if it remained unclear whether a U.S. nuclear response would be automatic. This could, moreover, be accomplished at a lower cost than the programs prescribed by NSC-68, meaning, in the words of Defense Secretary Charles Wilson, "more bang for a buck." The Eisenhower administration consequently invested deeply in building the U.S. nuclear stockpile, although it did not succeed in implementing major or enduring reductions in defense spending.

Just as the Korean War shaped perceptions of NSC-68, so did the Soviet launching of *Sputnik 1* (October 1957) impact massive retaliation. *Sputnik 1* was propelled into space by an intercontinental ballistic missile (ICBM), demonstrating that the continental United States was vulnerable to direct missile attack.

This event, coupled with the knowledge that the Soviet nuclear stockpile had increased significantly since 1949, forced many defense strategists to rethink the wisdom and prudence of massive retaliation. Although Eisenhower's policy was marginally more cost-effective, the ambiguity upon which much of the deterrent value was based also carried with it a heightened sense of brinkmanship and thus the possibility of nuclear war through miscalculation.

Eisenhower's political opponents, backed by several influential figures within his own military establishment, began calling for a more balanced military capability with a de-emphasis on nuclear weapons. By increasing NATO's conventional strength, the United States and its allies would be able to avoid the unpalatable choices of either nuclear annihilation or appeasement when responding to Soviet aggression. In what represented almost a direct throwback to NSC-68 and the Truman administration, John F. Kennedy's nomination as the Democratic presidential candidate saw him adopt the new doctrine of flexible response as the basis for national security policy.

Flexible response was implemented in 1961 following Soviet premier Nikita Khrushchev's ultimatum to end Western access rights to West Berlin. Conscious that the correlation of forces in conventional terms decidedly favored the Soviet Union and acutely aware that NATO's response to Soviet aggression lay between humiliation and all-out nuclear war, Kennedy employed the sword and shield concept by increasing the presence of tactical nuclear weapons and initiating a significant buildup of conventional forces in Europe. In turn, Khrushchev quietly dropped his ultimatum.

This shift toward flexible response played a significant role in the Cuban Missile Crisis, since NATO's conventional deterrent and its arsenal of tactical nuclear weapons allowed time for pauses in the escalatory process, maximized the possibility of a diplomatic settlement, and minimized the threat of war by miscalculation. Although the conflict was resolved peacefully, it highlighted the dangers of brinkmanship and the threat of full-scale nuclear conflict. With these lessons fresh in their minds, both the United States and the Soviet Union began to seek a Cold War détente. The Partial Test Ban Treaty, signed in August 1963, imposed mutual restraint on large-scale atmospheric nuclear tests, and perhaps most significantly, a direct hotline was established between the White House and the Kremlin.

By the early 1970s, the Cold War military balance entered its third and final stage: rough nuclear parity. As the decade progressed and both the United States and the Soviet Union increased their nuclear stockpiles, both sides recognized that a nuclear war was unwinnable. This underlay the concept of mutually assured destruction (MAD) and, paradoxically, the belief that mutual vulnerability was the key to stability and deterrence. This balance of strategic nuclear parity coupled with the Warsaw Pact's massive conventional forces and the sword and shield concept embraced by NATO gave rise to the Strategic Arms Limitation Talks (SALT) that began in November 1969 and set the tone for much of the remaining Cold War.

Josh Ushay

See also: Berlin Crises; Containment, Doctrine and Course of; Eisenhower, Dwight David; Kennedy, John Fitzgerald; Khrushchev, Nikita Sergeyevich; Missile Gap; Nuclear Arms Race; Partial Test Ban Treaty; U.S. Allies; Warsaw Pact

References

Bundy, McGeorge. *Danger and Survival: Choices about the Bomb in the First Fifty Years.* New York: Vintage, 1990.

Dockrill, Saki. *Eisenhower's New Look: National Security Policy, 1953–1961.* New York: St. Martin's Press, 1996.

Freedman, Lawrence. *The Evolution of Nuclear Strategy.* 3rd ed. Houndmills, UK: Palgrave Macmillan, 2003.

Gaddis, John Lewis. *Strategies of Containment: A Critical Appraisal of Postwar American National Security Policy.* New York: Oxford University Press, 1982.

Garthoff, Raymond L. *Soviet Strategy in the Nuclear Age.* Westport, CT: Greenwood Press, 1974.

Leffler, Melvyn P. *A Preponderance of Power: National Security, the Truman Administration, and the Cold War.* Stanford, CA: Stanford University Press, 1992.

Pierpaoli, Paul G., Jr. *Truman and Korea: The Political Culture of the Early Cold War.* Columbia and London: University of Missouri Press, 1999.

Williamson, Samuel R., Jr., and Steven L. Rearden. *The Origins of U.S. Nuclear Strategy, 1945–1953.* New York: St. Martin's Press, 1993.

Missile Gap

Alleged shortfall of U.S. intercontinental ballistic missiles (ICBMs) as compared to those of the Soviet Union during the late 1950s. Debate on this matter peaked in 1960 but began as early as 1956, when Democratic Missouri senator Stuart Symington charged that the United States lagged behind the Soviet Union in producing guided missiles. President Dwight D. Eisenhower's administration denied the allegations, but the Democrats refused to drop the issue. In August 1957 the Soviet Union launched the world's first ICBM. In October of the same year the Soviet Union launched the first satellite, *Sputnik 1. Sputnik 1* was propelled into space by a rocket, leading many Americans to believe the Soviet Union had taken the lead in rocket technology, and thus popular belief in a missile gap between the nations began in earnest. This development not only presented Americans with a public relations problem but also had national security ramifications, since the United States now faced a potential Soviet ICBM attack.

The findings of the 1957 Gaither Committee further increased this sense of technological inferiority and vulnerability. Among other things, the Gaither Report argued that the missile gap not only existed but could be expected to widen, with the Soviet Union moving well ahead of the United States in missile and rocket technology. Still worse, National Intelligence Estimate (NIE) reports seemed to support this evaluation, concluding that the Soviet Union had the capability to manufacture 100 ICBMs in 1960 and some 500 more during 1961–1962. These figures, however, represented nothing more than pure speculation.

Eisenhower tried to downplay *Sputnik 1* and the Gaither Report's findings, but the public reacted with fear and outrage. Furthermore, the matter became a partisan political issue, as the Democrats seized upon it to attack the president and the Republican Party for "complacency." Hard-line Democratic Cold Warriors viewed these developments as proof that the Eisenhower administration had not spent enough money on national defense. In fact, the Eisenhower administration had spent heavily to develop guided missiles, especially the Titan, Thor, Polaris, and Minuteman, but did so cautiously, seeking to find a middle ground among defense spending, domestic spending, and balanced budgets.

Even when the Central Intelligence Agency (CIA) presented Eisenhower with ominous estimates of the prospects of Soviet missile programs, the president remained unconvinced. The missile gap debate reignited in 1958, when Hanson W. Baldwin, military commentator for the *New York Times,* published the book *The Great Arms Race: A Comparison of Soviet and U.S. Power Today,* which criticized Eisenhower's reaction to *Sputnik 1.* This reinforced some voices from the Pentagon still warning of a missile gap and advocating increased defense spending. Another influential figure who joined the fray was the prominent journalist Joseph Alsop, who charged that the Soviet Union "will have unchallengeable superiority in the nuclear striking power that was once our specialty" and blamed Eisenhower.

Alsop's column provoked a striking reaction, especially given the upcoming 1958 congressional elections. Eisenhower then launched a countercampaign, asserting that no missile gap existed and the United States was still ahead in the missile race, but his efforts failed to convince the public. The missile gap furor helped the Democrats retake both houses of Congress in the November 1958 elections, leaving the Democrats poised to push through higher defense appropriations and thereby embarrass the president. Indeed, in 1959 Congress voted for a defense budget larger than Eisenhower had requested.

The controversy did not end there. Among those convinced of the existence of the missile gap was Massachusetts senator John F. Kennedy, a Democrat, who ran for reelection in 1958 in part by citing the missile gap as proof of Republican bungling. Kennedy easily won a second term but continued his crusade over the gap after his reelection, though much of his evidence for it apparently came from Alsop's columns on the subject, rather than from hard intelligence sources.

Predictably, the missile gap became a major issue in Kennedy's 1960 presidential campaign, when he attempted to portray his opponent, Vice President Richard M. Nixon, as soft on defense spending and communism. While Kennedy agreed with Eisenhower that the United States was militarily stronger than the Soviet Union, he was also convinced that the U.S. missile program was lagging behind that of the Soviets, which would pose grave future consequences. Reportedly, Eisenhower possessed fairly reliable intelligence data—much of it gathered by clandestine U-2 reconnaissance overflights of the Soviet Union—suggesting that the United States actually enjoyed superiority over the Soviets in ICBMs, but national security imperatives bound him to secrecy. Kennedy won a perilously thin victory over Nixon in the 1960 presidential election.

Once Kennedy became president, he quickly learned the truth: the missile gap was only a myth. Kennedy did not, however, reveal this information immediately. Robert McNamara, Kennedy's secretary of defense, quietly resolved the controversy during a February 1961 press conference, when he casually mentioned that no missile gap existed, whereupon the subject sank into relative obscurity. In practice, Kennedy conducted his national security policy on the basis that the United States enjoyed considerable strategic nuclear superiority over the Soviet Union. Soviet premier Nikita Khrushchev's desire to redress the imbalance between Soviet and U.S. missiles was probably one factor in the attempt to install Soviet short- and medium-range nuclear-capable missiles on Cuba, precipitating the Cuban Missile Crisis.

David Tal

See also: Central Intelligence Agency; Eisenhower, Dwight David; Kennedy, John Fitzgerald; Khrushchev, Nikita Sergeyevich; McNamara, Robert Strange; Military Balance; Nuclear Arms Race; U-2 Overflights

References

Divine, Robert. *The Sputnik Challenge.* New York: Oxford University Press, 1993.

Preble, Christopher A. *John F. Kennedy and the Missile Gap.* DeKalb: Northern Illinois University Press, 2004.

Roman, Peter J. *Eisenhower and the Missile Gap.* Ithaca, NY: Cornell University Press, 1996.

Snead, David L. *The Gaither Committee, Eisenhower, and the Cold War.* Columbus: Ohio State University Press, 1999.

MONGOOSE, Operation

U.S. covert operation, begun in 1961, to overthrow the Cuban government and assassinate Cuban leader Fidel Castro. Following the failed April 1961 Bay of Pigs invasion, communications between Castro and Soviet premier Nikita Khrushchev increased dramatically. Castro requested additional

Soviet military support, and the Kremlin responded to his appeal. Within a year, Moscow had approved a $148 million arms package, although Khrushchev stalled the support.

After a clandestine meeting between Richard Goodwin, President John F. Kennedy's representative to the Inter-American Economic and Social Council in Uruguay, and Ernesto "Che" Guevara, Cuban minister of the interior, on August 22, 1961, in which Goodwin laid out ways that Cuba could improve relations with the United States, he reported that he saw Guevara's views as symptomatic of a deteriorating Cuban economy and impatience with Moscow. Various U.S. agencies therefore started discussing programs to sabotage the Cuban economy, and Kennedy began exploring options to eliminate Castro. Kennedy's brother and attorney general, Robert Kennedy, did not want to involve the Central Intelligence Agency (CIA) because of the Bay of Pigs debacle. In November 1961, he approached President Kennedy with a plan to establish an interagency project against Cuba that would not rely on CIA experts. On November 30, President Kennedy named Brig. Gen. Edward Lansdale chief of operations for the project.

The interagency committee, known as Special Group, included Robert Kennedy and Treasury Secretary C. Douglas Dillon. The inclusion of Kennedy and Dillon changed the group's name to the Special Group Augmented (SGA). SGA members were CIA director John McCone, National Security Adviser McGeorge Bundy, Alexis Johnson from the State Department, Roswell Gilpatric from the Defense Department, Gen. Lyman Lemnitzer of the Joint Chiefs of Staff, and Gen. Maxwell D. Taylor. Also in attendance at meetings, although they were not members, were President Kennedy, Secretary of State Dean Rusk, and Secretary of Defense Robert McNamara.

In February 1962, Khrushchev finally agreed to provide enhanced arms support to Cuba after receiving intelligence reports that the White House was planning to destroy Castro.

Lansdale devised a two-phase plan to implement Operation MONGOOSE that included paramilitary, sabotage, and political propaganda programs. The SGA ordered an intensification of sabotage and intelligence activity, while President Kennedy continued to waver on the need for military action. Lacking support from U.S. forces, the stability of Operation MONGOOSE began to weaken. Instead, the CIA turned to the Mafia for assistance in assassination plots, and Lansdale used his experience in psychological warfare to devise propaganda strategies. Plans for sabotage and counterintelligence included the injection of untraceable poison into Castro's favorite brand of cigars, the poisoning of Castro's food and drinks, the retrofitting of Castro's fountain pen with a hidden needle capable of injecting a lethal toxin, airdropping anti-Castro propaganda over Cuba, spraying a television studio where Castro was about to appear with a hallucinogenic drug to undermine his popularity, contaminating Cuban sugar, and counterfeiting Cuban money and ration books.

In spring 1962, Robert Kennedy asked the SGA to consider the role of the Soviet Union as a factor in determining the outcome of Operation MONGOOSE. The group did not, however, act on this directive, viewing the idea of a Soviet military base on Cuba as too remote to consider. Yet only a few months earlier, Khrushchev had agreed to begin building up Cuban forces. Ultimately, SGA's nonchalance was a factor in the development of the Cuban Missile Crisis.

Lansdale's project was shut down in October 1962 following the Cuban Missile Crisis, but similar CIA psychological warfare projects against Castro continued well into 1963. These operations failed to win over a skeptical Cuban population.

Lacie A. Ballinger

See also: Bay of Pigs Invasion; Bundy, McGeorge; Castro, Fidel; Central Intelligence Agency; Dillon, C. Douglas; Gilpatric, Roswell Leavitt; Guevara de la Serna, Ernesto "Che"; Joint Chiefs of Staff; Kennedy, John Fitzgerald; Kennedy, Robert Francis; Khrushchev, Nikita Sergeyevich; Lansdale, Edward Geary; McCone, John Alex; McNamara, Robert Strange; Rusk, Dean David; Taylor, Maxwell Davenport

References

Beschloss, Michael R. *The Crisis Years: Kennedy and Khrushchev, 1960–1963.* New York: HarperCollins, 1991.

Bohning, Don. *The Castro Obsession: U.S. Covert Operations against Cuba, 1959–1965.* Washington, DC: Potomac Books, 2005.

Brugioni, Dino A. *Eyeball to Eyeball: Inside the Cuban Missile Crisis.* New York: Random House, 1993.

Fursenko, Aleksandr, and Timothy Naftali. *"One Hell of a Gamble": Khrushchev, Castro, and Kennedy, 1958–1964.* New York: Norton, 1997.

Monroe Doctrine (1823)

Promulgated on December 2, 1823, by U.S. President James Monroe, the Monroe Doctrine was a public declaration that the United States would oppose any efforts by European nations to obtain further colonial territory in the Americas or to reestablish control of colonies that had won independence. The statement, a unilateral announcement, effectively defined the Western Hemisphere as a U.S. sphere of influence. Throughout the 19th century, the United States tacitly relied heavily on the far stronger British fleet to enforce these principles. U.S. leaders nonetheless repeatedly invoked the Monroe Doctrine against British efforts to form alliances or acquire territory in the Americas. In 1842 President John Tyler extended the doctrine to the mid-Pacific islands of Hawai'i, then coveted by Britain. During the 1895 Venezuela Crisis U.S. Secretary of State Richard W. Olney cited the Monroe Doctrine when publicly exhorting Britain to submit to mediation a territorial dispute between its colony, British Guiana, and neighboring Venezuela. The Monroe Doctrine was also evoked to justify U.S. intervention against continued Spanish rule in Cuba in 1898.

Under the 1904 Roosevelt Corollary to the Monroe Doctrine, President Theodore Roosevelt asserted the right of the United States to intervene in the affairs of any Latin American nation that had fallen into disorder, a proviso the United States frequently used to prevent European naval expeditions collecting debts owed their nationals by insolvent Latin American governments. The United States invoked the Corollary to justify numerous unilateral interventions in Latin American nations, including Mexico, Nicaragua, Guatemala, Honduras, Cuba, Chile, the Dominican Republic, Panama, El Salvador, and Grenada. Critics characterized the Monroe Doctrine and Corollary as assertions of exclusive U.S. hegemony over the Americas. During the 1930s, President Franklin D. Roosevelt supposedly replaced these with a less intrusive "Good Neighbor Policy." In World War II and the Cold War years, extensive U.S. interventions in Latin America nonetheless occurred, usually combining the broad rubric of the Monroe Doctrine with the Cold War principle of containment of communism. Although President John F. Kennedy doubted the validity of the Monroe Doctrine as international law, he sought to apply its principles to U.S. actions against Cuba.

Priscilla Roberts

See also: Containment, Doctrine and Course of; Kennedy, John Fitzgerald; Organization of American States

References

Livingston, Grace. *America's Backyard: The United States and Latin America from the Monroe Doctrine to the War on Terror.* London: Zed Books, 2009.

May, Ernest R. *The Making of the Monroe Doctrine.* Cambridge, MA: Belknap Press, 1975.

Murphy, Gretchen. *Hemispheric Imaginings: The Monroe Doctrine and Narratives of U.S. Empire.* Durham, NC: Duke University Press, 2005.

Sexton, Jay. *The Monroe Doctrine: Empire and Nation in Nineteenth-Century America.* New York: Hill and Wang, 2011.

Smith, Gaddis. *The Last Years of the Monroe Doctrine, 1945–1993.* New York: Hill and Wang, 1994.

N

Nitze, Paul Henry (1907–2004)

Assistant secretary of defense for international security affairs, 1961–1963. Paul Nitze was born in Amherst, Massachusetts, on January 16, 1907. He entered investment banking in 1928, and during and after World War II held several government positions related to international trade and economics. In late 1949 he became director of the State Department's Policy Planning Staff. In January 1950, responding to the Soviet detonation of an atomic bomb and the fall of China to communism, Secretary of State Dean Acheson asked Nitze to chair an interdepartmental study group to conduct a full review of U.S. foreign and defense policy, the first such comprehensive survey. Nitze largely wrote its report, NSC-68, which was handed to President Harry S. Truman in April 1950, and argued that the Soviets were bent on world domination. Nitze recommended that, to meet this challenge, the United States should rebuild the West economically, while assuming primary responsibility for the entire non-Communist world's defense and security against outside attack. NSC-68 envisaged doubling to quadrupling U.S. defense spending, estimating that the United States could devote up to 20 percent of its gross national product to defense expenditures without major economic disruptions. When the Korean War began two months later, these recommendations were implemented. The U.S. defense budget rose from $13 billion to $50 billion. The broad framework of U.S. defense capabilities, commitments, and objectives laid out in NSC-68 would in many respects characterize U.S. strategy for the subsequent 40 years.

In 1961 President John F. Kennedy made Nitze assistant secretary of defense for international security affairs. Nitze participated in deliberations during crises over Berlin, in October 1961 even contemplating a preemptive strategic nuclear strike against the Soviet Union should West Berlin be threatened. During the Cuban Missile Crisis Nitze attended meetings of the Executive Committee (ExComm) of the president's advisers, but most of his work was done in small groups, on contingency planning related to Berlin and the potential withdrawal of NATO missiles from Turkey and Italy. Together with deputy undersecretary of state U. Alexis Johnson, he prepared detailed plans to implement a blockade. The existence of this blueprint helped tip the balance in favor of the quarantine option, even though Nitze himself believed this initial strategy might ultimately require reinforcement with air strikes and possibly a U.S. invasion of Cuba. Nitze strongly opposed the idea of removing NATO missiles in Turkey in return for the dismantling of Soviet missiles in Cuba, and he remained ignorant of the secret U.S.-Soviet understanding to this effect negotiated by Attorney General Robert F. Kennedy.

From 1963 to 1967 Nitze was secretary of the Navy, in which position he became a proponent of a negotiated Vietnam peace settlement and the de-escalation of the ground war. Nitze was one of the "Wise Men," the members of the President's Ad Hoc Task Force on Vietnam which in March 1968 recommended U.S. withdrawal from the Vietnam conflict. He was deputy secretary of defense from 1967 to 1969 and a leading figure in arms-control negotiations under Republican presidents Richard M. Nixon and Ronald Reagan. In the 1970s Nitze was a founder of the second Committee on the Present Danger, which argued that U.S. defenses were dangerously inadequate and attacked the SALT II arms-limitation treaty negotiated under Gerald Ford as ineffective. He died of pneumonia at his Georgetown, Washington, home on October 19, 2004.

Priscilla Roberts

See also: Berlin Crises; Containment, Doctrine and Course of; Jupiter Missiles (Turkey and Italy); Kennedy, John Fitzgerald; Kennedy, Robert Francis; Military Balance; Nuclear Arms Race

References

Callahan, David. *Dangerous Capabilities: Paul Nitze and the Cold War.* New York: Harper Collins, 1990.

Nitze, Paul H., with Ann M. Smith and Steven L. Rearden. *From Hiroshima to Glasnost at the Center of Decision: A Memoir.* New York: Grove Weidenfeld, 1989.

Rearden, Steven L. *The Evolution of American Strategic Doctrine: Paul H. Nitze and the Soviet Challenge.* Boulder, CO: Westview Press, 1984.

Talbott, Strobe. *The Master of the Game: Paul Nitze and the Nuclear Peace.* New York: Knopf, 1988.

Thompson, Nicholas. *The Hawk and the Dove: Paul Nitze, George Kennan, and the History of the Cold War.* New York: Henry Holt, 2009.

Nuclear Arms Race

General term for the undeclared Cold War contest in which the United States and the Soviet Union developed, tested, and deployed increasingly advanced nuclear weapons and delivery systems. The strategic motivation behind the arms race was each nation's drive to ensure that its adversary did not gain any measurable advantage in nuclear-strike capability. Also at play was the evolving concept of nuclear deterrence, which held that a nation must retain adequate nuclear capabilities to deter the enemy from launching a preemptive nuclear attack. This concept became known as mutually assured destruction (MAD) and held that any preemptive attack would result in an overwhelming and catastrophic retaliatory strike.

The nuclear arms race traces its origins to World War II, when the U.S. government learned that Germany had the capacity and desire to build an atomic bomb. Spurred by this threat, the Americans raced the Germans to build the first nuclear weapon, although it was hardly a competitive endeavor. The Germans paid less attention to atomic weapons development than the Americans, who poured considerable sums into their Manhattan Project, while Germany focused on apparently more pragmatic weapons systems.

The race continued beyond World War II. With its first test explosion in July 1945, the United States possessed an atomic monopoly, and the Soviet Union, with which the Americans found themselves increasingly at odds, understandably feared the U.S. nuclear threat, especially given the demonstrated ability of the United States to conduct long-range strategic bombing. Thus, the Soviets pursued their own atomic bomb extremely vigorously. Soviet spies who had infiltrated the Manhattan Project and a skilled scientific community allowed the Soviet Union to detonate its first nuclear weapon in August 1949.

The Americans sought to retain their nuclear lead and, in an action-reaction cycle that would typify the arms race, pursued the next nuclear

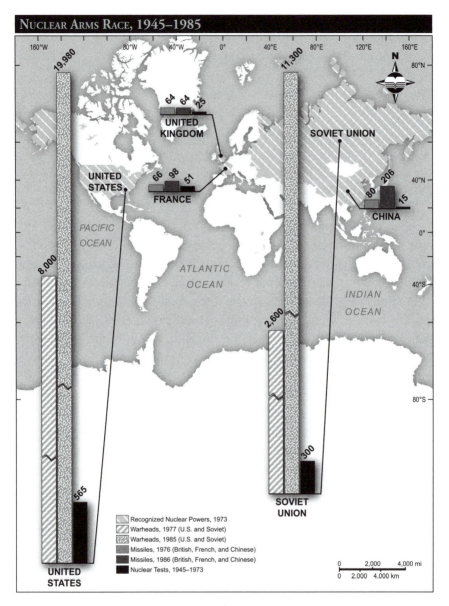

Nuclear Arms Race, 1945–1985

development—in this case, a thermonuclear (or hydrogen) bomb. U.S. success in developing the hydrogen bomb in 1952 was followed by Soviet success in 1955. The nuclear arms race now entered its most recognizable form, wherein the superpowers pursued weapons that were smaller in size, more powerful, and increasingly accurate, while delivery systems became faster, more accurate, and more difficult for enemy surveillance to locate.

During the late 1940s and early 1950s, the primary delivery vehicle for nuclear weapons was the strategic bomber. More advanced aircraft were needed to carry more than one nuclear weapon, and indeed, nuclear weapons needed to be smaller to enable a variety of aircraft to carry them. The U.S. B-29 bomber was matched by the Soviet TU-4, but neither proved adequate, and ultimately the B-52 and the TU-20 were developed, both intercontinental bombers capable of delivering large payloads to multiple targets.

The next step in the nuclear arms race was missile development. Advances in rocketry led to the development of ballistic missiles in both the United States and the Soviet Union. The first U.S. intercontinental ballistic missile (ICBM), the Atlas D, was deployed on October 31, 1959. The Soviets followed suit with their own ICBM, the SS-6 Sapwood of North Atlantic Treaty Organization (NATO) designation, on January 20, 1960. ICBMs were a step up from their cousins, medium-range ballistic missiles (MRBMs) and intermediate-range ballistic missiles (IRBMs), and became the most popular delivery system because of their range and relative invulnerability to enemy air defenses. ICBMs had a maximum range of 10,000 miles and could be stationed on the other side of the world from their targets.

In the 1950s, both superpowers came to rely on nuclear weapons as the primary weapon for any major Cold War engagement. The nuclear arms race created ever-larger arsenals and increasingly effective delivery systems, leaving both sides vulnerable to an enemy attack. This vulnerability perpetuated the arms race during the decade and beyond. Neither side was willing to give up its weapons, and the newer weapons now meant that the nation that launched a first strike might be able to avoid a retaliatory strike if its nuclear advantage were enough to allow it to destroy most of the enemy's nuclear forces in the first blow. Any large gap in nuclear arms made one nation vulnerable, and only nuclear parity could ensure nuclear stability. Scientific advances by one nation consequently had to be matched by the other, since otherwise a gap would result, advantaging one side. The Cuban Missile Crisis can be understood as an attempt by the Soviet Union to take a shortcut and reduce an asymmetrical nuclear balance greatly favoring the United States, by stationing assorted tactical, intermediate-range, and medium-range nuclear-capable missiles within 100 miles of the United States.

In the 1960s the evolution of the counterforce (or no cities) doctrine aggravated this situation. Advocates of the doctrine suggested a general agreement between the superpowers to use nuclear weapons only against military installations, sparing population centers. Adopting this policy meant accepting the reality that in order to sustain the ability to launch an effective counterstrike, a nation must deploy sufficient weapons to ensure that the enemy could not destroy them all in a preemptive strike, mandating more and better weapons.

Arms-control talks and treaties during the 1970s and arms-reduction agreements during the 1980s slowed but did not halt the nuclear arms race. When the Cold War ended, so did the nuclear arms race in its original form. Because nuclear weapons remain a strategic force for some nations, a new and different nuclear arms race can be anticipated.

Brian Madison Jones

See also: Containment, Doctrine and Course of; Military Balance; Missile Gap; Partial Test Ban Treaty

References

Bottome, Edgar M. *The Balance of Terror: A Guide to the Arms Race.* Boston: Beacon, 1971.

Powaski, Ronald E. *March to Armageddon: The United States and the Nuclear Arms Race, 1939 to the Present.* New York: Oxford University Press, 1987.

Powaski, Ronald E. *Return to Armageddon: The United States and the Nuclear Arms Race, 1981–1999.* New York: Oxford University Press, 2000.

O

Organization of American States

Multinational institution established in 1948 by the U.S. and Latin American governments to promote international cooperation within the Western Hemisphere. The concept of an organization to encourage cooperation among Western Hemispheric nations originated in the early 19th century, when the South American revolutionary war hero Simón Bolivar unsuccessfully proposed a league of Latin American republics. Decades later, the United States revived the idea with more success and with a different agenda: the promotion of trade. At a conference in Washington, D.C., during 1889–1890, 18 Western Hemispheric nations founded the Commercial Bureau of the American Republics (later transformed into the Pan-American Union), with headquarters in Washington, D.C.

After 1945 various pressures, many related to the Cold War, led the U.S. and Latin American governments to seek closer cooperation through new institutions. Latin American leaders, worried by declining U.S. economic engagement following World War II, sought to open new channels to encourage U.S. aid and investment. President Harry Truman's administration, anxious about worsening Cold War tensions, hoped to consolidate U.S. authority in the hemisphere.

In 1947 the United States and 19 Latin American governments signed the Rio Pact, a mutual defense treaty that advanced the long-standing U.S. effort to make enforcement of the 1823 Monroe Doctrine a multilateral responsibility. A year later, 21 Western Hemispheric nations gathered in Bogotá, Colombia, to discuss economic and political relations. On April 30, 1948, the attending nations signed the Charter of the Organization of American States (OAS).

The OAS called for efforts to promote peace, prosperity, and democracy in the hemisphere and established mechanisms for resolving disputes among member states. Members were committed to opposing communism within the Western Hemisphere. At the insistence of Latin American governments keenly aware of the long record of U.S. intervention in their nations, the OAS also declared the principle of nonintervention. Adopted over U.S. objections, Article 15 of the OAS Charter asserted that "no State or group of States has the right to intervene, directly or indirectly, for any reason whatever, in the internal or external affairs of any other State."

In subsequent decades, U.S. leaders repeatedly overcame this limitation by using the OAS as a means to attain U.S. geopolitical objectives behind a façade of regional solidarity. President Dwight Eisenhower's administration established this pattern in 1954 when it used the OAS to help oust the left-leaning government of Jacobo Arbenz in Guatemala, in the following way. In March 1954, at an OAS meeting in Caracas, U.S. officials successfully pushed for a resolution committing OAS members to take joint action against any communist regime in the Western Hemisphere. The Eisenhower administration had calculated that an OAS resolution condemning Arbenz as a communist would give a veneer of legitimacy to U.S. action against his regime. The U.S. government told Latin American governments that the episode was a "test case" of the OAS's ability to defend the hemisphere and threatened to act alone if the organization failed to take a stand. With only Guatemala in opposition, 16 Latin American governments grudgingly supported the United States. In June 1954, as a military operation sponsored by the Central Intelligence Agency (CIA) overthrew Arbenz, U.S. leaders claimed to be acting in the interests of the OAS.

The OAS performed a similar function when the United States sought to apply pressure on Cuba during 1959 and the early 1960s. One reason why Cuban leader Fidel Castro was initially cagey about committing himself openly to the communist camp was his apprehension that this would allow the United States to invoke the Caracas Resolution and cloak any action against his government in OAS legitimacy. Similar reasons impelled Cuban officials to conceal how from mid-1959 onward they received substantial quantities of arms from Czechoslovakia, Poland, and eventually the Soviet Union. When Cuban leaders complained to the United Nations (UN) about U.S. hostility, U.S. officials convinced the UN Security Council that the OAS, not the UN, was the appropriate body to consider the issue. Under the guise of regional cooperation, the United States then maneuvered to exclude Cuba from the OAS. At a ministerial meeting in Punta del Este, Uruguay, in January 1962, President John Kennedy's administration won OAS approval—by a one-vote margin—of a statement declaring Marxism-Leninism incompatible with the American system. Technically, Cuba remained a member state, but its existing government was excluded from attending OAS meetings and participating in the body's activities.

During the Cuban Missile Crisis, after several days' deliberations Kennedy decided to impose a naval quarantine or blockade to prevent any further Soviet weapons shipments reaching Cuba. The Kennedy administration decided to do so under OAS auspices, entrusting Secretary of State Dean Rusk and Edwin Martin, undersecretary of state for Latin American affairs, with steering the resolution through the OAS, which they did on October 23, winning unanimous support for the quarantine. The blockade became operative at 10:00 a.m. on October 24 and remained in force until November 20, 1962.

Despite periodic protests from Castro's government, Cuba's suspension from the OAS lasted much longer, in part because he openly promoted revolution in other Latin American states. In 1964, after Cuba began supporting revolutionary movements in Venezuela and elsewhere, all Latin American nations except Mexico broke diplomatic relations with Cuba. In June 2009 the OAS Assembly voted to lift Cuba's suspension, but made this conditional on Cuban compliance with all treaties signed by OAS member states, including the Inter-American Democratic Charter of 2001.

Mark Atwood Lawrence

See also: Castro, Fidel; Central Intelligence Agency; Containment, Doctrine and Course of; Eisenhower, Dwight David; Kennedy, John Fitzgerald; Monroe Doctrine; Rusk, Dean David; United Nations

References

Herz, Mônica. *The Organization of American States (OAS): Global Governance Away from the Media.* New York: Routledge, 2011.

Schoultz, Lars. *Beneath the United States: A History of U.S. Policy toward Latin America.* Cambridge, MA: Harvard University Press, 1998.

Shaw, Carolyn M. *Cooperation, Conflict, and Consensus in the Organization of American States.* New York: Palgrave Macmillan, 2004.

Smith, Gaddis. *The Last Years of the Monroe Doctrine, 1945–1993.* New York: Hill and Wang, 1994.

Smith, Peter H. *Talons of the Eagle: Dynamics of U.S.–Latin American Relations.* 3rd ed. New York: Oxford University Press, 2007.

P

Partial Test Ban Treaty

Treaty banning all nuclear tests, except underground trials. The Partial Test Ban Treaty (PTBT), also known as the Limited Test Ban Treaty (LTBT), was signed in Moscow on August 5, 1963, by representatives of Great Britain, the United States, and the Soviet Union and entered into force on October 10, 1963, with unlimited duration. The PTBT was the result of five years of intense negotiations concerning the limiting of nuclear weapons tests. Some 125 nations have since signed the document, although France and the People's Republic of China (PRC) refused to sign, arguing that the test ban was a means of preserving the superiority of the three initial nuclear powers.

The PTBT was clearly an attempt to make nuclear weapons programs more difficult to sustain, thus limiting nuclear proliferation. Signatories agreed that they would no longer carry out any nuclear test explosion in the atmosphere, underwater, in outer space, or in any other environment that would allow radioactive fallout to spread beyond the territorial borders of the state conducting the test. There was a precedent for an agreement of this kind, namely the 1959 Antarctic Treaty, the first major international arms-control treaty following World War II. Its goal was to prevent the use of Antarctica for military purposes in the belief that it was in humankind's interest to keep the continent pristine and open to scientific research.

World public opinion was already attuned to the dangers of atmospheric nuclear testing as a result of the 1954 *Castle Bravo* incident, when a thermonuclear weapons test at Bikini Island in the Pacific unwittingly exposed to nuclear fallout 28 Americans, 236 Marshall Islanders, and 23 crew members of the Japanese fishing boat *Castle Bravo*. France's decision to conduct atmospheric tests in Polynesia in 1962 further inflamed public opinion.

Furthermore, in the United States support for a test ban increased throughout the summer of 1963. In early July that year, 52 percent of Americans signaled unqualified support for a test ban. After the treaty had been signed, 81 percent of those polled approved the ban. During the early 1960s, two developments were influential in pushing forward a test ban. Considerable radioactive materials were being poured into the atmosphere as a result of atmospheric nuclear testing, and the world's nuclear states had advanced their nuclear technology to the point where a combination of underground tests and physical calculations gave them sufficient information to design and test their strategic weapons without risking radioactive fallout.

In 1962, the newly established Eighteen-Nation Disarmament Committee (ENDC) within the United Nations (UN) became the principal forum for discussions concerning a test ban. After protracted negotiations, an agreement emerged on the use of seismic stations and on-site inspections for verification purposes, but disagreement on the acceptable number of inspections continued. In July 1963 the United States, Britain, and the Soviet Union initiated tripartite talks on the cessation of nuclear tests in the atmosphere, in outer space, and underwater. Agreement on a partial test-ban treaty emerged from those discussions after about three weeks of talks.

The PTBT seemed to offer hope for future disarmament agreements. In 1968 the Nuclear Non-Proliferation Treaty (NPT) was signed, restricting the flow of weapons, technical knowledge, and fissile materials to states that did not already have nuclear weapons. The United States and the Soviet Union went a step further in 1974 when they signed the Threshold Test Ban Treaty (TTBT), limiting underground testing, which entered into force in 1990.

Jérôme Dorvidal and Jeffrey Larsen

See also: Kennedy, John Fitzgerald; Khrushchev, Nikita Sergeyevich; Military Balance; Nuclear Arms Race; U.S. Allies

References

Dean, Arthur H. *Test Ban and Disarmament: The Path of Negotiation.* New York: Harper and Row, 1966.

Oliver, Kendrick. *Kennedy, Macmillan, and the Nuclear Test-Ban Debate, 1961–63.* New York: St. Martin's Press, 1998.

Seaborg, Glenn, with Benjamin S. Loeb. *Kennedy, Khrushchev, and the Test Ban.* Berkeley: University of California Press, 1981.

Sobel, Lester A. *Disarmament and Nuclear Tests, 1960–1963.* New York: Facts on File Series, Library of Congress, 1964.

Terchek, Ronald J. *The Making of the Test Ban Treaty.* The Hague: Martinus Nijhoff, 1970.

Walker, John R. *British Nuclear Weapons and the Test Ban 1954–73.* Farnham, Surrey, UK: Ashgate, 2010.

Pliyev, Issa Alexandrovich (1903–1979)

Soviet general, commander of Soviet forces on Cuba, July–December 1961. Issa Pliyev was born on November 25, 1903, in Stari Batakoyurt, North Ossetia, in the Russian Empire. After fighting in the Russian Civil War, he joined the Red Army in 1922, graduating from the Leningrad Cavalry School in 1926, the Frunze Military Academy in 1933, and the Soviet General Staff Academy in 1941. He joined the Soviet Communist Party in 1926. A cavalry and tank commander, during World War II Pliyev took part in the battles of Moscow, Stalingrad, and Debrecen (Hungary), and the Budapest and Prague offensives. In August 1945 he commanded the Soviet-Mongolian Cavalry-Mechanized Group in Manchuria, fighting the Japanese Kwantung Army. For his wartime service, Pliyev was twice named a Hero of the Soviet Union. After World War II, Pliyev held several important military commands. From 1955 to 1962 he served as deputy commander and then commander of the North Caucasus Military District. In 1962, after suppressing popular riots in Novocherkassk in the Caucasus, he was appointed general of the army.

In July 1962 the Soviet Presidium selected Pliyev, a longtime associate of Defense Minister Rodion Malinovsky, under whom he had served in Hungary and Manchuria during World War II, to command the forces selected to install nuclear-capable missiles in Cuba. Bearing a false passport under the assumed name Pavlov, he left by air for Cuba on July 10. Pliyev, who suffered from a recurrent kidney ailment, possessed a dour personality and few diplomatic skills. He developed little rapport with Cuban officials, especially Premier Fidel Castro. Maj. Gen. Aleksei Alekseyevich Dementyev, head of the group of Soviet military advisers in Cuba, largely handled relations with Cuban authorities. Pliyev was also on poor terms with many of his subordinates. Under his supervision, 41,000 Soviet personnel nonetheless moved swiftly to construct 24 R-12 medium-range ballistic missile (MRBM) (range 1,100–1,400 miles) sites and 16 R-14 intermediate-range ballistic missile (IRBM) (range up to 2,800 miles) sites, together with 16 coastal batteries, each equipped with 5 short-range FKR cruise missiles.

In a verbal briefing in July 1962, Soviet premier Nikita Khrushchev reportedly gave Pliyev permission to use battlefield nuclear weapons, namely the cruise missiles, should he be unable to contact Moscow in a combat situation, but emphasized that he should not employ any of the strategic MRBMs or IRBMs without explicit Kremlin orders. In early September 1962, however, Malinovsky failed to confirm this authorization when sending Pliyev written instructions, in connection with further deployments of a squadron of Il-28 light bombers, equipped with six atomic bombs, and three detachments of Luna short-range missiles, with a total of 12 two-kiloton warheads. In mid-October the Soviet Ministry of Defense, concerned that the U.S. government appeared increasingly suspicious of the presence of Soviet forces in Cuba, dispatched a mission headed by Maj. Gen. Anatoli I. Gribkov, deputy head of the Soviet General Staff's Main Operations Directorate. On Malinovsky's orders Gribkov, who arrived on the island on October 18, reiterated and emphasized Kremlin insistence that the R-12 and R-14 missiles must not be used. Even the short-range Luna missiles were to be employed only if U.S. forces actually attacked and invaded, and there should be no haste to do so. Malinovsky also stressed the need to maintain strict control of all missiles.

On October 22, when President John F. Kennedy publicly announced that the United States would not tolerate the presence of Soviet missiles in Cuba, Pliyev had completed construction of the R-12 sites but not the R-14 installations. He controlled 36 R-12 warheads, all the Luna missiles, the Il-28s and their bombs, and 36 cruise missile FKR warheads. After Kennedy's speech, construction of missile sites continued at full speed, and one Soviet ship, the *Alexandrovsk,* carrying 24 nuclear warheads for R-14 IRBMs and 44 warheads for FKR land-based cruise missiles, reached Cuba just before the United States imposed a naval blockade, though several other vessels bearing R-14 missiles turned back. The Presidium tentatively considered allowing Pliyev to use tactical nuclear-armed missiles to resist a U.S. invasion, while forbidding him to launch the MRBMs against targets in the United States without direct authorization from Moscow. On October 22 Pliyev received instructions "to be in full readiness" but not to employ any nuclear weapons, including the Lunas and FKR cruise missiles, in combat situations, effectively a tightening of Kremlin control.

On October 23 Pliyev stepped up preparations for war, accelerating the uncrating and assembly of Il-28s capable of carrying nuclear payloads. It seems likely that on October 26 he moved nuclear warheads on or close to missile sites, though it is uncertain whether any missiles were actually armed. On the night of October 26–27 Pliyev informed Moscow of his intention to use "all available means of air defense" against anticipated U.S. air strikes. Malinovsky and Khrushchev approved this decision. Shortly afterward, however, as a negotiated settlement with the United States seemed likely, the Presidium instructed Pliyev to refrain from installing nuclear warheads on short-range cruise missiles or atomic bombs on the Il-28s without specific authorization.

On the morning of October 27, a U.S. U-2 reconnaissance plane piloted by Maj. Rudolf Anderson overflew Cuba, where a Soviet SA-2 surface-to-air missile (SAM) battery spotted it. The commander, Capt. N. Antonyets, tried to call Pliyev at his headquarters but failed to reach him. Unable to contact Pliyev by telephone, his deputy, Lt. Gen. Stepan Grechko, authorized Antonyets to fire at the U-2, which he did, downing it and killing Anderson. On learning of the incident, Pliyev sent a report to the Ministry of Defense, and although Malinovsky characterized the response as "too hasty," given that negotiations to resolve the crisis peacefully were already under way, no reprimands were subsequently issued. On October 28 the Presidium, still concerned that the United States might launch air strikes on the missile sites, decided to permit Pliyev to use force to defend himself in such an eventuality, leaving it ambivalent whether or not he might employ tactical nuclear-armed weapons. Later that day, as the outlines of a settlement with the United States became clearer, Khrushchev sent Pliyev a warning forbidding him to use either missiles or fighter jets to attack U-2s. Shortly afterward, Pliyev was ordered to begin dismantling the MRBM sites, which were already operational. On October 30, he received instructions to load all the R-12 warheads onto the *Alexandrovsk,* to be returned to the Soviet Union together with the R-14s. Between November 20 and 22, Malinovsky ordered Pliyev to ship out all remaining tactical nuclear warheads on Cuba, an operation completed on December 25, 1962.

Pliyev soon followed, though around 18,000 Soviet troops remained on Cuba. The Soviet government awarded Pliyev the Order of Lenin for his service in Cuba. He subsequently wrote two volumes of memoirs on his World War II service. In 1968 the Defense Ministry appointed him a military inspector and adviser to its General Inspectors Group. Pliyev died on February 2, 1979.

Priscilla Roberts

See also: ANADYR, Operation; Castro, Fidel; Gribkov, Anatoli Ivanovich; Kennedy, John Fitzgerald; Khrushchev, Nikita Sergeyevich; Malinovsky, Rodion Yakovlevich; U-2 Overflights

References

Blight, James G., Bruce J. Allyn, and David A. Welch. *Cuba on the Brink: Castro, the Missile Crisis, and the Soviet Collapse.* New York: Pantheon Books, 1993.

Fursenko, Aleksandr, and Timothy Naftali. *One Hell of a Gamble: Khrushchev, Castro, and Kennedy, 1958–1964.* New York: Norton, 1997.

Gribkov, Anatoli I., and William Y. Smith. *Operation ANADYR: U.S. and Soviet Generals Recount the Cuban Missile Crisis.* Edited by Alfred Friendly, Jr. Chicago, Berlin, Tokyo, and Moscow: edition q, 1994.

Polmar, Norman, and John D. Gresham. *DEFCON-2: Standing on the Brink of Nuclear War During the Cuban Missile Crisis.* New York: John Wiley, 2006.

R

Rostow, Walt Whitman (1916–2003)

Chairman, State Department Policy Planning Council, 1961–1966. Walt Rostow was born in New York City on October 7, 1916, and studied economics at Yale University and as a Rhodes Scholar at Oxford University. During World War II, he served in the Office of Strategic Services (OSS), and from 1945 to 1949 he held positions in the State Department and the Economic Commission for Europe. Returning to academic life in 1950, for a decade he taught economics at the Massachusetts Institute of Technology. He was also associated with the Institute's Central Intelligence Agency–supported Center for International Studies. Rostow's research centered upon modernization theory and sought to provide an alternative to Marxist models and historical theories of economic development.

Rostow informally advised Sen. John F. Kennedy during his presidential campaign. As deputy special assistant to the president for national security affairs, from early February 1961 onward Rostow enthusiastically supported substantially expanding U.S. programs in South Vietnam. Immediately after the failed April 1961 Bay of Pigs invasion of Cuba, Rostow warned Kennedy against allowing resentment of Cuba to dominate U.S. foreign policymaking to the detriment of U.S. interests in Southeast Asia. In August 1961 he nonetheless urged that, to safeguard its own credibility and standing in the Western Hemisphere, the United States should employ covert means to overthrow Fidel Castro's government while providing massive developmental aid to Latin American nations.

Appointed chairman of the State Department's Policy Planning Council in November 1961, Rostow was only indirectly involved in resolving the Cuban Missile Crisis. Rostow counseled National Security Adviser

McGeorge Bundy—who differed strongly with him—against offering the Soviet Union any concessions or bargains in order to avoid nuclear warfare and recommended air strikes on Cuba, hoping that these would overturn Castro's regime. On October 25, he also unsuccessfully recommended that the United States embargo all petroleum imports to Cuba. Rostow further proposed deploying tactical nuclear weapons in Berlin, though this suggestion never reached the president. Unaware of Kennedy's secret understanding with the Soviets to remove NATO Jupiter nuclear missiles from Turkey, Rostow thought that U.S. firmness alone had forced the Soviets to back down, a belief that reinforced his existing proclivity to advocate the continuing expansion of U.S. commitments in South Vietnam. During Lyndon B. Johnson's presidency, Rostow—who succeeded Bundy as national security adviser in March 1966—became the administration's staunchest advocate of this position.

In January 1969, Rostow moved to the University of Texas at Austin, teaching economics and history. In voluminous writings, he consistently defended U.S. involvement in the Vietnam War, arguing that this gave other Southeast Asian nations the breathing space needed to develop strong economies and become staunch regional bastions of anticommunism. He died in Austin, Texas, on February 14, 2003.

Priscilla Roberts

See also: Bay of Pigs Invasion; Berlin Crises; Bundy, McGeorge; Castro, Fidel; Central Intelligence Agency; Johnson, Lyndon Baines; Jupiter Missiles (Turkey and Italy); Kennedy, John Fitzgerald

References

Halberstam, David. *The Best and the Brightest.* New York: Random House, 1973.

Milne, David. *America's Rasputin: Walt Rostow and the Vietnam War.* New York: Hill and Wang, 2008.

Peace, Charles Kimber. *Rostow, Kennedy, and the Rhetoric of Foreign Aid.* Lansing: Michigan State University Press, 2001.

Rostow, Walt W. *The Diffusion of Power, 1957–1972: An Essay in Recent History.* New York: Macmillan, 1972.

Rusk, Dean David (1909–1994)

U.S. secretary of state (1961–1969). Born in Cherokee County, Georgia, on February 9, 1909, Dean Rusk graduated from Davidson College, then won a Rhodes Scholarship to Oxford University. In 1934 he became professor of government and dean at Mills College, California. An Army Reserve officer, he was called to active duty in 1940, ending the war as a colonel on the War Department General Staff. He then became special assistant to Secretary of War Robert P. Patterson. In 1947 incoming secretary of state George C. Marshall invited Rusk to head the State Department's Office of Special Political Affairs. In spring 1949 Rusk became deputy undersecretary of state. Major policy initiatives during his tenure included the Marshall Plan, the establishment of a separate West German state, and negotiating the North Atlantic Treaty.

In March 1950 Rusk became assistant secretary of state for Far Eastern affairs, formulating policy on the People's Republic of China (PRC), the Republic of China (ROC) (Taiwan), and the Koreas. When the Democratic People's Republic of Korea (DPRK) (North Korea) invaded the Republic

President John F. Kennedy's Executive Committee (ExComm) of top advisers met daily during the Cuban Missile Crisis, discussing and trying to decide on the best policies to pursue. The meeting of October 29, 1962, included President Kennedy and (clockwise) Secretary of Defense Robert S. McNamara; Deputy Secretary of Defense Roswell Gilpatric; Chairman of the Joint Chiefs of Staff Gen. Maxwell Taylor; Assistant Secretary of Defense Paul Nitze; Deputy USIA Director Donald Wilson; Special Counsel Theodore Sorensen; Special Assistant McGeorge Bundy; Secretary of the Treasury Douglas Dillon; Attorney General Robert F. Kennedy; Vice President Lyndon B. Johnson (hidden); Ambassador Llewellyn Thompson; Arms Control and Disarmament Agency Director William C. Foster; CIA Director John McCone (hidden); Undersecretary of State George Ball; and Secretary of State Dean Rusk. (John F. Kennedy Presidential Library)

of Korea (ROK) (South Korea) in June 1950, Rusk recommended firm action and military intervention under international United Nations (UN) auspices. His varied experiences reinforced his conviction that aggressive totalitarian powers, whether leftist or rightist, must be uncompromisingly opposed. During 1951–1961 Rusk headed the Rockefeller Foundation, greatly expanding aid programs to the developing world.

In 1961 President John F. Kennedy appointed Rusk secretary of state. Rusk placed special emphasis on improving relations with the Soviet Union, pushing arms-control agreements—including the 1963 Partial Test Ban Treaty (PTBT) and the 1968 Non-Proliferation Treaty (NPT)—and increasing aid to developing countries.

Although he had reservations regarding the feasibility of the April 1961 Bay of Pigs invasion attempt against Cuba, doubts he privately shared with Kennedy, to his later regret Rusk failed to express these forcefully in meetings of Kennedy's advisers or to coordinate potential opposition to the scheme within the Kennedy administration. As the invasion encountered major resistance, Rusk refused requests from its Central Intelligence Agency (CIA) planners to permit further U.S. air strikes against Cuban airfields. In January 1962, Rusk headed the U.S. delegation that persuaded the Organization of American States (OAS) to suspend Cuba's participation and impose economic and diplomatic sanctions on Castro's government.

Generally speaking, Rusk counseled moderation during both the ongoing Berlin Crisis and the Cuban Missile Crisis. Although often silent during the deliberations of the Executive Committee (ExComm) of presidential advisers that debated how best to counter the Soviet installation of nuclear-capable missiles in Cuba, Rusk favored the naval quarantine/blockade approach rather than immediate air strikes and helped develop a consensus for it. Unannounced air strikes would, he warned forcibly, contravene international law. Rusk led the delegation that obtained OAS endorsement of the blockade on October 23. Rusk was among the few Kennedy advisers privy to efforts by the president's brother, Attorney General Robert F. Kennedy, to negotiate an understanding with Soviet officials whereby the United States would decommission NATO Jupiter nuclear missiles in Turkey in exchange for the withdrawal of Soviet missiles from Cuba. Had this approach failed, he and John Kennedy were ready to ask the secretary general of the United Nations to propose a similar arrangement.

Initially skeptical of Kennedy's growing troop commitments to South Vietnam, under President Lyndon B. Johnson, who relied far more heavily on his advice, Rusk became increasingly convinced that the United States must resist communist aggression there. He soon became the war's most ardent official defender, backing subsequent troop increases and heavy U.S. bombing raids on North Vietnam. His reputation tarnished by exhausting years in office, a deeply scarred Rusk left the State Department in 1969, teaching international law at the University of Georgia until 1984 and eventually writing his memoirs. He died in Athens, Georgia, on December 20, 1994.

Priscilla Roberts

See also: Bay of Pigs Invasion; Berlin Crises; Central Intelligence Agency; Johnson, Lyndon Baines; Jupiter Missiles (Turkey and Italy); Kennedy, John Fitzgerald; Kennedy, Robert Francis; Organization of American States; Partial Test Ban Treaty; United Nations

References

Cohen, Warren I. *Dean Rusk.* Totowa, NJ: Cooper Square, 1980.

Papp, Daniel S., ed. *As I Saw It: By Dean Rusk As Told to Richard Rusk.* New York: Norton, 1990.

Schoenbaum, Thomas J. *Waging Peace and War: Dean Rusk in the Truman, Kennedy, and Johnson Years.* New York: Simon and Schuster, 1988.

Zeiler, Thomas W. *Dean Rusk: Defending the American Mission Abroad.* Wilmington, DE: Scholarly Resources, 2000.

S

Schlesinger, Arthur Meier, Jr. (1917–2007)

U.S. historian, special assistant to the president, 1960–1964. Arthur Schlesinger, Jr., was born on October 15, 1917, in Columbus, Ohio, the son of a distinguished professor of history who moved to Harvard University in 1924. Educated at Phillips Exeter Academy, Harvard University, and Peterhouse College, Cambridge, he was appointed a Junior Fellow of Harvard's elite Society of Fellows in September 1939. He served in the Office of War Information from 1942 to 1943 and then transferred to the Office of Strategic Services (OSS) as an analyst, spending two years in Britain and France. Schlesinger, a diligent researcher and prolific writer of highly readable history, rejoined Harvard's History Department in 1947. A committed Democrat, he produced several volumes focusing upon the presidencies of Andrew Jackson and Franklin D. Roosevelt. Schlesinger quickly became a leading figure in the anticommunist U.S. left and in 1947 helped to found Americans for Democratic Action, an organization embodying this outlook.

During the 1960 presidential campaign Schlesinger worked to elect the young, Harvard-educated senator John F. Kennedy, whom he considered the embodiment of pragmatic liberalism. In late 1960, Kennedy appointed Schlesinger to the ill-defined position of special assistant to the president, which he remained until two months after Kennedy's assassination in November 1963. With Kennedy's knowledge, from his vantage point Schlesinger gathered raw material for his subsequent memoir of the Kennedy presidency, *A Thousand Days* (1965). He functioned as the president's contact to intellectuals and his liaison with United Nations (UN) ambassador Adlai Stevenson, whose earlier presidential bids Schlesinger had supported.

Schlesinger also advised Kennedy on Latin America, a long-standing interest of his own, and wrote some of his speeches. In 1961 he was among the few administration officials to oppose the disastrous Bay of Pigs invasion attempt in Cuba, though afterward he publicly defended this venture. Schlesinger did not join the Executive Committee (ExComm) of senior officials that debated U.S. policy during the October 1962 crisis over the installation of Soviet missiles in Cuba. Stevenson, who handled the issue at the United Nations, confided in him and Schlesinger joined Stevenson in New York, assisting the ambassador in drafting speeches for the UN Security Council. On October 24 Schlesinger also passed on to Kennedy advice from W. Averell Harriman, assistant secretary of state for Far Eastern affairs, that Soviet leader Nikita Khrushchev was seeking a peaceful solution and the United States should cooperate with him to achieve this. At this time Schlesinger remained unaware of the secret U.S.-Soviet understanding that NATO Jupiter missiles in Turkey would be removed, negotiated by Attorney General Robert F. Kennedy, the president's younger brother.

Schlesinger, who settled in Manhattan and accepted the Albert Schweitzer Chair in the Humanities at the City University of New York Graduate School in 1967, was closely identified with the Kennedy family. He supported Robert in his 1968 presidential bid, cut short by assassination. Ten years later, Schlesinger published the massive *Robert Kennedy and His Times* (1978), which won the National Book Award. Although important sources, Schlesinger's two somewhat hagiographical volumes on the Kennedy brothers reflected his deep attachment to them and tended to interpret history in their favor while ignoring less flattering evidence. He continued to write prolifically, producing numerous short pieces on history and politics, many later published in book form. Over time, Schlesinger turned against the U.S. military intervention in Vietnam he had originally supported and watched apprehensively the growing strength of U.S. conservatism in the later 20th century. On February 27, 2007, he died of a heart attack in Manhattan.

Priscilla Roberts

See also: Bay of Pigs Invasion; Harriman, William Averell; Jupiter Missiles; Kennedy, John Fitzgerald; Kennedy, Robert Francis; Khrushchev, Nikita Sergeyevich; Stevenson, Adlai Ewing II; United Nations

References

Depoe, Stephen P. *Arthur M. Schlesinger, Jr., and the Ideological History of American Liberalism.* Tuscaloosa: University of Alabama Press, 1994.

Diggins, John Patrick, ed. *The Liberal Persuasion: Arthur Schlesinger, Jr., and the Challenge of the American Past.* Princeton, NJ: Princeton University Press, 1997.

Schlesinger, Arthur M., Jr. *Journals 1952–2000.* Edited by Andrew Schlesinger and Stephen Schlesinger. New York: Penguin Press, 2007.

Schlesinger, Arthur M., Jr. *Robert Kennedy and His Times.* Boston: Houghton Mifflin, 1978.

Schlesinger, Arthur M., Jr. *A Thousand Days: John F. Kennedy in the White House.* Boston: Houghton Mifflin, 1965.

Sorensen, Theodore Chaikin (1928–2010)

Special counsel to President John F. Kennedy, 1961–1963. Theodore Sorensen was born on May 8, 1928, in Lincoln, Nebraska, where his father was active in progressive Republican politics. After earning bachelor's and law degrees from the University of Nebraska, he moved to Washington, D.C., working first for the Farm Security Administration, then as a congressional aide.

In 1953 the youthful senator John F. Kennedy of Massachusetts hired Sorensen as a legislative assistant. Sorensen remained with Kennedy until the latter's death, his duties expanding to include speechwriting; many of Kennedy's best-known lines and jokes originated with him. He also drafted numerous articles for Kennedy, did significant research and writing on Kennedy's prize-winning book *Profiles in Courage* (1956), and accompanied the senator as he traveled across the United States campaigning for the presidency.

Once elected, Kennedy immediately appointed Sorensen special counsel to the president, expecting him to be a major adviser on domestic affairs as well as chief speechwriter. Sorensen had no involvement in planning the abortive April 1961 Bay of Pigs invasion of Cuba. After this event, Kennedy began to consult Sorensen on foreign policies, including such sensitive issues as the ongoing German crisis over the status of West Berlin.

In October 1962 Sorensen attended virtually all deliberations of the Executive Committee (ExComm) of advisers whom Kennedy consulted on the Cuban Missile Crisis. He also joined the smaller group with whom Kennedy discussed concurrent secret negotiations with Soviet officials regarding the removal of NATO Jupiter missiles from Turkey in exchange for dismantling of Soviet missile installations in Cuba. Kennedy entrusted Sorensen with drafting several presidential letters to Soviet premier Nikita Khrushchev. His failure to produce an acceptable draft of an initial communication on October 18 may have helped tip the balance toward the imposition of a U.S. naval blockade (quarantine) on Cuba, rather than air strikes against missile installations. Sorensen himself favored the quarantine option as less likely "to precipitate general war while still causing the Soviets...to back down."

Sorensen drafted Kennedy's October 22 speech, informing the American people of the presence of Soviet nuclear-capable missiles in Cuba and demanding their withdrawal. Together with Robert F. Kennedy, he helped draft the president's response to Khrushchev's letters of October 26 and 27, setting out terms on which the Soviet Union would remove the Cuban missiles. He also joined in drafting a secret letter to Khrushchev on the scrapping of the Turkish missiles. Robert McNamara, Kennedy's secretary of defense, later credited him with helping hold the members of ExComm together.

Three months after Kennedy's assassination in November 1963, a devastated Sorensen submitted his resignation to President Lyndon B. Johnson, who had asked him to remain and utilized Sorensen's speechwriting talents for his first State of the Union Address. Sorensen wrote a memoir of the Kennedy administration and had a successful career with a prominent international law firm. He also remained active in Democratic Party politics, a recognized standard-bearer of liberal values, and wrote extensively on domestic and international affairs. On October 31, 2010, he died of a stroke in Manhattan.

Priscilla Roberts

See also: Bay of Pigs Invasion; Berlin Crises; Johnson, Lyndon Baines; Jupiter Missiles (Turkey and Italy); Kennedy, John Fitzgerald; Kennedy, Robert Francis; Khrushchev, Nikita Sergeyevich; McNamara, Robert Strange

References

Goduti, Philip A., Jr. *Kennedy's Kitchen Cabinet and the Pursuit of Peace: The Shaping of American Foreign Policy, 1961–1963.* Jefferson, NC: McFarland Press, 2009.

Sorensen, Theodore C. *Counselor: A Life at the Edge of History.* New York: Harper, 2008.

Sorensen, Theodore C. *Kennedy.* With new preface. New York: Harper, 2009.

Stevenson, Adlai Ewing, II (1900–1965)

U.S. politician, 1952 and 1956 Democratic Party presidential candidate, and ambassador to the United Nations (UN), 1961–1965. Born in Los Angeles on February 5, 1900, Adlai Stevenson attended Princeton University and Northwestern University Law School. Joining the leading Chicago law firm of Cutting, Moore and Sidley, he rapidly won social prominence and a wide circle of intellectual friends, serving on many public service organizations, most notably the Chicago Council on Foreign Relations, becoming its president in 1935. He soon won a reputation as a stellar public speaker.

From 1941 to 1944, Stevenson worked in the U.S. Navy Department. He then spent three years in the State Department as a special assistant to the secretary of state, serving on the U.S. team at the 1945 San Francisco conference that created the UN and attending several UN General Assemblies. In 1948 he was elected governor of Illinois on the Democratic ticket. In 1952 and again in 1956 Stevenson ran unsuccessfully as the Democratic candidate for the U.S. presidency, losing twice by wide margins to the Republican Dwight D. Eisenhower.

In 1961 the newly elected Democratic president, John F. Kennedy, made Stevenson ambassador to the UN, a position he held for the rest of his life. The president and his closest adviser, his brother Robert, both considered Stevenson overly liberal, weak, and indecisive, and treated him rather contemptuously. Left ignorant of planning for the April 1961 Bay of Pigs invasion of Cuba, Stevenson at first erroneously informed the UN that his country had played no part in it, a humiliating indication of his exclusion from the administration's inner circle.

Stevenson's finest hour came during the Cuban Missile Crisis. Speaking before the UN Security Council in an emergency debate on October 25, he displayed photographic evidence of Soviet missile bases on Cuba and aggressively demanded that Valerian Zorin, the Soviet UN representative, confirm whether or not his country had deployed nuclear-capable missiles there. Participating sporadically in the deliberations of the Executive Committee (ExComm) of Kennedy's senior advisers, sometimes in person, sometimes by telephone from New York, during the crisis Stevenson consistently counseled moderation and resolving issues through negotiations. Shown pictures of the missile installations by Kennedy on October 16, Stevenson advised against air strikes on them. By October 20, he supported the option of a blockade of Cuba, which he hoped would lead to negotiations "in an atmosphere free of threat." Even if Soviet premier Nikita

Khrushchev remained intransigent, Stevenson still hoped to avoid resorting to air strikes against Cuba. More conciliatory than other U.S. officials, on October 24 he inclined to favor a proposal by UN secretary general U Thant suggesting that the Soviet Union suspend all further nuclear and other weaponry shipments for two or three weeks while the United States dropped its quarantine and both sides embarked on peaceful discussions. Once the Soviet Union had agreed to withdraw the missiles, Stevenson participated in lengthy UN-supervised negotiations with Soviet representatives settling the details of these arrangements.

In a sour aftermath, in December 1962 the *Saturday Evening Post* published an article by the journalists Stewart Alsop and Charles Bartlett depicting Stevenson as so eager to conciliate the Soviets during the crisis by jettisoning NATO missiles in Italy and Turkey in exchange for those in Cuba that he "wanted a Munich," a reference to the 1938 agreement whereby Britain and France pressured Czechoslovakia to cede much of its territory to Nazi Germany. Ironically, Robert Kennedy, who had secretly negotiated an arrangement along these lines with Soviet officials, was the unnamed source for this story. It probably represented an attempt on his part to force Stevenson, whom he disliked intensely, to resign from his brother's administration. Stevenson retained his post until July 14, 1965, when he died suddenly of a heart attack in London.

Priscilla Roberts

See also: Bay of Pigs Invasion; Eisenhower, Dwight David; Jupiter Missiles (Turkey and Italy); Kennedy, John Fitzgerald; Kennedy, Robert Francis; Khrushchev, Nikita Sergeyevich; Schlesinger, Arthur M., Jr; U Thant; United Nations; Zorin, Valerian Aleksandrovich

References

Broadwater, Jeff. *Adlai Stevenson and American Politics: The Odyssey of a Cold War Liberal.* New York: Twayne, 1994.

Johnson, Walter, ed. *The Papers of Adlai E. Stevenson.* 8 vols. Boston: Little, Brown, 1972–1979.

Liebling, Alvin, ed. *Adlai Stevenson's Lasting Legacy.* New York: Palgrave Macmillan, 2007.

Martin, John Bartlow. *Adlai Stevenson and the World: The Life of Adlai E. Stevenson.* Garden City, NY: Doubleday, 1977.

McKeever, Porter. *Adlai Stevenson: His Life and Legacy.* New York: William Morrow, 1989.

T

Taylor, Maxwell Davenport (1901–1987)

U.S. military officer, chairman of the Joint Chiefs of Staff, 1962–1964. Maxwell Taylor was born on August 26, 1901, in Keytesville, Missouri. He graduated from the U.S. Military Academy, West Point, in 1922. In February 1955 he became chief of staff of the U.S. Army. Although Taylor served out his four-year term and did not, as often alleged, resign in protest, he differed with President Dwight D. Eisenhower over army policy: whereas Taylor favored building up conventional forces to enable the United States to fight limited wars—the strategy of "flexible response"—the budget-conscious president preferred to rely on massive but probably unusable "New Look" nuclear retaliation. In his 1959 book *The Uncertain Trumpet* Taylor publicly aired his views, winning the attention and approval of Eisenhower's successor, John F. Kennedy, and a reputation as a "political general."

The 1961 Bay of Pigs fiasco left Kennedy disillusioned with the Joint Chiefs of Staff (JCS), who had, he believed, left him inadequately briefed on the risks of the operation, assuming that, faced with potential failure, the president would simply authorize direct assistance by U.S. military forces. Shortly afterward, Kennedy brought Taylor in to investigate that episode and then appointed Taylor his principal military adviser, to serve as liaison with the JCS and as chairman of the Special Group (Augmented) on Cuba. Taylor also developed an extremely close relationship with Attorney General Robert F. Kennedy, the president's brother. In August 1962 Taylor, commenting on Operation MONGOOSE proposals to destabilize Cuba devised by Edward Lansdale, deputy assistant secretary of defense for special operations, in collaboration with the Central Intelligence Agency, recognized that internal opposition to Fidel Castro's government was unlikely to overthrow his regime. Taylor favored an expanded program of intelligence gathering and economic warfare against Cuba, together with efforts to discredit Castro domestically and internationally. On October 1, 1962, Kennedy appointed Taylor chairman of the Joint Chiefs of Staff, a post he held until mid-1964.

Once photographic evidence revealed the presence of nuclear-capable missile launching sites in Cuba, Taylor was a key member of the Executive Committee (ExComm) of senior officials the Kennedy administration established on October 16, 1962, to handle the crisis. Initially he recommended a surgical strike against the bases, followed by a naval blockade to prevent the arrival of further weapons. Later that day, after speaking to the Joint Chiefs of Staff (JCS), he recommended massive air strikes on Cuban military facilities over several days but hoped to avoid outright U.S. invasion. By October 19 the rest of the JCS unanimously supported the full program of air strikes plus invasion, a position to which Taylor eventually converted as evidence of numerous additional Soviet missile sites on Cuba emerged. Both Kennedy brothers initially leaned toward the option of air strikes, rather than a less provocative limited naval blockade of Cuba, but by October 20 they had come around to favoring the blockade (or "quarantine"). Taylor expressed disagreement on behalf of the JCS but pledged their complete backing for the president's decision. After Kennedy's public announcement of the quarantine on October 22, Taylor continued to support massive air strikes targeting all identified nuclear-capable and surface-to-air missile sites, plus all Soviet and Cuban airplanes and airfields.

In late 1961 Taylor was an early advocate of the expansion of U.S. troop commitments in South Vietnam, together with military and economic aid. As JCS chairman from 1962 to 1964, and then as U.S. ambassador to South Vietnam, Taylor opposed the commitment of further U.S. ground forces to Vietnam but supported escalation of the war through U.S. air strikes within Vietnam and bombing raids on North Vietnam. In March 1968 Taylor was one of only three senior advisers or "Wise Men" to dissent from the view that the United States should seek a negotiated settlement to end the war. For the rest of his life Taylor continued to defend U.S. policies in Vietnam and to blame his country's defeat largely upon criticism by the media and public opinion, which in his view had sapped American resolve to win. He died in Washington, D.C., on April 19, 1987.

Priscilla Roberts

See also: Bay of Pigs Invasion; Castro, Fidel; Central Intelligence Agency; Eisenhower, Dwight David; Joint Chiefs of Staff; Kennedy,

John Fitzgerald; Kennedy, Robert Francis; Lansdale, Edward Geary; Military Balance; MONGOOSE, Operation; U-2 Overflights

References

Buzzanco, Robert. *Masters of War: Military Dissent and Politics in the Vietnam Era.* New York: Cambridge University Press, 1996.

Goduti, Philip A., Jr. *Kennedy's Kitchen Cabinet and the Pursuit of Peace: The Shaping of American Foreign Policy, 1961–1963.* Jefferson, NC: McFarland Press, 2009.

Kinnard, Douglas. *The Certain Trumpet: Maxwell Taylor and the American Experience in Vietnam.* Washington, DC: Brassey's, 1991.

McMaster, H. R. *Dereliction of Duty: Lyndon Johnson, Robert McNamara, the Joint Chiefs of Staff, and the Lies That Led to Vietnam.* New York: HarperPerennial, 1998.

Taylor, John M. *General Maxwell Taylor: The Sword and the Pen.* New York: Doubleday, 1989. Reissued as *An American Soldier: The Wars of General Maxwell Taylor.* Novato, CA: Presidio, 2001.

Taylor, Maxwell D. *Swords and Plowshares.* New York: Norton, 1972.

Thompson, Llewellyn Edward, Jr. (1904–1972)

U.S. career diplomat and one of the premier Cold War Soviet experts. Born the son of a sheep rancher on August 24, 1904, in Las Animas, Colorado, Llewellyn Thompson graduated from the University of Colorado in 1928 and joined the Foreign Service the following year. His first appointment to Moscow came in 1941. He endeared himself to Muscovites by staying on during the grim Nazi siege of 1941–1942. In 1944 he was sent to London, and in 1946 he returned to Washington to take on senior posts in Eastern European and European affairs.

In 1950 Thompson went to Rome and was then appointed high commissioner and ambassador to Austria (1952–1956). He went on to serve during 1957–1961 as ambassador to the Soviet Union, where he secured Soviet leader Nikita Khrushchev's personal trust. This served Thompson well as an adviser to presidents Dwight D. Eisenhower and John F. Kennedy during Cold War crises over Berlin and Cuba between 1958 and 1962.

Thompson facilitated Khrushchev's visit to the United States in 1959 as well as U.S.-Soviet summits in Paris (1960) and Vienna (1961). Thompson returned to Washington in 1962 and was appointed ambassador-at-large. During the Cuban Missile Crisis, he exerted a moderating influence in White House Executive Committee (ExComm) meetings, in which President Kennedy relied particularly heavily on his expertise on the Soviet Union. In 1966 President Lyndon B. Johnson appointed Thompson—who was involved in many crucial nuclear arms talks—ambassador to the Soviet Union for a second time, a post he held until 1969, making him the longest-serving U.S. ambassador to the Soviet Union in history. Thompson died in Bethesda, Maryland, on February 6, 1972.

Günter Bischof

See also: Berlin Crises; Eisenhower, Dwight David; Johnson, Lyndon Baines; Kennedy, John Fitzgerald; Nuclear Arms Race

References

Beschloss, Michael R. *The Crisis Years: Kennedy and Khrushchev, 1960–1963.* New York: HarperCollins, 1991.

Garthoff, Raymond L. *A Journey through the Cold War: A Memoir of Containment and Coexistence.* Washington, DC: Brookings Institution Press, 2001.

Mayers, David. *The Ambassadors and America's Soviet Policy.* New York: Oxford University Press, 1995.

U

U Thant (1909–1974)

Burmese politician, secretary general of the United Nations (UN), 1961–
1971. Born in Pantanaw, Burma, on January 22, 1909, U Thant worked
as an educator and freelance journalist before going into government service. During 1947–1957 he served as press director of the government of
Burma, director of national broadcasting, secretary to the Ministry of Information, secretary of projects in the Prime Minister's Office, and executive secretary of Burma's Economic and Social Board. In 1957 he became
Burma's representative to the UN. He quickly became a leading figure in
the UN effort to broker a solution to the war in Algeria. As a moderate neu-
tralist, he was elected to complete the term of UN secretary general Dag
Hammarskjöld, who died in a September 1961 plane crash. He served two
further terms in his own right, from November 1962 until December 1971.

As secretary general, Thant preferred quiet diplomacy and tended
to rely more heavily on superpower initiatives than had his predecessor.
But he could also be quite forceful in policy implementation, sending UN
forces in November 1961 and again in December 1962 to end the seces-
sion crisis involving the Congolese province of Katanga.

His most notable successes included sending UN peacekeeping forces
to Cyprus in 1964 and his 1965 brokering of a cease-fire in the 1965 Indo-
Pakistani war over Kashmir.

At the height of the Cuban Missile Crisis, Thant sent identical appeals
to U.S. president John F. Kennedy and Soviet leader Nikita Khrushchev
to end the dispute through negotiations, suggesting that the United States
lift the naval quarantine and the Soviet Union halt work on the missile
sites. Those appeals were ignored. It seems, however, that if U.S.-Soviet

negotiations for a peaceful resolution failed, Kennedy intended to seek UN mediation, a strategy he considered greatly preferable to outright nuclear warfare. Once a settlement was reached in principle, on October 30 and 31, 1962, Thant led a delegation that visited Cuba and inspected some of the missile installations. As a conciliatory gesture, the United States ceased surveillance overflights during his visit. Thant also allowed U.S. and Soviet representatives to work under UN auspices in finalizing the sometimes contentious details of the agreement to remove the missiles and other weaponry from Cuba.

Thant's attempts after 1963 to sponsor negotiations among the United States, the Democratic Republic of Vietnam (DRV) (North Vietnam), and the Soviet Union were less successful. He retired from the UN in December 1971, when his term of office ended. Thant died on November 25, 1974, in New York City.

Lise Namikas

See also: Kennedy, John Fitzgerald; Khrushchev, Nikita Sergeyevich; U-2 Overflights; United Nations

References

Firestone, Bernard J. *The United Nations under U Thant, 1961–1971.* Lanham, MD: Scarecrow Press, 2001.

Fursenko, Aleksandr, and Timothy Naftali. *One Hell of a Gamble: Khrushchev, Castro, and Kennedy, 1958–1964.* New York: Norton, 1997.

May, Ernest R., and Philip D. Zelikow, eds. *The Kennedy Tapes: Inside the White House during the Cuban Missile Crisis.* Cambridge, MA: Harvard University Press, 1997.

Nassif, Ramses. *U Thant in New York, 1961–1971: Portrait of the Third U.N. General-Secretary.* New York: St. Martin's Press, 1988.

U Thant. *View from the UN.* New York: Doubleday, 1977.

U-2 Overflights

In the 1950s, the U.S. defense contractor and aircraft manufacturer Lockheed developed light jet-powered sailplanes that could undertake photographic reconnaissance missions at high altitude, designated U-2s. As part of a program beginning in 1956 under direction from the Central Intelligence Agency (CIA), pilots who came from the U.S. military but were officially employed by Lockheed and attached to a Weather Observation Squadron based in Turkey and making heavy use of bases in Pakistan flew 24 U-2 surveillance flights over Soviet territory along an arc running from Pakistan to Norway. These clandestine flights, which violated Soviet airspace, provided the CIA with vital information on the number, strength, and location of Soviet nuclear missiles and other weapons. The program was ended with the 24th such flight in 1960, after the U-2 Affair, in which Soviet surface-to-air missiles (SAMs) shot down a U-2 deep over Soviet territory, capturing the pilot, Francis Gary Powers, alive and obtaining his public confession that he had been engaged in an espionage mission. One casualty of the U-2 Affair was a summit meeting in Paris between U.S. president Dwight D. Eisenhower and Soviet premier Nikita Khrushchev, an encounter originally intended to defuse international tensions and make some progress toward halting the nuclear arms race.

No further flights were made over Soviet territory, but U-2s still undertook reconnaissance missions over other hostile states, such as China

At the height of the Cuban Missile Crisis, on October 27, 1962, a Soviet missile battery shot down a U-2 surveillance aircraft conducting reconnaissance over Cuba. The pilot, Rudolph Martin Anderson, Jr., was killed. Fearing that any retaliation would further escalate the situation and possibly result in outright war, President John F. Kennedy deliberately chose not to retaliate with an air strike against the antiaircraft battery responsible for downing the U-2. (Getty Images)

and Cuba, where the danger of interception was considered small. From August 1962, CIA director John McCone, who had heard reports that unusual quantities of Soviet military equipment were arriving in Cuba and rumors that these included nuclear warheads, pressed to resume U-2 missions over Cuba. This was allowed in October 1962. At the insistence of Secretary of Defense Robert S. McNamara, uniformed military officers rather than civilians piloted the airplanes involved.

Analysis of photographic data collected by several flights on October 14 and 15 revealed the existence of several nuclear-capable missile sites in Cuba, some equipped for intermediate-range ballistic missiles (IRBMs) and others intended for medium-range ballistic missiles (MRBMs), as well as crates holding Il-28 medium-range light bombers. On the evening of October 15 Ray Cline, the CIA's deputy director of intelligence, passed on this information to McGeorge Bundy, President John F. Kennedy's national security adviser. The following morning Bundy in turn told Kennedy. The news marked the beginning of the Cuban Missile Crisis, triggering 13 days of deliberations among Kennedy and his senior diplomatic and military advisers.

Further U-2 sorties over the next week identified numerous additional missile sites on Cuba, with no certainty that the reconnaissance revealed all existing installations. On October 25, in an emergency debate at the United Nations, U.S. ambassador Adlai Stevenson displayed sample photographs and demanded that Valerian Zorin, his Soviet counterpart, confirm or deny the presence of Soviet nuclear-capable missiles on Cuba. When French newspapers expressed doubts over the validity of the photographic evidence, CIA officials flew to France bearing sets of the photographs to verify their allegations.

U-2 overflights had the potential to escalate the crisis. Soviet forces tracked overflights on October 14, 15, and 17, but had been ordered not to fire on U.S. aircraft unless attacked. On October 27, as negotiations between U.S. and Soviet officials continued, a Soviet SAM battery in Cuba shot down a U-2, killing the pilot, Maj. Rudolph Anderson. Other lower-flying naval reconnaissance aircraft over Cuba also came under fire; one was damaged but returned safely to base. Kennedy and other U.S. officials had previously agreed that any attacks on U.S. airplanes would trigger U.S. air strikes against the batteries responsible for these. In the event, Kennedy and McNamara decided against immediate retaliation, choosing instead to assume that lower-level Soviet military personnel in Cuba had acted without specific authorization from their superiors in Moscow.

The same day, another U-2 collecting atmospheric samples from Soviet nuclear testing near the North Pole strayed off course into Soviet airspace. Soviet MiG fighter jets tried to intercept it, and nuclear-armed U.S. fighter jets based in Alaska escorted the U-2 back once it reentered U.S. airspace. All these incidents revealed the potential for trigger-happy military forces to spark an incident that could easily spiral into a full-scale nuclear exchange. The Pentagon hastily stated that any interference with U.S. surveillance would provoke a response. Khrushchev—who apparently initially believed that Cuban rather than Soviet troops had shot down the U-2—instructed his military commanders in Cuba to exercise restraint and avoid further attacks on U.S. aircraft. At this point the bellicose Cuban leader Fidel Castro was urging Khrushchev to initiate a nuclear first strike against the United States. Fearful that Castro might try to incite Soviet and Cuban military officers manning missile batteries to further hostile action against U.S. targets, Khrushchev begged him to resist the temptation to respond forcibly to U.S. overflights.

Once Soviet officials had agreed to remove the missiles from Cuba, throughout November and December 1962 U-2 overflights as well as lower-level air reconnaissance flights monitored the progress of these operations, provoking sharp protests from Castro. The Soviet government bluntly warned him that Soviet troops would no longer assist in shooting down such aircraft. Eventually, U.S. officials decided to suspend the noisy and disruptive low-level flights and restrict their surveillance to high-altitude U-2 missions. U-2 flights over Cuba continued until the late 1970s, and thereafter were reintroduced during times of tension in U.S.-Cuban relations.

Priscilla Roberts

See also: Bundy, McGeorge; Castro, Fidel; Central Intelligence Agency; Eisenhower, Dwight David; Kennedy, John Fitzgerald; Khrushchev, Nikita Sergeyevich; McCone, John Alex; McNamara, Robert Strange; Stevenson, Adlai Ewing II; United Nations; U.S. Allies; Zorin, Valerian Aleksandrovich

References

Brugioni, Dino. *Eyeball to Eyeball: The Inside Story of the Cuban Missile Crisis.* Edited by Robert F. McCort. New York: Random House, 1991.

Dobbs, Michael. *One Minute to Midnight: Kennedy, Khrushchev, and Castro on the Brink of Nuclear War.* New York: Knopf, 2008.

Pedlow, Gregory W., and Donald E. Welzenbach. *The CIA and the U-2 Program 1954–1974.* Washington, DC: Central Intelligence Agency, Center for the Study of Intelligence, 1998.

Pocock, Chris. *The U-2 Spyplane: Toward the Unknown: A New History of the Early Years.* Atglen, PA: Schiffer Publishing, 2000.

Polmar, Norman, and John D. Gresham. *DEFCON-2: Standing on the Brink of Nuclear War during the Cuban Missile Crisis.* New York: John Wiley, 2006.

Prados, John. *Presidents' Secret Wars: CIA and Pentagon Covert Operations from World War II through the Persian Gulf.* Rev. ed. Chicago: Ivan R. Dee, 1996.

United Nations

Multinational organization established in 1945 and designed to promote four primary objectives: collective security, international economic and cultural cooperation, multilateral humanitarian assistance, and human rights. The creation of the United Nations (UN) represented an attempt by the World War II Allies to establish an international organization more effective than the interwar League of Nations, which had failed to mitigate the worldwide economic depression of the 1930s or prevent a second world war. UN architects were heavily influenced by the belief that during the 1930s, nationalist policies, economic and political rivalries, and the absence of international collaboration to help resolve outstanding disputes had contributed substantially to the outbreak of World War II.

The UN soon became an arena for Cold War contests and disputes in which the major powers tested their strength, while Third World nations came to see the UN as a forum where, given their growing numbers, the concerns of less-developed countries could be voiced and made effective, especially in the General Assembly, which was empowered to discuss all international questions of interest to members. In the Cold War context, the UN became a venue where communist and Western-led camps contended for power. Despite its stated security role, the organization proved largely unsuccessful in defusing the growing tensions that, during the second half of the 1940s, rapidly came to divide the former World War II Allies, with the Western powers—Britain, France, and the United States—soon fiercely at odds with the Soviet Union.

When the UN was founded, it was anticipated that peacekeeping and the restoration of international security and order, if necessary by military means, would be among its major functions. Under Article 43 of the

Debate on the Cuban Missile Crisis at the United Nations (UN) on October 25, 1962. During the meeting, U.S. ambassador to the UN Adlai Stevenson dramatically confronted his Soviet counterpart Valerian Zorin, challenging him to confirm or deny the presence of Soviet missiles in Cuba. Stevenson displayed U-2 surveillance photographs documenting the existence of these missiles. (United Nations)

UN's charter, member states were originally expected to agree to make specified military forces available to the UN for deployment under the organization's control, for use on occasions when military intervention was required to maintain or reestablish international peace and security. In practice, no nation signed any such agreement relinquishing control of any military forces to UN authority.

The UN General Assembly was the stage for some of the most significant pronouncements and dramatic confrontations of the Cold War, providing a backdrop to the saga of Cuba in the late 1950s and 1960s. U.S. diplomats soon noted that under Fidel Castro Cuba frequently voted with the Soviet bloc, a disturbing indication of its new international alignment. On September 26, 1960, Castro addressed the UN General Assembly in New York, denouncing U.S. policies toward Cuba. The audience included Soviet premier Nikita Khrushchev, who loudly affirmed his country's support for Cuba. A month later, on October 25, 1960, as fears that the United States was covertly planning military intervention against Cuba mounted, both Cuban and Soviet representatives appealed to the United Nations to prevent this. Washington convinced the UN Security Council that the

Organization of American States, not the UN, was the appropriate body to consider the issue. Embarrassingly for the United States, during the U.S.-backed Bay of Pigs invasion attempt against Cuba in April 1961, U.S. ambassador to the UN Adlai Stevenson initially denied that his country was involved, a statement he was later forced to retract.

Eighteen months later, in an emergency debate in the Security Council on October 25, 1962, Stevenson dramatically challenged his Soviet counterpart Valerian Zorin to confirm the presence of Soviet nuclear-capable missiles in Cuba, displaying photographic evidence of these installations. One day earlier, UN secretary general U Thant sent identical messages to both parties, suggesting that the Soviet Union suspend all further nuclear and conventional weapons shipments for two or three weeks while the United States dropped its quarantine and both sides embarked on peaceful negotiations. He offered to mediate a settlement, an offer that President John F. Kennedy might well have accepted had his own efforts for a peaceful resolution proved futile. On October 30 and 31, 1962 a UN delegation headed by U Thant visited Havana to inspect the missile sites. Initially, Soviet and U.S. negotiators anticipated UN inspectors would provide verification once the missiles had left, but the resentful Castro refused to allow such inspections on Cuban soil. After the broad lines of an agreement to remove the missiles and other assorted weaponry in exchange for a U.S. pledge not to invade Cuba had been reached, U.S. representatives led by arms-control negotiator John J. McCloy and Soviet deputy foreign minister Vasili Kuznetsov spent two months working under UN auspices to finalize details of these arrangements, completing their work in late December 1962. In late 1963 William Attwood, an adviser to Stevenson, and Carlos Lechuga, Cuban ambassador to the UN, served as conduits for preliminary feelers from Castro to Kennedy on a possible normalization of Cuban-U.S. relations, approaches cut short by Kennedy's assassination in November 1963.

Priscilla Roberts

See also: Bay of Pigs Invasion; Castro, Fidel; Cordier, Andrew Wellington; Kennedy, John Fitzgerald; Khrushchev, Nikita Sergeyevich; Kuznetsov, Vasili Vasilyevich; McCloy, John Jay; Organization of American States; Stevenson, Adlai Ewing II; U Thant; Zorin, Valerian Aleksandrovich

References

Firestone, Bernard J. *The United Nations under U Thant, 1961–1971.* Lanham, MD: Scarecrow Press, 2001.

Heller, Peter B. *The United Nations under Dag Hammarskjöld, 1953–1961*. Lanham, MD: Scarecrow Press, 2001.

Kennedy, Paul. *The Parliament of Man: The Past, Present, and Future of the United Nations*. New York: Random House, 2006.

Lechuga, Carlos M. *In the Eye of the Storm: Castro, Kennedy, Khrushchev, and the Missile Crisis*. Translated by Mary Todd. Melbourne, Victoria, Australia: Ocean Press, 1995.

Luard, Evan. *A History of the United Nations*. 2 vols. New York: St. Martin's Press, 1982–1989.

Meisler, Stanley. *The United Nations: A History*. 2nd ed. New York: Grove, 2011.

Ostrower, Gary B. *The United Nations and the United States*. New York: Twayne, 1998.

U.S. Allies

The emergence in Cuba in January 1959 of a radical revolutionary government led by Fidel Castro had implications for U.S. relations with its allies, particularly those in the North Atlantic Treaty Organization (NATO). Most U.S. allies considered U.S. hostility toward Castro's Cuba excessive. The British Conservative government under Prime Minister Harold Macmillan thought U.S. economic sanctions against Cuba liable to prove counterproductive by inclining Castro toward the communist bloc, though during 1959–1960 U.S. pressure impelled Britain to refuse to sell Hunter warplanes or other arms to Castro. Canadian prime minister John Diefenbaker, reluctant to simply endorse U.S. policies toward Cuba and elsewhere, refused to end trade or break diplomatic relations with revolutionary Cuba and also rejected Canadian membership in the Organization of American States (OAS).

By mid-1960 British officials sympathized with U.S. president Dwight D. Eisenhower's desire to oust Castro, but urged caution in avoiding the appearance of U.S. interventionism. In April 1961 Macmillan loyally backed President John F. Kennedy's actions during the abortive U.S.-sponsored Bay of Pigs invasion attempt—in which NATO allies played no official role—but the episode drew widespread condemnation from the British press, public, and political elite. Internationally, popular and media reaction from most U.S. allies in Western Europe and Canada was generally unfavorable, especially when U.S. officials sought to deceive the United Nations over their country's involvement.

During the Cuban Missile Crisis, NATO states in Western Europe were acutely conscious that U.S. aerial bombing or invasion of Cuba might easily bring Soviet retaliation against West Berlin and the escalation of the dispute into a full-scale nuclear conflict. On October 19, the CIA formally briefed British officials on the developing crisis, and from then onward Kennedy consulted frequently with Macmillan by telephone and in person with his old friend Sir David Ormsby-Gore, the British ambassador in Washington. Asked whether he preferred the options of U.S. air strikes against Cuban missile bases or the imposition of a naval blockade, Ormsby-Gore selected the latter, the alternative Kennedy ultimately chose. On October 22 Kennedy dispatched personal emissaries to inform Macmillan, President Charles de Gaulle of France, West German chancellor Konrad Adenauer, and the North Atlantic Council of his anticipated response to the Soviet missiles in Cuba. With some reservations over the blockade's legality and fears the confrontation might escalate into full-scale war involving both Berlin and British thermonuclear forces, Macmillan offered his support, as did de Gaulle, though much British and French media opinion was initially skeptical of U.S. allegations that nuclear-capable missiles were present on Cuba.

As the crisis developed, U.S. and Soviet officials secretly agreed that the United States would within a few months remove obsolete NATO Jupiter nuclear missiles in Turkey and Italy, close to Soviet borders, in exchange for Soviet withdrawal of nuclear-capable weapons in Cuba. Soviet diplomats in London apparently suggested a bargain on these lines. Before offering this concession, Kennedy consulted Macmillan, who was willing to contribute 60 Thor intermediate-range ballistic missiles (IRBMs), based in Eastern England and already scheduled for removal in 1963. Eventually, it proved unnecessary to add these to the package. Formally, the Turkish and Italian missiles were under NATO control, requiring the United States to convince its allies, especially the reluctant Turks, that relinquishing these weapons would not affect those countries' security. U.S. defense officials, fearful of diminishing the credibility of their commitment to Europe's defense, agreed to compensate for their loss by stationing nuclear-armed Polaris submarines in the Mediterranean, a deployment Soviet premier Nikita Khrushchev eventually but unavailingly protested. Turkey and Italy also received substantial quantities of substitute U.S. conventional and dual-purpose weaponry.

In some respects, the Cuban Missile Crisis encouraged anti-American tendencies among U.S. allies. Kennedy's failure to notify Canada before taking action during the crisis led Diefenbaker, angered by this omission, to refuse U.S. requests that Canada participate in the blockade of Cuba or place the Canadian armed forces in heightened readiness. President de Gaulle's sense that U.S. officials had informed rather than consulted him during the crisis intensified his conviction that French policy should be more independent of both NATO and the United States. The U.S. decision to remove Jupiter missiles from Turkey and Italy likewise impelled France to develop its own independent nuclear deterrent, free from U.S. control. Although Britain, the United States, and the Soviet Union, all sobered by the crisis, negotiated a Partial Nuclear Test Ban Treaty in spring 1963, an agreement that most U.S. allies quickly signed, France refused to be a party to it. The fact that Western Europe came uncomfortably close to enduring thermonuclear devastation over distant bases on a Caribbean island helped boost European peace organizations, including the Campaign for Nuclear Disarmament.

Most U.S. allies greeted the peaceful resolution of the crisis with relief. Yet when news of the crisis became public on October 22, many in the South Korean military were eager to see it escalate into full-scale war, as they believed this would offer an ideal opportunity to invade North Korea and unify the country. U.S. forces in the Demilitarized Zone separating the two Koreas turned their artillery south toward their own ally, and on the insistence of the U.S. government South Korean air force planes were grounded, to prevent any attack on the north. The episode was one example of just how far the implications of the Cuban Missile Crisis extended and how volatile and explosive its impact on the international situation might easily have become.

Priscilla Roberts

See also: Acheson, Dean Gooderham; Bay of Pigs Invasion; Berlin Crises; Castro, Fidel; Eisenhower, Dwight David; Kennedy, John Fitzgerald; Jupiter Missiles (Turkey and Italy); Military Balance; Nuclear Arms Race; Organization of American States; Partial Test Ban Treaty; United Nations

References

Glazov, Jamie. *Canadian Policy toward Khrushchev's Soviet Union.* Montreal and Kingston: McGill-Queen's University Press, 2002.

Mahan, Erin R. *Kennedy, de Gaulle, and Western Europe.* New York: Palgrave Macmillan, 2002.

Mayer, Frank A. *Adenauer and Kennedy: A Study in German-American Relations, 1961–1963.* New York: St. Martin's Press, 1996.

McMahon, Patricia I. *Essence of Indecision: Diefenbaker's Nuclear Policy, 1957–1963.* Montreal: McGill-Queen's University Press, 2009.

Scott, L. V. *Macmillan, Kennedy and the Cuban Missile Crisis: Political, Military and Intelligence Aspects.* New York: St. Martin's Press, 1999.

U.S. Congress

When dealing with Cuban issues, U.S. president John F. Kennedy was always conscious that he needed to maintain congressional support for his policies. Usually, strongly anticommunist senators and congresspersons tended to attack his administration for being too weak on Cuba. An exception to this pattern came when the president informed J. William Fulbright, chairman of the Senate Foreign Relations Committee, of the planned April 1961 Bay of Pigs invasion. Fulbright forcefully condemned the venture as a hypocritical affront to stated American principles of national self-determination.

As Cuba moved ever further into the Soviet camp, Republican criticism of Kennedy's policies mounted, spearheaded by such conservative stalwarts as Arizona senator Barry Goldwater. News that massive Soviet shipments of arms were reaching Cuba provoked allegations by New York senator Kenneth Keating, a Republican, made on the Senate floor on August 31, 1962, that Soviet troops were building nuclear-capable missile bases in Cuba. Indiana senator Homer Capehart, also a Republican, made similar charges, suggesting that the United States should move to impose a blockade on Cuba. In response, on September 4 Kennedy, Secretary of State Dean Rusk, and Defense Secretary Robert McNamara met with 15 congressional leaders and stated that U.S. surveillance had so far revealed only defensive weaponry on Cuba. Kennedy then issued a public statement that the United States would take action should Soviet combat troops, military bases, or offensive ground-to-ground or nuclear-capable missiles be present on Cuba. Recognizing that the forthcoming midterm congressional elections exposed Kennedy to political pressures to take a tough anti-Soviet line, on October 4 Soviet premier Nikita Khrushchev informally sent a message that he would do nothing provocative until mid-November, after these had taken place. A few days later, on October 10, as the Kennedy administration accelerated its U-2 surveillance overflights of Cuba, Keating again claimed to possess evidence that six launching pads for intermediate-range ballistic missiles (IRBMs) were under construction there.

On October 16, Kennedy and his chief advisers began discussing how best to respond to the discovery that these allegations were true. On October 22 Kennedy publicly announced the presence of Soviet nuclear-capable missiles on Cuba. Two hours earlier, he had briefed 20 Republican and Democratic congressional leaders on the situation and informed them he initially intended to impose a blockade. Most—including Fulbright, Richard Russell (D-GA), chairman of the Senate Armed Services Committee, and Carl Vinson (D-GA), chairman of the House Armed Services Committee— tended to favor air strikes or an invasion, the more provocative options. After Kennedy's speech that evening, Congress adopted a resolution supporting his policies, especially his unequivocal demand that the Soviets remove the missiles. The following day Central Intelligence Agency (CIA) director John McCone met again with selected congressional leaders, including Fulbright and Russell. On October 24—as U.S.-Soviet negotiations continued, the blockade came into force, and U.S. officials waited to see whether Soviet ships would turn back—Kennedy once more met congressional leaders, who were broadly supportive. The successful resolution of the crisis rebounded to Kennedy's political advantage. Noting with some satisfaction that hardline Republicans fared poorly in the November 1962 midterm congressional elections, while former vice president Richard Nixon, a strong anticommunist, lost his gubernatorial race in California, and Democrats gained four Senate seats overall, Khrushchev congratulated Kennedy on this political outcome of recent events.

Fears of adverse political repercussions were a major reason Kennedy administration officials insisted on keeping secret the informal U.S.-Soviet agreement that NATO would remove nuclear missiles from Turkey. In February 1963, Kennedy faced renewed allegations from suspicious Republican congressmen, especially Keating, that up to 40 Soviet medium-range nuclear-capable ballistic missiles remained concealed on Cuba. On February 7 McNamara publicly denied these allegations, providing U-2 surveillance photographic evidence. He was less forthcoming over continued stationing of Soviet troops in Cuba, which lasted throughout the Cold War, provoking congressional complaints in 1979. Congressional pressure was one factor limiting Kennedy's options during the Cuban Missile Crisis, since failure on his part to ensure the withdrawal of Soviet missiles from the island would almost certainly have been extremely politically damaging to him.

Priscilla Roberts

See also: Bay of Pigs Invasion; Castro, Fidel; Central Intelligence Agency; Jupiter Missiles (Turkey and Italy); Kennedy, John Fitzgerald; Khrushchev,

Nikita Sergeyevich; McCone, John Alex; McNamara, Robert Strange; Rusk, Dean David; U-2 Overflights

References

Freedman, Lawrence. *Kennedy's Wars: Berlin, Cuba, Laos, and Vietnam.* New York: Oxford University Press, 2000.

Fursenko, Aleksandr, and Timothy Naftali. *One Hell of a Gamble: Khrushchev, Castro, and Kennedy, 1958–1964.* New York: Norton, 1997.

George, Alice L. *Awaiting Armageddon: How Americans Faced the Cuban Missile Crisis.* Chapel Hill: University of North Carolina Press, 2006.

May, Ernest R., and Philip D. Zelikow, eds. *The Kennedy Tapes: Inside the White House during the Cuban Missile Crisis.* Cambridge, MA: Harvard University Press, 1997.

V

Vienna Conference (June 3–4, 1961)

Summit meeting between U.S. president John F. Kennedy and Soviet premier Nikita Khrushchev in Vienna, Austria, on June 3–4, 1961. Shortly after Kennedy took office in January 1961, Khrushchev suggested a meeting with his American counterpart. After the embarrassing and abortive Cuban Bay of Pigs invasion in April, Kennedy's advisers adamantly opposed the conference, believing that Khrushchev would exploit the failed invasion either by berating the president or by using it as a propaganda ploy. Kennedy rejected their advice.

Kennedy wanted the meeting to focus on a nuclear test ban treaty and the neutralization of Laos, where a communist insurgency was threatening the government. The president believed that these agreements would be important steps toward easing Cold War tensions, which had intensified since the May 1960 U-2 Affair. He also hoped that the summit might encourage a wider détente.

Khrushchev had little interest in a test ban and almost none in Laos, however. His primary concern was the fate of Berlin. He wanted an agreement that would stanch the flow of East Germans fleeing to the West via the divided city. His earlier attempt to pressure President Dwight D. Eisenhower into accepting a settlement on Berlin by threatening to sign a peace treaty with the German Democratic Republic (GDR) (East Germany), which would have given the GDR full control of the city, had failed embarrassingly.

Following President Kennedy's death in 1963, his brother, Attorney General Robert F. Kennedy, reported that he had laid the groundwork for the summit during secret meetings with Khrushchev's conduit Georgi

Bolshakov, a Soviet intelligence officer who worked undercover as a reporter. Kennedy later claimed that Khrushchev had used this channel to trick his brother into believing that he would limit the Vienna discussions to Laos and the test ban treaty, which Khrushchev hinted could be verified by numerous on-site inspections. Robert Kennedy had not saved the messages, but the Soviets had. Their records verified that Khrushchev was not interested in either Laos or a nuclear test ban and that he had never agreed to on-site inspections. Instead, Khrushchev's notes to Kennedy focused on Berlin, reiterating his earlier threats.

Khrushchev's recalcitrance alarmed the president. Hoping to make the summit a success, President Kennedy sent the attorney general to Bolshakov, offering concessions and assurances that he wanted a good working relationship. Shortly before leaving for Vienna, Khrushchev met with his advisers, berating those who suggested that he work seriously with Kennedy and telling them that the president was weak and would buckle under his threats.

During the conference the president was in constant pain from a recent back injury, which many suggested meant he was not in top form. The summit had no formal agenda, allowing the two men to roam from topic to topic. Kennedy told aides that when he broached the subject of the dangers of war through miscalculation, Khrushchev became almost uncontrollably hostile. The Soviet leader also rebuffed Kennedy's efforts to discuss the nuclear test ban, responding that it "meant nothing" outside the context of total nuclear disarmament. As predicted by Kennedy's advisers and ignoring the president's earlier request, Khrushchev taunted Kennedy over Cuba. On Berlin, Khrushchev again threatened to sign a peace treaty if Kennedy did not agree to neutralize the city. Although badgered, Kennedy did not back down.

The following day, Khrushchev hinted at possible future discussions on Laos, although no progress was made on the test ban. In his last meeting with the president that day, Khrushchev told Kennedy that he intended to give East Germany control over West Berlin's access routes, adding that if the United States used force to keep them open, war would result. Kennedy icily replied, "Then there will be war, Mr. Chairman. It's going to be a very cold winter." Despite Kennedy's bold counterpunch, Khrushchev believed that he had sufficiently cowed the president.

Although Kennedy's aides told him that the meeting had been typical for Khrushchev, the president refused to believe it and began to prepare for war over Berlin. In a July 25, 1961, speech, Kennedy announced that he was dramatically expanding the armed forces, reinforcing Berlin, and seeking increased congressional appropriations for civil defense. The administration even advised Americans to build backyard bomb shelters.

Khrushchev soon realized that he had badly miscalculated by bullying Kennedy. Believing that Kennedy had lost control of his government to militarists, Khrushchev concluded that the only way to solve the Berlin Crisis and avoid a war was to construct a wall separating the halves of the city. Nevertheless, largely because of Vienna, Khrushchev continued to view Kennedy as weak. This probably contributed to his decision in summer 1962 to offer to install nuclear-capable missiles in Cuba.

Robert Anthony Waters, Jr.

See also: Bay of Pigs Invasion; Berlin Crises; Bohlen, Charles Eustis; Bolshakov, Georgi Nikitovich; Eisenhower, Dwight David; Kennedy, John Fitzgerald; Kennedy, Robert Francis; Khrushchev, Nikita Sergeyevich; Partial Test Ban Treaty; U.S. Allies

References

Beschloss, Michael R. *The Crisis Years: Kennedy and Khrushchev, 1960–1963.* New York: HarperCollins, 1991.

Dallek, Robert. *An Unfinished Life: John F. Kennedy, 1917–1963.* Boston: Little, Brown, 2003.

Fursenko, Aleksandr, and Timothy Naftali. *One Hell of a Gamble: Khrushchev, Castro, and Kennedy, 1958–1964.* New York: Norton, 1997.

Kempe, Frederick. *Berlin 1961: Kennedy, Khrushchev, and the Most Dangerous Place on Earth.* New York: G. P. Putnam's Sons, 2011.

Reeves, Richard. *President Kennedy: Profile of Power.* New York: Simon and Schuster, 1993.

Reynolds, David. *Summits: Six Meetings That Shaped the Twentieth Century.* New York: Basic Books, 2007.

W

Warsaw Pact

Politico-military alliance among the Soviet Union and its Eastern European satellite states. The multilateral Treaty of Friendship, Cooperation, and Mutual Assistance signed on May 14, 1955, in Warsaw, Poland, formally institutionalized the Eastern European alliance system, the Warsaw Treaty Organization, known as the Warsaw Pact. The Warsaw Treaty was identical to bilateral treaties concluded during 1945–1949 between the Soviet Union and its Eastern European client states to assure Moscow's continued military presence on their territory. The Soviet Union, Albania, Bulgaria, Romania, the German Democratic Republic (GDR) (East Germany), Hungary, Poland, and Czechoslovakia pledged to defend each other if one or more of the members were attacked.

The Warsaw Pact was created as a political instrument for Soviet leader Nikita S. Khrushchev's Cold War policy in Europe. The immediate trigger was the admission of the Federal Republic of Germany (FRG) (West Germany) into the North Atlantic Treaty Organization (NATO) on May 5, 1955, and the Austrian State Treaty of May 15, 1955, which provided for Austrian neutrality and the withdrawal of Soviet troops. The creation of the Warsaw Pact sent important signals to both Eastern Europe and the West. On the one hand, the Soviet Union made clear to its satellite states that Austria's neutral status would not likewise be granted to them. On the other hand, Khrushchev allured the West with a standing offer to disband the Warsaw Pact in conjunction with the dissolution of NATO, contingent upon East-West agreement on a new collective security system in Europe.

The Political Consultative Committee (PCC) was established as the alliance's highest governing body, consisting of the member states' party leaders. The PCC met almost annually in one of the capitals of the Warsaw Pact states. On the military side, a unified command and a joint staff were created to organize the actual defense of the Warsaw Treaty states.

Behind the façade of unity, however, growing differences hounded the Eastern alliance. Following Khrushchev's campaign of de-Stalinization, Poles and Hungarians in the fall of 1956 demanded a reform of the Warsaw Pact to reduce overwhelming Soviet dominance within the alliance. Polish generals issued a memorandum that proposed modeling the Warsaw Pact more after NATO, while Hungary's new Communist Party leader, Imre Nagy, declared his country's neutrality and plans to leave the Warsaw Pact. In November 1956, the Soviet Army invaded Hungary and soon crushed all resistance.

In 1958, Romania demanded the withdrawal from its territory of all Soviet troops and military advisers. To cover Soviet embarrassment, Khrushchev termed this a unilateral troop reduction contributing to greater European security. At the height of the Berlin Crisis (1961), the Warsaw Pact's weakest and least strategically important country, Albania, stopped supporting the pact and formally withdrew from the alliance in 1968.

From December 1958 onward Fidel Castro's revolutionary government in Cuba sought to purchase substantial armaments from Czechoslovakia, Poland, and other Warsaw Pact countries, requests that those states carefully cleared with the Soviet Union before dispatching any military equipment. The Warsaw Pact was left in ignorance when Khrushchev provoked the Cuban Missile Crisis. Only after the crisis ended did Eastern European leaders learn, in a secret meeting, that nuclear war had been narrowly avoided. Romania reacted promptly to Moscow's nonconsultation in such a serious matter. In 1963, the Romanian government gave secret assurances to the United States that it would remain neutral in the event of a confrontation between the superpowers. In 1963 Castro, seeking additional assurance that the United States would not invade Cuba in future, asked Khrushchev to admit Cuba as a Warsaw Pact member, a request the Soviet leader rejected.

Christian Nuenlist

See also: Berlin Crises; Castro, Fidel; Khrushchev, Nikita Sergeyevich

References

Heiss, Mary Ann, and S. Victor Papacosma, eds. *NATO and the Warsaw Pact: Intrabloc Conflicts.* Kent, OH: Kent State University Press, 2008.

Holden, Gerard. *The Warsaw Pact: The WTO and Soviet Security Policy.* Oxford, UK: Blackwell, 1989.

Jones, Christopher D. *Soviet Influence in Eastern Europe: Political Autonomy and the Warsaw Pact.* Brooklyn: Praeger, 1981.

Mastny, Vojtech, and Malcolm Byrne, eds. *A Cardboard Castle? An Inside History of the Warsaw Pact, 1955–1991.* Budapest, Hungary, and New York: Central European Press, 2005.

Mastny, Vojtech, Sven Holtsmark, and Andreas Wenger, eds. *War Plans and Alliances in the Cold War: Threat Perceptions in the East and West.* New York: Routledge, 2006.

Z

Zorin, Valerian Aleksandrovich (1902–1986)

Soviet diplomat. Born in Novocherkassk in the Rostov Oblast on January 14, 1902, Valerian Zorin joined the Communist Party of the Soviet Union (CPSU) in 1922. He taught and served as a party official in several posts until joining the People's Commissariat of Foreign Affairs in 1941. He served as assistant secretary general during 1941–1942, deputy commissar during 1942–1943, and head of the Fourth (Central European) Department during 1943–1945.

In March 1945, Zorin was appointed Soviet ambassador to Czechoslovakia, where he served until the spring of 1947. He then served as Soviet representative to the United Nations (UN) Economic Commission for Europe and later served on the Soviet delegation to the UN before returning to Moscow in November 1947 as deputy foreign minister, a post he held until 1955. He was dispatched to Prague to help oversee the February 1948 coup that installed a communist government.

From October 1952 to April 1953, Zorin was Soviet ambassador to the UN while retaining his foreign ministry post. In 1955 he was named Soviet ambassador to the Federal Republic of Germany (FRG) (West Germany) before returning as deputy foreign minister the following year, a position he held until 1965. In 1959, when the new radical government of Cuba sought to buy arms from Poland and Czechoslovakia, both Soviet satellites, the two Eastern European governments consulted Soviet officials. Speaking for the Foreign Ministry, Zorin expressed misgivings that such arms sales might harm the recent rapprochement negotiated by U.S. president Dwight D. Eisenhower and Soviet premier Nikita Khrushchev. Cuba nonetheless soon received substantial Soviet arms shipments.

From 1960 to 1963 Zorin also served once more as Soviet ambassador to the UN, representing his country in inconclusive 1961 disarmament negotiations with the United States for a nuclear test ban treaty. In October 1960, with rumors rife that the United States planned to invade Cuba and overthrow Castro, Zorin urged all nations to implement "urgent measures to prevent military action against Cuba." Two years later, during the Cuban Missile Crisis, he engaged in a dramatic exchange with U.S. ambassador to the UN Adlai Stevenson on October 25, 1962, as Stevenson pressed the recalcitrant Zorin to confirm or deny the presence of Soviet nuclear-capable missiles in Cuba. Once the Soviet Union had agreed to remove the missiles, Zorin participated in negotiations with U.S. and UN representatives to hammer out the details of implementation.

In 1965, Zorin was named Soviet ambassador to France, where he served until retiring in 1971. Subsequently, he served occasionally as an ambassador-at-large with responsibility for human rights issues. Elected a candidate member of the CPSU Central Committee in 1956, he became a full member in 1965. He died in Moscow on January 14, 1986.

Steven W. Guerrier

See also: Castro, Fidel; Eisenhower, Dwight David; Khrushchev, Nikita Sergeyevich; Stevenson, Adlai Ewing II; United Nations; Warsaw Pact

References

Brugioni, Dino A. *Eyeball to Eyeball: Inside the Cuban Missile Crisis.* Edited by Robert F. McCort. New York: Random House, 1993.

Dobrynin, Anatoly. *In Confidence: Moscow's Ambassador to America's Six Cold War Presidents, 1962–1986.* New York: Times Books, 1995.

Friedman, Norman. *The Fifty-Year War: Conflict and Strategy in the Cold War.* Annapolis, MD: Naval Institute Press, 2000.

Fursenko, Aleksandr, and Timothy Naftali. *One Hell of a Gamble: Khrushchev, Castro, and Kennedy, 1958–1964.* New York: Norton, 1997.

Meisler, Stanley. *The United Nations: A History.* 2nd ed. New York: Grove, 2011.

Primary Documents

1. President John F. Kennedy, Report to the American People on the Soviet Arms Buildup in Cuba, October 22, 1962

**The first public acknowledgment that the United States govern-
ment knew of the presence of Soviet nuclear-capable missiles in
Cuba came when President John F. Kennedy addressed the nation on
October 22, 1962. He demanded the withdrawal of these weapons
and announced the imposition of a naval blockade (or "quarantine")
on Cuba.**

This Government, as promised, has maintained the closest surveillance of
the Soviet military buildup on the island of Cuba. Within the past week,
unmistakable evidence has established the fact that a series of offensive
missile sites is now in preparation on that imprisoned island. The purpose
of these bases can be none other than to provide a nuclear strike capability
against the Western Hemisphere.

Upon receiving the first preliminary hard information of this nature last
Tuesday morning at 9 A.M., I directed that our surveillance be stepped up.
And having now confirmed and completed our evaluation of the evidence
and our decision on a course of action, this Government feels obliged to
report this new crisis to you in fullest detail.

The characteristics of these new missile sites indicate two distinct
types of installations. Several of them include medium range ballistic missiles, capable of carrying a nuclear warhead for a distance of more than
1,000 nautical miles. Each of these missiles, in short, is capable of striking

Washington, D.C., the Panama Canal, Cape Canaveral, Mexico City, or any other city in the southeastern part of the United States, in Central America, or in the Caribbean area.

Additional sites not yet completed appear to be designed for intermediate range ballistic missiles—capable of traveling more than twice as far—and thus capable of striking most of the major cities in the Western Hemisphere, ranging as far north as Hudson Bay, Canada, and as far south as Lima, Peru. In addition, jet bombers, capable of carrying nuclear weapons, are now being uncrated and assembled in Cuba, while the necessary air bases are being prepared.

This urgent transformation of Cuba into an important strategic base— by the presence of these large, long-range, and clearly offensive weapons of sudden mass destruction—constitutes an explicit threat to the peace and security of all the Americas, in flagrant and deliberate defiance of the Rio Pact of 1947, the traditions of this Nation and hemisphere, the joint resolution of the 87th Congress, the Charter of the United Nations, and my own public warnings to the Soviets on September 4 and 13. This action also contradicts the repeated assurances of Soviet spokesmen, both publicly and privately delivered, that the arms buildup in Cuba would retain its original defensive character, and that the Soviet Union had no need or desire to station strategic missiles on the territory of any other nation.

The size of this undertaking makes clear that it has been planned for some months. Yet only last month, after I had made clear the distinction between any introduction of ground-to-ground missiles and the existence of defensive antiaircraft missiles, the Soviet Government publicly stated on September 11 that, and I quote, "the armaments and military equipment sent to Cuba are designed exclusively for defensive purposes," that, and I quote the Soviet Government, "there is no need for the Soviet Government to shift its weapons. for a retaliatory blow to any other country, for instance Cuba," and that, and I quote their government, "the Soviet Union has so powerful rockets to carry these nuclear warheads that there is no need to search for sites for them beyond the boundaries of the Soviet Union." That statement was false.

Only last Thursday, as evidence of this rapid offensive buildup was already in my hand, Soviet Foreign Minister Gromyko told me in my office that he was instructed to make it clear once again, as he said his government had already done, that Soviet assistance to Cuba, and I quote, "pursued solely the purpose of contributing to the defense capabilities of

Cuba," that, and I quote him, "training by Soviet specialists of Cuban nationals in handling defensive armaments was by no means offensive, and if it were otherwise," Mr. Gromyko went on, "the Soviet Government would never become involved in rendering such assistance." That statement also was false.

Neither the United States of America nor the world community of nations can tolerate deliberate deception and offensive threats on the part of any nation, large or small. We no longer live in a world where only the actual firing of weapons represents a sufficient challenge to a nation's security to constitute maximum peril. Nuclear weapons are so destructive and ballistic missiles are so swift, that any substantially increased possibility of their use or any sudden change in their deployment may well be regarded as a definite threat to peace.

For many years, both the Soviet Union and the United States, recognizing this fact, have deployed strategic nuclear weapons with great care, never upsetting the precarious status quo which insured that these weapons would not be used in the absence of some vital challenge. Our own strategic missiles have never been transferred to the territory of any other nation under a cloak of secrecy and deception; and our history—unlike that of the Soviets since the end of World War II—demonstrates that we have no desire to dominate or conquer any other nation or impose our system upon its people. Nevertheless, American citizens have become adjusted to living daily on the bull's-eye of Soviet missiles located inside the U.S.S.R. or in submarines.

In that sense, missiles in Cuba add to an already clear and present danger—although it should be noted the nations of Latin America have never previously been subjected to a potential nuclear threat.

But this secret, swift, and extraordinary buildup of Communist missiles—in an area well known to have a special and historical relationship to the United States and the nations of the Western Hemisphere, in violation of Soviet assurances, and in defiance of American and hemispheric policy—this sudden, clandestine decision to station strategic weapons for the first time outside of Soviet soil—is a deliberately provocative and unjustified change in the status quo which cannot be accepted by this country, if our courage and our commitments are ever to be trusted again by either friend or foe.

The 1930's taught us a clear lesson: aggressive conduct, if allowed to go unchecked, ultimately leads to war. This nation is opposed to war. We are also true to our word. Our unswerving objective, therefore, must be to prevent the use of these missiles against this or any other country, and to secure their withdrawal or elimination from the Western Hemisphere.

Our policy has been one of patience and restraint, as befits a peaceful and powerful nation, which leads a worldwide alliance. We have been determined not to be diverted from our central concerns by mere irritants and fanatics. But now further action is required—and it is under way; and these actions may only be the beginning. We will not prematurely or unnecessarily risk the costs of worldwide nuclear war in which even the fruits of victory would be ashes in our mouth—but neither will we shrink from that risk at any time it must be faced.

Acting, therefore, in the defense of our own security and of the entire Western Hemisphere, and under the authority entrusted to me by the Constitution as endorsed by the Resolution of the Congress, I have directed that the following *initial* steps be taken immediately:

First: To halt this offensive buildup, a strict quarantine on all offensive military equipment under shipment to Cuba is being initiated. All ships of any kind bound for Cuba from whatever nation or port will, if found to contain cargoes of offensive weapons, be turned back. This quarantine will be extended, if needed, to other types of cargo and carriers. We are not at this time, however, denying the necessities of life as the Soviets attempted to do in their Berlin blockade of 1948.

Second: I have directed the continued and increased close surveillance of Cuba and its military buildup. The foreign ministers of the OAS, in their communiqué of October 6, rejected secrecy on such matters in this hemisphere. Should these offensive military preparations continue, thus increasing the threat to the hemisphere, further action will be justified. I have directed the Armed Forces to prepare for any eventualities; and I trust that in the interest of both the Cuban people and the Soviet technicians at the sites, the hazards to all concerned of continuing this threat will be recognized.

Third: It shall be the policy of this Nation to regard any nuclear missile launched from Cuba against any nation in the Western Hemisphere as an attack by the Soviet Union on the United States, requiring a full retaliatory response upon the Soviet Union.

Fourth: As a necessary military precaution, I have reinforced our base at Guantanamo, evacuated today the dependents of our personnel there, and ordered additional military units to be on a standby alert basis.

Fifth: We are calling tonight for an immediate meeting of the Organ of Consultation under the Organization of American States, to consider this threat to hemispheric security and to invoke articles 6 and 8 of the Rio Treaty in support of all necessary action. The United Nations Charter allows for regional security arrangements-and the nations of this hemisphere decided long ago against the military presence of outside powers. Our other allies around the world have also been alerted.

Sixth: Under the Charter of the United Nations, we are asking tonight that an emergency meeting of the Security Council be convoked without delay to take action against this latest Soviet threat to world peace. Our resolution will call for the prompt dismantling and withdrawal of all offensive weapons in Cuba, under the supervision of U.N. observers, before the quarantine can be lifted.

Seventh and finally: I call upon Chairman Khrushchev to halt and eliminate this clandestine, reckless, and provocative threat to world peace and to stable relations between our two nations. I call upon him further to abandon this course of world domination, and to join in an historic effort to end the perilous arms race and to transform the history of man. He has an opportunity now to move the world back from the abyss of destruction—by returning to his government's own words that it had no need to station missiles outside its own territory, and withdrawing these weapons from Cuba—by refraining from any action which will widen or deepen the present crisis-and then by participating in a search for peaceful and permanent solutions.

This Nation is prepared to present its case against the Soviet threat to peace, and our own proposals for a peaceful world, at any time and in any forum—in the OAS, in the United Nations, or in any other meeting that could be useful-without limiting our freedom of action. We have in the past made strenuous efforts to limit the spread of nuclear weapons. We have proposed the elimination of all arms and military bases in a fair and effective disarmament treaty. We are prepared to discuss new proposals for the removal of tensions on both sides—including the possibilities of a genuinely independent Cuba, free to determine its own destiny. We have no wish to war with the Soviet Union—for we are a peaceful people who desire to live in peace with all other peoples.

But it is difficult to settle or even discuss these problems in an atmosphere of intimidation. That is why this latest Soviet threat—or any other threat which is made either independently or in response to our actions this week—must and will be met with determination. Any hostile move anywhere in the world against the safety and freedom of peoples to whom we are committed—including in particular the brave people of West Berlin—will be met by whatever action is needed.

Finally, I want to say a few words to the captive people of Cuba, to whom this speech is being directly carried by special radio facilities. I speak to you as a friend, as one who knows of your deep attachment to your fatherland, as one who shares your aspirations for liberty and justice for all. And I have watched and the American people have watched with deep sorrow how your nationalist revolution was betrayed—and how your fatherland fell under foreign domination. Now your leaders are no longer Cuban leaders inspired by Cuban ideals. They are puppets and agents of an international conspiracy which has turned Cuba against your friends and neighbors in the Americas—and turned it into the first Latin American country to become a target for nuclear war—the first Latin American country to have these weapons on its soil.

These new weapons are not in your interest. They contribute nothing to your peace and well-being. They can only undermine it. But this country has no wish to cause you to suffer or to impose any system upon you. We know that your lives and land are being used as pawns by those who deny your freedom. Many times in the past, the Cuban people have risen to throw out tyrants who destroyed their liberty. And I have no doubt that most Cubans today look forward to the time when they will be truly free-free from foreign domination, free to choose their own leaders, free to select their own system, free to own their own land, free to speak and write and worship without fear or degradation. And then shall Cuba be welcomed back to the society of free nations and to the associations of this hemisphere.

My fellow citizens: let no one doubt that this is a difficult and dangerous effort on which we have set out. No one can foresee precisely what course it will take or what costs or casualties will be incurred. Many months of sacrifice and self-discipline lie ahead—months in which both our patience and our will will be tested—months in which many threats and denunciations will keep us aware of our dangers. But the greatest danger of all would be to do nothing.

The path we have chosen for the present is full of hazards, as all paths are—but it is the one most consistent with our character and courage as a nation and our commitments around the world. The cost of freedom is always high—but Americans have always paid it. And one path we shall never choose, and that is the path of surrender or submission.

Our goal is not the victory of might, but the vindication of right—not peace at the expense of freedom, but both peace *and* freedom, here in this hemisphere, and, we hope, around the world. God willing, that goal will be achieved.

Source: Kennedy, John F. *Public Papers of the Presidents of the United States: John F. Kennedy, 1962* (Washington, DC: Government Printing Office, 1963).

Available at *The American Presidency Project,* http://www.presidency.ucsb.edu/ws/?pid=8986.

2. Kennedy-Khrushchev Exchanges during the Cuban Missile Crisis, October 22–28, 1962

When he publicly announced that the United States would not accept the presence of Soviet nuclear-capable missiles in Cuba, President John F. Kennedy had already dispatched a letter to Soviet premier Nikita Khrushchev, demanding their withdrawal. For four days, through October 25, Khrushchev and Kennedy traded intransigent letters in which neither showed any sign of backing down. On October 26, Khrushchev dispatched a lengthy letter, suggesting that the Soviets might be willing to remove their missiles if the United States promised not to invade Cuba in the future. The following day, he supplemented this with demands that the United States remove intermediate-range ballistic missiles (IRBMs) recently installed in Turkey, a U.S. NATO ally, which could be used to attack targets in the Soviet Union. On October 27 Kennedy responded publicly to the first letter, accepting its terms in principle. He did not publicize a response to the second letter but privately authorized his brother Robert to explore with Soviet officials the possibility of an informal understanding on the removal of intermediate-range NATO missiles in both Turkey and Italy. On October 27, Soviet surface-to-air batteries shot down a U.S. U-2 reconnaissance plane overflying Cuba, killing the pilot, while another U-2 strayed into Soviet airspace over Siberia but returned safely. U.S. and Soviet officials feared that such these episodes might easily escalate into outright war. In further correspondence on October 28, Khrushchev and Kennedy discussed these incidents. In a message broadcast over Soviet radio to ensure that it would reach the United States as fast as possible, Khrushchev complained of the overflights, pointing out their potential to overturn any peaceful Soviet-U.S. resolution of the crisis. On October 28, Kennedy went so far as to apologize for the October 27 intrusion into Soviet airspace. At this point, neither mentioned the U-2 brought down over Cuba. Instead, both focused upon the need to end the crisis through negotiations rather than war and expressed their hopes for further progress in this direction.

President Kennedy to Chairman Khrushchev, Washington, October 22, 1962

Dear Mr. Chairman: A copy of the statement I am making tonight concerning developments in Cuba and the reaction of my Government thereto has been handed to your Ambassador in Washington. In view of the gravity of the developments to which I refer, I want you to know immediately and accurately the position of my Government in this matter.

In our discussions and exchanges on Berlin and other international questions, the one thing that has most concerned me has been the possibility that your Government would not correctly understand the will and determination of the United States in any given situation, since I have not assumed that you or any other sane man would, in this nuclear age, deliberately plunge the world into war which it is crystal clear no country could win and which could only result in catastrophic consequences to the whole world, including the aggressor.

At our meeting in Vienna and subsequently, I expressed our readiness and desire to find, through peaceful negotiation, a solution to any and all problems that divide us. At the same time, I made clear that in view of the objectives of the ideology to which you adhere, the United States could not tolerate any action on your part which in a major way disturbed the existing over-all balance of power in the world. I stated that an attempt to force abandonment of our responsibilities and commitments in Berlin would constitute such an action and that the United States would resist with all the power at its command.

It was in order to avoid any incorrect assessment on the part of your Government with respect to Cuba that I publicly stated that if certain developments in Cuba took place, the United States would do whatever must be done to protect its own security and that of its allies.

Moreover, the Congress adopted a resolution expressing its support of this declared policy. Despite this, the rapid development of long-range missile bases and other offensive weapons systems in Cuba has proceeded. I must tell you that the United States is determined that this threat to the security of this hemisphere be removed. At the same time, I wish to point out that the action we are taking is the minimum necessary to remove the threat to the security of the nations of this hemisphere. The fact of this minimum response should not be taken as a basis, however, for any mis-judgment on your part.

I hope that your Government will refrain from any action which would widen or deepen this already grave crisis and that we can agree to resume the path of peaceful negotiation.

Sincerely,

John F. Kennedy

Source: U.S. Department of State, *Foreign Relations of the United States 1961–1963,* Vol. XI: *The Cuban Missile Crisis and Its Aftermath* (Washington, DC: Government Printing Office, 1996), Document 44, http://www.state.gov/www/about_state/history/frusXI/26_50.html; also Department of State *Bulletin,* November 19, 1973, pp. 635–636.

Chairman Khrushchev to President Kennedy, Moscow, October 23, 1962 [translated by U.S. Embassy, Moscow]

Mr. President.

I have just received your letter, and have also acquainted myself with text of your speech of October 22 regarding Cuba.

I should say frankly that measures outlined in your statement represent serious threat to peace and security of peoples. United States has openly taken path of gross violation of Charter of United Nations, path of violation of international norms of freedom of navigation on high seas, path of aggressive actions both against Cuba and against Soviet Union.

Statement of Government of United States America cannot be evaluated in any other way than as naked interference in domestic affairs of Cuban Republic, Soviet Union, and other states. Charter of United Nations and international norms do not give right to any state whatsoever to establish in international waters control of vessels bound for shores of Cuban Republic.

It is self-understood that we also cannot recognize right of United States to establish control over armaments essential to Republic of Cuba for strengthening of its defensive capacity.

We confirm that armaments now on Cuba, regardless of classification to which they belong, are destined exclusively for defensive purposes, in order to secure Cuban Republic from attack of aggressor.

I hope that Government of United States will show prudence and renounce actions pursued by you, which would lead to catastrophic consequences for peace throughout world.

Viewpoint of Soviet Government with regard to your statement of October 22 is set forth in statement of Soviet Government, which is being conveyed to you through your Ambassador in Moscow.

N. Khrushchev

Source: U.S. Department of State, *Foreign Relations of the United States 1961–1963,* Vol. XI: *The Cuban Missile Crisis and Its Aftermath* (Washington, DC: Government Printing Office, 1996), Document 48, http://www.state.gov/www/about_state/history/frusXI/26_50.html.

President Kennedy to Chairman Khrushchev, Washington, October 23, 1962

Dear Mr. Chairman:

I have received your letter of October twenty-third. I think you will recognize that the steps which started the current chain of events was [sic] the action of your Government in secretly furnishing offensive weapons to Cuba. We will be discussing this matter in the Security Council. In the meantime, I am concerned that we both show prudence and do nothing to allow events to make the situation more difficult to control than it already is.

I hope that you will issue immediately the necessary instructions to your ships to observe the terms of the quarantine, the basis of which was established by the vote of the Organization of American States this afternoon, and which will go into effect at 1400 hours Greenwich time October twenty-four.

Sincerely,

John F. Kennedy

Source: U.S. Department of State, *Foreign Relations of the United States 1961–1963,* Vol. XI: *The Cuban Missile Crisis and Its Aftermath* (Washington, DC: Government Printing Office, 1996), Document 52, http://www.state.gov/www/about_state/history/frusXI/51_75.html.

Chairman Khrushchev to President Kennedy,
Moscow, October 24, 1962

Dear Mr. President:

I have received your letter of October 23, have studied it, and am answering you.

Just imagine, Mr. President, that we had presented you with the conditions of an ultimatum which you have presented us by your action. How would you have reacted to this? I think that you would have been indignant at such a step on our part. And this would have been understandable to us.

In presenting us with these conditions, you, Mr. President, have flung a challenge at us. Who asked you to do this? By what right did you do this? Our ties with the Republic of Cuba, like our relations with other states, regardless of what kind of states they may be, concern only the two countries between which these relations exist. And if we now speak of the quarantine to which your letter refers, a quarantine may be established, according to accepted international practice, only by agreement of states between themselves, and not by some third party. Quarantines exist, for example, on agricultural goods and products. But in this case the question is in no way one of quarantine, but rather of far more serious things, and you yourself understand this.

You, Mr. President, are not declaring a quarantine, but rather are setting forth an ultimatum and threatening that if we do not give in to your demands you will use force. Consider what you are saying! And you want to persuade me to agree to this! What would it mean to agree to these demands? It would mean guiding oneself in one's relations with other countries not by reason, but by submitting to arbitrariness. You are no longer appealing to reason, but wish to intimidate us.

No, Mr. President, I cannot agree to this, and I think that in your own heart you recognize that I am correct. I am convinced that in my place you would act the same way.

Reference to the decision of the Organization of American States cannot in any way substantiate the demands now advanced by the United States. This Organization has absolutely no authority or basis for adopting decisions such as the one you speak of in your letter. Therefore, we do not recognize these decisions. International law exists and universally recognized norms of conduct exist. We firmly adhere to the principles of international law and observe strictly the norms which regulate navigation on the high seas, in international waters. We observe these norms and enjoy the rights recognized by all states.

You wish to compel us to renounce the rights that every sovereign state enjoys, you are trying to legislate in questions of international law, and you are violating the universally accepted norms of that law. And you are doing all this not only out of hatred for the Cuban people and its government, but also because of considerations of the election campaign in the United States. What morality, what law can justify such an approach by the American Government to international affairs? No such morality or law can be found, because the actions of the United States with regard to Cuba constitute outright banditry or, if you like, the folly of degenerate imperialism. Unfortunately, such folly can bring grave suffering to the peoples of all countries, and to no lesser degree to the American people themselves, since the United States has completely lost its former isolation with the advent of modern types of armament.

Therefore, Mr. President, if you coolly weigh the situation which has developed, not giving way to passions, you will understand that the Soviet Union cannot fail to reject the arbitrary demands of the United States. When you confront us with such conditions, try to put yourself in our place and consider how the United States would react to these conditions. I do not doubt that if someone attempted to dictate similar conditions to you—the United States—you would reject such an attempt. And we also say—no.

The Soviet Government considers that the violation of the freedom to use international waters and international air space is an act of aggression which pushes mankind toward the abyss of a world nuclear-missile war. Therefore, the Soviet Government cannot instruct the captains of Soviet vessels bound for Cuba to observe the orders of American naval forces blockading that Island. Our instructions to Soviet mariners are to observe strictly the universally accepted norms of navigation in international waters and not to retreat one step from them. And if the American side violates these rules, it must realize what responsibility will rest upon it in that case. Naturally we will not simply be bystanders with regard to piratical acts by American ships on the high seas. We will then be forced on our part to take the measures we consider necessary and adequate in order to protect our rights. We have everything necessary to do so.

Respectfully,

N. Khrushchev

Source: U.S. Department of State, *Foreign Relations of the United States 1961–1963,* Vol. XI: *The Cuban Missile Crisis and Its Aftermath* (Washington, DC: Government Printing Office, 1996), Document 61, http://www.state.gov/www/about_state/history/frusXI/51_75.html.

President Kennedy to Chairman Khrushchev, Washington, October 25, 1962

Dear Mr. Chairman:

I have received your letter of October 24, and I regret very much that you still do not appear to understand what it is that has moved us in this matter.

The sequence of events is clear. In August there were reports of important shipments of military equipment and technicians from the Soviet Union to Cuba. In early September I indicated very plainly that the United States would regard any shipment of offensive weapons as presenting the gravest issues. After that time, this Government received the most explicit assurance from your Government and its representatives, both publicly and privately, that no offensive weapons were being sent to Cuba. If you will review the statement issued by TASS in September, you will see how clearly this assurance was given.

In reliance on these solemn assurances I urged restraint upon those in this country who were urging action in this matter at that time. And then I learned beyond doubt what you have not denied—namely, that all these public assurances were false and that your military people had set out recently to establish a set of missile bases in Cuba. I ask you to recognize clearly, Mr. Chairman, that it was not I who issued the first challenge in this case, and that in the light of this record these activities in Cuba required the responses I have announced.

I repeat my regret that these events should cause a deterioration in our relations. I hope that your Government will take the necessary action to permit a restoration of the earlier situation.

Sincerely yours,

John F. Kennedy

Source: U.S. Department of State, *Foreign Relations of the United States 1961–1963,* Vol. XI: *The Cuban Missile Crisis and Its Aftermath* (Washington, DC: Government Printing Office, 1996), Document 68, http://www.state.gov/www/about_state/history/frusXI/51_75.html.

Chairman Khrushchev to President Kennedy, Moscow, October 26, 1962 [translated by U.S. Embassy, Moscow]

Dear Mr. President:

I have received your letter of October 25. From your letter, I got the feeling that you have some understanding of the situation which has developed and a sense of responsibility. I value this.

Now we have already publicly exchanged our evaluations of the events around Cuba and each of us has set forth his explanation and his understanding of these events. Consequently, I would think that, apparently, a continuation of an exchange of opinions at such a distance, even in the form of secret letters, will hardly add anything to that which one side has already said to the other.

I think you will understand me correctly if you are really concerned about the welfare of the world. Everyone needs peace: both capitalists, if they have not lost their reason, and, still more, Communists, people who know how to value not only their own lives but, more than anything, the lives of the peoples. We, Communists, are against all wars between states in general and have been defending the cause of peace since we came into the world. We have always regarded war as a calamity, and not as a game nor as a means for the attainment of definite goals, nor, all the more, as a goal in itself. Our goals are clear, and the means to attain them is labor. War is our enemy and a calamity for all the peoples.

It is thus that we, Soviet people, and, together with US, other peoples as well, understand the questions of war and peace. I can, in any case, firmly say this for the peoples of the socialist countries, as well as for all progressive people who want peace, happiness, and friendship among peoples.

I see, Mr. President, that you too are not devoid of a sense of anxiety for the fate of the world and not without an understanding of what war entails. What would a war give you? You are threatening us with war. But you well know that the very least which you would receive in reply would be that you would experience the same consequences as those which you sent us. And that must be clear to us, people invested with authority, trust, and responsibility. We must not succumb to intoxication and petty passions, regardless of whether elections are impending in this or that country, or not impending. These are all transient things, but if indeed war should break out, then it would not be in our power to contain or stop it, for such is the logic of war. I have participated in two wars and know that war ends when it has rolled through cities and villages, everywhere sowing death and destruction.

In the name of the Soviet Government and the Soviet people, I assure you that your arguments regarding offensive weapons on Cuba are groundless. It is apparent from what you have written me that our conceptions are different on this score, or rather, we have different definitions for these or those military means, indeed, in reality, the same forms of weapons can have different interpretations.

You are a military man and, I hope, will understand me. Let us take for example a simple cannon. What sort of means is this: offensive or defensive? A cannon is a defensive means if it is set up to defend boundaries or a fortified area. But if one concentrates artillery, and adds to it the necessary number of troops, then the same cannons do become an offensive means, because they prepare and clear the way for infantry to advance. The same happens with missile-nuclear weapons as well, with any type of this weapon.

You are mistaken if you think that any of our means on Cuba are offensive. However, let us not argue now, it is apparent that I will not be able to convince you of this, but I say to you: You, Mr. President, are a military man and should understand: can one advance, if one has on one's territory even an enormous quantity of missiles of various effective radiuses and various power, but using only these means. These missiles are a means of extermination and destruction, but one cannot advance with these missiles, even nuclear missiles of a power of 100 megatons because only people, troops, can advance, without people, any means however powerful cannot be offensive.

How can one, consequently, give such a completely incorrect interpretation as you are now giving, to the effect that some sort of means on Cuba are offensive. All the means located there, and I assure you of this, have a defensive character, are on Cuba solely for the purposes of defense, and we have sent them to Cuba at the request of the Cuban Government. You, however, say that these are offensive means.

But, Mr. President, do you really seriously think that Cuba can attack the United States and that even we together with Cuba can advance upon you from the territory of Cuba? Can you really think that way? How is it possible? We do not understand this. Has something so new appeared in military strategy that one can think that it is possible to advance thus. I say precisely advance, and not destroy, since barbarians, people who have lost their sense, destroy.

I believe that you have no basis to think this way. You can regard us with distrust, but, in any case, you can be calm in this regard, that we are of sound mind and understand perfectly well that if we attack you, you will respond the same way. But you too will receive the same that you hurl against us. And I think that you also understand this. My conversation with you in Vienna gives me the right to talk to you this way.

This indicates that we are normal people, that we correctly understand and correctly evaluate the situation. Consequently, how can we permit the incorrect actions which you ascribe to us? Only lunatics or suicides, who themselves want to perish and to destroy the whole world before they die, could do this. We, however, want to live and do not at all want to destroy your country. We want something quite different: to compete with your country on a peaceful endeavor. We quarrel with you, we have differences in ideological questions. But our view of the world consists in this, that ideological questions, as well as economic problems, should be solved not by military means, they must be solved on the basis of peaceful competition, i.e., as this is understood in capitalist society, on the basis of competition. We have proceeded and are proceeding from the fact that the peaceful co-existence of the two different social-political systems, now existing in the world, is necessary, that it is necessary to assure a stable peace. That is the sort of principle we hold.

You have now proclaimed piratical measures, which were employed in the Middle Ages, when ships proceeding in international waters were attacked, and you have called this "a quarantine" around Cuba. Our vessels, apparently, will soon enter the zone which your Navy is patrolling. I assure you that these vessels, now bound for Cuba, are carrying the most innocent peaceful cargoes. Do you really think that we only occupy ourselves with the carriage of so-called offensive weapons, atomic and hydrogen bombs? Although perhaps your military people imagine that these (cargoes) are some sort of special type of weapon, I assure you that they are the most ordinary peaceful products.

Consequently, Mr. President, let us show good sense. I assure you that on those ships, which are bound for Cuba, there are no weapons at all. The weapons which were necessary for the defense of Cuba are already there. I do not want to say that there were not any shipments of weapons at all.

No, there were such shipments. But now Cuba has already received the necessary means of defense.

I don't know whether you can understand me and believe me. But I should like to have you believe in yourself and to agree that one cannot give way to passions; it is necessary to control them. And in what direction are events now developing? If you stop the vessels, then, as you yourself know, that would be piracy. If we started to do that with regard to your ships, then you would also be as indignant as we and the whole world now are. One cannot give another interpretation to such actions, because one cannot legalize lawlessness. If this were permitted, then there would be no peace, there would also be no peaceful coexistence. We should then be forced to put into effect the necessary measures of a defensive character to protect our interest in accordance with international law. Why should this be done? To what would all this lead?

Let us normalize relations. We have received an appeal from the Acting Secretary General of the UN, U Thant, with his proposals. I have already answered him. His proposals come to this, that our side should not transport armaments of any kind to Cuba during a certain period of time, while negotiations are being conducted—and we are ready to enter such negotiations—and the other side should not undertake any sort of piratical actions against vessels engaged in navigation on the high seas. I consider these proposals reasonable. This would be a way out of the situation which has been created, which would give the peoples the possibility of breathing calmly. You have asked what happened, what evoked the delivery of weapons to Cuba? You have spoken about this to our Minister of Foreign Affairs. I will tell you frankly, Mr. President, what evoked it.

We were very grieved by the fact—I spoke about it in Vienna—that a landing took place, that an attack on Cuba was committed, as a result of which many Cubans perished. You yourself told me then that this had been a mistake. I respected that explanation. You repeated it to me several times, hinting that not everybody occupying a high position would acknowledge his mistakes as you had done. I value such frankness. For my part, I told you that we too possess no less courage; we also acknowledged those mistakes which had been committed during the history of our state, and not only acknowledged, but sharply condemned them.

If you are really concerned about the peace and welfare of your people, and this is your responsibility as President, then I, as the Chairman of the Council of Ministers, am concerned for my people. Moreover, the preservation of world peace should be our joint concern, since if, under contemporary conditions, war should break out, it would be a war not only between the Soviet Union and the United States which have no contentions between them, but a worldwide cruel and destructive war.

Why have we proceeded to assist Cuba with military and economic aid? The answer is: we have proceeded to do so only for reasons of humanitarianism. At one time, our people itself had a revolution, when Russia was still a backward country, we were attacked then. We were the target of attack by many countries. The USA participated in that adventure. This has been recorded by participants in the aggression against our country. A whole book has been written about this by General Graves, who, at that time, commanded the US Expeditionary Corps. Graves called it "The American Adventure in Siberia."

We know how difficult it is to accomplish a revolution and how difficult it is to reconstruct a country on new foundations. We sincerely sympathize with Cuba and the Cuban people, but we are not interfering in questions of domestic structure, we are not interfering in their affairs. The Soviet Union desires to help the Cubans build their life as they themselves wish and that others should not hinder them.

You once said that the United States was not preparing an invasion. But you also declared that you sympathized with the Cuban counter-revolutionary emigrants, that you support them and would help them to realize their plans against the present Government of Cuba. It is also not a secret to anyone that the threat of armed attack, aggression, has constantly hung, and continues to hang over Cuba. It was only this which impelled us to respond to the request of the Cuban Government to furnish it aid for the strengthening of the defensive capacity of this country.

If assurances were given by the President and the Government of the United States that the USA itself would not participate in an attack on Cuba and would restrain others from actions of this sort, if you would recall your fleet, this would immediately change everything. I am not speaking for Fidel Castro, but I think that he and the Government of Cuba, evidently, would declare demobilization and would appeal to the people to get down to peaceful labor. Then, too, the question of armaments would disappear, since, if there is no threat, then armaments are a burden for every people. Then, too, the question of the destruction, not only of the armaments which you call offensive, but of all other armaments as well, would look different.

I spoke in the name of the Soviet Government in the United Nations and introduced a proposal for the disbandment of all armies and for the destruction of all armaments. How then can I now count on those armaments?

Armaments bring only disasters. When one accumulates them, this damages the economy, and if one puts them to use, then they destroy people on both sides. Consequently, only a madman can believe that armaments are the principal means in the life of society. No, they are an enforced loss of human energy, and what is more are for the destruction of man himself. If people do not show wisdom, then in the final analysis they will come to a clash, like blind moles, and then reciprocal extermination will begin.

Let us therefore show statesmanlike wisdom. I propose: we, for our part, will declare that our ships, bound for Cuba, are not carrying any armaments. You would declare that the United States will not invade Cuba with its forces and will not support any sort of forces which might intend to carry out an invasion of Cuba. Then the necessity for the presence of our military specialists in Cuba would disappear.

Mr. President, I appeal to you to weigh well what the aggressive, piratical actions, which you have declared the USA intends to carry out in international waters, would lead to. You yourself know that any sensible man simply cannot agree with this, cannot recognize your right to such actions.

If you did this as the first step towards the unleashing of war, well then, it is evident that nothing else is left to us but to accept this challenge of yours. If, however, you have not lost your self-control and sensibly conceive what this might lead to, then, Mr. President, we and you ought not now to pull on the ends of the rope in which you have tied the knot of war, because the more the two of us pull, the tighter that knot will be tied. And a moment may come when that knot will be tied so tight that even he who tied it will not have the strength to untie it, and then it will be necessary to cut that knot. And what that would mean is not for me to explain to you, because you yourself understand perfectly of what terrible forces our countries dispose.

Consequently, if there is no intention to tighten that knot and thereby to doom the world to the catastrophe of thermonuclear war, then let us not only relax the forces pulling on the ends of the rope, let us take measures to untie that knot. We are ready for this.

We welcome all forces which stand on positions of peace. Consequently, I both expressed gratitude to Mr. Bertrand Russell, who manifests alarm and concern for the fate of the world, and readily responded to the appeal of the Acting Secretary General of the UN, U Thant.

There, Mr. President, are my thoughts, which, if you agreed with them, could put an end to that tense situation which is disturbing all peoples.

These thoughts are dictated by a sincere desire to relieve the situation, to remove the threat of war.

Respectfully yours,

N. Khrushchev

Source: U.S. Department of State, *Foreign Relations of the United States 1961–1963,* Vol. XI: *The Cuban Missile Crisis and Its Aftermath* (Washington, DC: Government Printing Office, 1996), Document 84, http://www.state.gov/www/about_state/history/frusXI/76_100.html; also printed in Department of State *Bulletin,* November 19, 1973, pp. 640–643.

Chairman Khrushchev to President Kennedy, Moscow, October 27, 1962 [translation by Language Services, U.S. Department of State]

DEAR MR. PRESIDENT,

I have studied with great satisfaction your reply to Mr. Thant concerning measures that should be taken to avoid contact between our vessels and thereby avoid irreparable and fatal consequences. This reasonable step on your part strengthens my belief that you are showing concern for the preservation of peace, which I note with satisfaction.

I have already said that our people, our Government, and I personally, as Chairman of the Council of Ministers, are concerned solely with having our country develop and occupy a worthy place among all peoples of the world in economic competition, in the development of culture and the arts, and in raising the living standard of the people. This is the most noble and necessary field for competition, and both the victor and the vanquished will derive only benefit from it, because it means peace and an increase in the means by which man lives and finds enjoyment.

In your statement you expressed the opinion that the main aim was not simply to come to an agreement and take measures to prevent contact between our vessels and consequently a deepening of the crisis which could, as a result of such contacts, spark a military conflict, after which all negotiations would be superfluous because other forces and other laws would then come into play—the laws of war. I agree with you that this is only the first step. The main thing that must be done is to normalize and stabilize the state of peace among states and among peoples.

I understand your concern for the security of the United States, Mr. President, because this is the primary duty of a President. But we too are disturbed about these same questions; I bear these same obligations as Chairman of the Council of Ministers of the U.S.S.R. You have been alarmed by the fact that we have aided Cuba with weapons, in order to strengthen its defense capability—precisely defense capability—because whatever weapons it may possess, Cuba cannot be equated with you since the difference in magnitude is so great, particularly in view of modern means of destruction. Our aim has been and is to help Cuba, and no one can dispute the humanity of our motives, which are oriented toward enabling Cuba to live peacefully and develop in the way its people desire.

You wish to ensure the security of your country, and this is understandable. But Cuba, too, wants the same thing; all countries want to maintain their security. But how are we, the Soviet Union, our Government, to assess your actions which are expressed in the fact that you have surrounded the Soviet Union with military bases; surrounded our allies with military bases; placed military bases literally around our country; and stationed your missile armaments there? This is no secret. Responsible American personages openly declare that it is so. Your missiles are located in Britain, are located in Italy, and are aimed against us. Your missiles are located in Turkey.

You are disturbed over Cuba. You say that this disturbs you because it is 90 miles by sea from the coast of the United States of America. But Turkey adjoins us; our sentries patrol back and forth and see each other. Do you consider, then, that you have the right to demand security for your own country and the removal of the weapons you call offensive, but do not accord the same right to us? You have placed destructive missile weapons, which you call offensive, in Turkey, literally next to us. How then can recognition of our equal military capacities be reconciled with such unequal relations between our great states? This is irreconcilable.

It is good, Mr. President, that you have agreed to have our representatives meet and begin talks, apparently through the mediation of U Thant, Acting Secretary General of the United Nations. Consequently, he to some degree has assumed the role of a mediator and we consider that he will be able to cope with this responsible mission, provided, of course, that each party drawn into this controversy displays good will.

I think it would be possible to end the controversy quickly and normalize the situation, and then the people could breathe more easily, considering that statesmen charged with responsibility are of sober mind and have an awareness of their responsibility combined with the ability to solve complex questions and not bring things to a military catastrophe.

I therefore make this proposal: We are willing to remove from Cuba the means which you regard as offensive. We are willing to carry this out and to make this pledge in the United Nations. Your representatives will make a declaration to the effect that the United States, for its part, considering the uneasiness and anxiety of the Soviet State, will remove its analogous means from Turkey. Let us reach agreement as to the period of time needed by you and by us to bring this about. And, after that, persons entrusted by the United Nations Security Council could inspect on the spot the fulfillment of the pledges made. Of course, the permission of the Governments of Cuba and of Turkey is necessary for the entry into those countries of these representatives and for the inspection of the fulfillment of the pledge made by each side. Of course it would be best if these representatives enjoyed the confidence of the Security Council, as well as yours and mine—both the United States and the Soviet Union—and also that of Turkey and Cuba. I do not think it would be difficult to select people who would enjoy the trust and respect of all parties concerned.

We, in making this pledge, in order to give satisfaction and hope of the peoples of Cuba and Turkey and to strengthen their confidence in their security, will make a statement within the framework of the Security Council to the effect that the Soviet Government gives a solemn promise to respect the inviolability of the borders and sovereignty of Turkey, not to interfere in its internal affairs, not to invade Turkey, not to make available our territory as a bridgehead for such an invasion, and that it would also restrain those who contemplate committing aggression against Turkey, either from the territory of the Soviet Union or from the territory of Turkey's other neighboring states.

The United States Government will make a similar statement within the framework of the Security Council regarding Cuba. It will declare that the United States will respect the inviolability of Cuba's borders and its sovereignty, will pledge not to interfere in its internal affairs, not to invade Cuba itself or make its territory available as a bridgehead for such an invasion, and will also restrain those who might contemplate committing aggression against Cuba, either from the territory of the United States or from the territory of Cuba's other neighboring states.

Of course, for this we would have to come to an agreement with you and specify a certain time limit. Let us agree to some period of time, but without unnecessary delay—say within two or three weeks, not longer than a month.

The means situated in Cuba, of which you speak and which disturb you, as you have stated, are in the hands of Soviet officers. Therefore, any accidental use of them to the detriment of the United States is excluded. These means are situated in Cuba at the request of the Cuban Government and are only for defense purposes. Therefore, if there is no invasion of Cuba, or attack on the Soviet Union or any of our other allies, then of course these means are not and will not be a threat to anyone. For they are not for purposes of attack.

If you are agreeable to my proposal, Mr. President, then we would send our representatives to New York, to the United Nations, and would give them comprehensive instructions in order that an agreement may be reached more quickly. If you also select your people and give them the corresponding instructions, then this question can be quickly resolved.

Why would I like to do this? Because the whole world is now apprehensive and expects sensible actions of us. The greatest joy for all peoples would be the announcement of our agreement and of the eradication of the controversy that has arisen. I attach great importance to this agreement in so far as it could serve as a good beginning and could in particular make it easier to reach agreement on banning nuclear weapons tests. The question of the tests could be solved in parallel fashion, without connecting one with the other, because these are different issues. However, it is important that agreement be reached on both these issues so as to present humanity with a fine gift, and also to gladden it with the news that agreement has been reached on the cessation of nuclear tests and that consequently the atmosphere will no longer be poisoned. Our position and yours on this issue are very close together.

All of this could possibly serve as a good impetus toward the finding of mutually acceptable agreements on other controversial issues on which you and I have been exchanging views. These views have so far not been resolved, but they are awaiting urgent solution, which would clear up the international atmosphere. We are prepared for this.

These are my proposals, Mr. President.

Respectfully yours,

N. Khrushchev

Source: U.S. Department of State, *Foreign Relations of the United States 1961–1963*, Vol. XI: *The Cuban Missile Crisis and Its Aftermath* (Washington, DC: Government Printing Office, 1996), Document 91, http://www.state.gov/www/

about_state/history/frusXI/76_100.html; also printed in Department of State
Bulletin, November 19, 1962, pp. 646–649.

President Kennedy to Chairman Khrushchev, Washington, October 27, 1962

Dear Mr. Chairman:

I have read your letter of October 26 with great care and welcomed the statement of your desire to seek a prompt solution to the problem. The first thing that needs to be done, however, is for work to cease on offensive missile bases in Cuba and for all weapons systems in Cuba capable of offensive use to be rendered inoperable, under effective United Nations arrangements.

Assuming this is done promptly, I have given my representatives in New York instructions that will permit them to work out this week and—in cooperation with the Acting Secretary General and your representative—an arrangement for a permanent solution to the Cuban problem along the lines suggested in your letter of October 26. As I read your letter, the key elements of your proposals—which seem generally acceptable as I under-stand them—are as follows:

1. You would agree to remove these weapons systems from Cuba under appropriate United Nations observation and supervision; and undertake, with suitable safeguards, to halt the further introduction of such weapons systems into Cuba.
2. We, on our part, would agree—upon the establishment of adequate arrangements through the United Nations to ensure the carrying out and continuation of these commitments—(a) to remove promptly the quarantine measures now in effect and (b) to give assurances against an invasion of Cuba and I am confident that other nations of the Western Hemisphere would be prepared to do likewise.

If you will give your representative similar instructions, there is no reason why we should not be able to complete these arrangements and announce them to the world within a couple of days. The effect of such a settlement on easing world tensions would enable us to work toward a more general arrangement regarding "other armaments", as proposed in your second letter which you made public. I would like to say again that the United States is very much interested in reducing tensions and halting the arms race; and if your letter signifies that you are prepared to discuss a detente affecting NATO and the Warsaw Pact, we are quite prepared to consider with our allies any useful proposals.

But the first ingredient, let me emphasize, is the cessation of work on missile sites in Cuba and measures to render such weapons inoperable, under effective international guarantees. The continuation of this threat, or a prolonging of this discussion concerning Cuba by linking these problems to the broader questions of European and world security, would surely lead to an intensification of the Cuban crisis and a grave risk to the peace of the world. For this reason I hope we can quickly agree along the lines outlined in this letter and in your letter of October 26.

John F. Kennedy

Source: U.S. Department of State, *Foreign Relations of the United States 1961–1963,* Vol. XI: *The Cuban Missile Crisis and Its Aftermath* (Washington, DC: Government Printing Office, 1996), Document 95, http://www.state.gov/www/about_state/history/frusXI/76_100.html; also printed in *American Foreign Policy: Current Documents, 1962,* pp. 441–442.

Chairman Khrushchev to President Kennedy, Moscow, October 28, 1962 [Translated by U.S. Embassy, Moscow]

DEAR MR. PRESIDENT:

I have received your message of October 27. I express my satisfaction and thank you for the sense of proportion you have displayed and for realization of the responsibility which now devolves on you for the preservation of the peace of the world.

I regard with great understanding your concern and the concern of the United States people in connection with the fact that the weapons you describe as offensive are formidable weapons indeed. Both you and we understand what kind of weapons these are.

In order to eliminate as rapidly as possible the conflict which endangers the cause of peace, to give an assurance to all people who crave peace, and to reassure the American people, who, I am certain, also want peace, as do the people of the Soviet Union, the Soviet Government, in addition to earlier instructions on the discontinuation of further work on weapons construction sites, has given a new order to dismantle the arms which you described as offensive, and to crate and return them to the Soviet Union.

Mr. President, I should like to repeat what I had already written to you in my earlier messages—that the Soviet Government has given economic assistance to the Republic of Cuba, as well as arms, because Cuba and the Cuban people were constantly under the continuous threat of an invasion of Cuba.

A piratic vessel had shelled Havana. They say that this shelling was done by irresponsible Cuban émigrés. Perhaps so, however, the question is from where did they shoot. It is a fact that these Cubans have no territory, they are fugitives from their country, and they have no means to conduct military operations.

This means that someone put into their hands these weapons for shelling Havana and for piracy in the Caribbean in Cuban territorial waters. It is impossible in our time not to notice a piratic ship, considering the concentration in the Caribbean of American ships from which everything can be seen and observed.

In these conditions, pirate ships freely roam around and shell Cuba and make piratic attacks on peaceful cargo ships. It is known that they even shelled a British cargo ship. In a word, Cuba was under the continuous threat of aggressive forces, which did not conceal their intention to invade its territory.

The Cuban people want to build their life in their own interests without external interference. This is their right, and they cannot be blamed for wanting to be masters of their own country and disposing of the fruits of their own labor.

The threat of invasion of Cuba and all other schemes for creating tension over Cuba are designed to strike the Cuban people with a sense of insecurity, intimidate them, and prevent them from peacefully building their new life.

Mr. President, I should like to say clearly once more that we could not remain indifferent to this. The Soviet Government decided to render assistance to Cuba with the means of defense against aggression—only with means for defense purposes. We have supplied the defense means which you describe as offensive means. We have supplied them to prevent an attack on Cuba—to prevent rash acts.

I regard with respect and trust the statement you made in your message of October 27, 1962, that there would be no attack, no invasion of

Cuba, and not only on the part of the United States, but also on the part of other nations of the Western Hemisphere, as you said in your same message. Then the motives which induced us to render assistance of such a kind to Cuba disappear.

It is for this reason that we instructed our officers—these means as I had already informed you earlier are in the hands of the Soviet officers—to take appropriate measures to discontinue construction of the aforementioned facilities, to dismantle them, and to return them to the Soviet Union. As I had informed you in the letter of October 27, we are prepared to reach agreement to enable United Nations Representatives to verify the dismantling of these means.

Thus in view of the assurances you have given and our instructions on dismantling, there is every condition for eliminating the present conflict.

I note with satisfaction that you have responded to the desire I expressed with regard to elimination of the aforementioned dangerous situation, as well as with regard to providing conditions for a more thoughtful appraisal of the international situation, fraught as it is with great dangers in our age of thermonuclear weapons, rocketry, spaceships, global rockets, and other deadly weapons. All people are interested in insuring peace.

Therefore, vested with trust and great responsibility, we must not allow the situation to become aggravated and must stamp out the centers where a dangerous situation fraught with grave consequences to the cause of peace has arisen. If we, together with you, and with the assistance of other people of good will, succeed in eliminating this tense atmosphere, we should also make certain that no other dangerous conflicts which could lead to a world nuclear catastrophe would arise.

In conclusion, I should like to say something about a detente between NATO and the Warsaw Treaty countries that you have mentioned. We have spoken about this long since and are prepared to continue to exchange views on this question with you and to find a reasonable solution.

We should like to continue the exchange of views on the prohibition of atomic and thermonuclear weapons, general disarmament, and other problems relating to the relaxation of international tension.

Although I trust your statement, Mr. President, there are irresponsible people who would like to invade Cuba now and thus touch off a war. If we do take practical steps and proclaim the dismantling and evacuation of the means in question from Cuba, in so doing we, at the same time, want the Cuban people to be certain that we are with them and are not absolving ourselves of responsibility for rendering assistance to the Cuban people.

We are confident that the people of all countries, like you, Mr. President, will understand me correctly. We are not threatening. We want nothing but peace. Our country is now on the upsurge.

Our people are enjoying the fruits of their peaceful labor. They have achieved tremendous successes since the October Revolution, and created the greatest material, spiritual, and cultural values. Our people are enjoying these values; they want to continue developing their achievements and insure their further development on the way of peace and social progress by their persistent labor.

I should like to remind you, Mr. President, that military reconnaissance planes have violated the borders of the Soviet Union. In connection with this there have been conflicts between us and notes exchanged. In 1960 we shot down your U-2 plane, whose reconnaissance flight over the USSR wrecked the summit meeting in Paris. At that time, you took a correct position and denounced that criminal act of the former U.S. Administration.

But during your term of office as President another violation of our border has occurred, by an American U-2 plane in the Sakhalin area. We wrote you about that violation on 30 August. At that time you replied that that violation had occurred as a result of poor weather, and gave assurances that this would not be repeated. We trusted your assurances, because the weather was indeed poor in that area at that time.

But had not your planes been ordered to fly about our territory, even poor weather could not have brought an American plane into our airspace. Hence, the conclusion that this is being done with the knowledge of the Pentagon, which tramples on international norms and violates the borders of other states.

A still more dangerous case occurred on 28 October, when one of your reconnaissance planes intruded over Soviet borders in the Chukotka Peninsula area in the north and flew over our territory. The question is, Mr. President: How should we regard this? What is this: A provocation? One of your planes violates our frontier during this anxious time we are both experiencing, when everything has been put into combat readiness. Is it not a fact that an intruding American plane could be easily taken for a nuclear bomber, which might push us to a fateful step? And all the more so since the U.S. Government and Pentagon long ago declared that you are maintaining a continuous nuclear bomber patrol.

Therefore, you can imagine the responsibility you are assuming, especially now, when we are living through such anxious times.

I should like to express the following wish; it concerns the Cuban people. You do not have diplomatic relations. But through my officers in Cuba, I have reports that American planes are making flights over Cuba.

We are interested that there should be no war in the world, and that the Cuban people should live in peace. And besides, Mr. President, it is no secret that we have our people in Cuba. Under such a treaty with the Cuban Government we have sent there officers, instructors, mostly plain people: specialists, agronomists, zoo technicians, irrigators, land reclamation specialists, plain workers, tractor drivers, and others. We are concerned about them.

I should like you to consider, Mr. President, that violation of Cuban airspace by American planes could also lead to dangerous consequences. And if you do not want this to happen, it would be better if no cause is given for a dangerous situation to arise.

We must be careful now and refrain from any steps which would not be useful to the defense of the states involved in the conflict, which could only cause irritation and even serve as a provocation for a fateful step. Therefore, we must display sanity, reason, and refrain from such steps.

We value peace perhaps even more than other peoples because we went through a terrible war with Hitler. But our people will not falter in the face of any test. Our people trust their Government, and we assure our people and world public opinion that the Soviet Government will not allow itself to be provoked. But if the provocateurs unleash a war, they will not evade responsibility and the grave consequences a war would bring upon them. But we are confident that reason will triumph, that war will not be unleashed and peace and the security of the peoples will be insured.

In connection with the current negotiations between Acting Secretary General U Thant and representatives of the Soviet Union, the United States, and the Republic of Cuba, the Soviet Government has sent First Deputy Foreign Minister V.V. Kuznetsov to New York to help U Thant in his noble efforts aimed at eliminating the present dangerous situation.

Respectfully yours,

N. Khrushchev

Source: U.S. Department of State, *Foreign Relations of the United States 1961–1963*, Vol. XI: *The Cuban Missile Crisis and Its Aftermath* (Washington, DC: Government Printing Office, 1996), Document 102, http://www.state.gov/www/about_state/history/frusXI/101_125.html; also printed in Department of State *Bulletin*, November 19, 1973, pp. 650–654.

President Kennedy to Chairman Khrushchev, Washington, October 28, 1962

DEAR MR. CHAIRMAN:

I am replying at once to your broadcast message of October twenty-eight even though the official text has not yet reached me because of the great importance I attach to moving forward promptly to the settlement of the Cuban crisis. I think that you and I, with our heavy responsibilities for the maintenance of peace, were aware that developments were approaching a point where events could have become unmanageable. So I welcome this message and consider it an important contribution to peace.

The distinguished efforts of Acting Secretary General U Thant have greatly facilitated both our tasks. I consider my letter to you of October twenty-seventh and your reply of today as firm undertakings on the part of both our governments which should be promptly carried out. I hope that the necessary measures can at once be taken through the United Nations as your message says, so that the United States in turn can remove the quarantine measures now in effect. I have already made arrangements to report all these matters to the Organization of American States, whose members share a deep interest in a genuine peace in the Caribbean area.

You referred in your letter to a violation of your frontier by an American aircraft in the area of the Chukotsk Peninsula. I have learned that this plane, without arms or photographic equipment, was engaged in an air sampling mission in connection with your nuclear tests. Its course was direct from Eielson Air Force Base in Alaska to the North Pole and return. In turning south, the pilot made a serious navigational error which carried him over Soviet territory. He immediately made an emergency call on open radio for navigational assistance and was guided back to his home base by the most direct route. I regret this incident and will see to it that every precaution is taken to prevent recurrence.

Mr. Chairman, both of our countries have great unfinished tasks and I know that your people as well as those of the United States can ask for nothing better than to pursue them free from the fear of war. Modern science and technology have given us the possibility of making labor fruitful beyond anything that could have been dreamed of a few decades ago.

I agree with you that we must devote urgent attention to the problem of disarmament, as it relates to the whole world and also to critical areas. Perhaps now, as we step back from danger, we can together make real progress in this vital field. I think we should give priority to questions relating to the proliferation of nuclear weapons, on earth and in outer space, and to the great effort for a nuclear test ban. But we should also work hard to see if wider measures of disarmament can be agreed and put into operation at an early date. The United States Government will be prepared to discuss these questions urgently, and in a constructive spirit, at Geneva or elsewhere.

John F. Kennedy

Source: U.S. Department of State, *Foreign Relations of the United States 1961–1963,* Vol. XI: *The Cuban Missile Crisis and Its Aftermath* (Washington, DC: Government Printing Office, 1996), Document 104, http://www.state.gov/www/about_state/history/frusXI/101_125.html.

3. Meeting between U.S. Attorney General Robert F. Kennedy and Soviet Ambassador Anatoly Dobrynin, October 27, 1962

President John F. Kennedy was unwilling to agree publicly to decommission NATO intermediate-range nuclear missile bases in Turkey and Italy in exchange for the removal of Soviet missiles from Cuba. Privately, however, he thought such an arrangement, which Soviet premier Nikita Khrushchev proposed in a letter to Kennedy broadcast over Soviet radio on October 27, an acceptable means of ending the crisis. That same evening Kennedy sent Attorney General Robert F. Kennedy, his brother and closest adviser, to discuss the possibility of such a bargain with Anatoly Dobrynin, the Soviet ambassador in Washington. Robert Kennedy stressed that such an understanding would be strictly contingent on the immediate cessation of further Soviet work on the missile bases in Cuba. Both men left a record of this meeting. Dobrynin immediately cabled a description of it to Soviet leaders in Moscow, while Robert Kennedy, who reported back to his brother and Secretary of State Dean Rusk, set down his recollections of their encounter three days later. All concerned kept their discussions extremely confidential, as they wished the negotiations to remain completely secret.

Ambassador Dobrynin's Cable to the
Soviet Foreign Ministry, October 27, 1962

TOP SECRET Making Copies Prohibited Copy No. I
CIPHERED TELEGRAM

Late tonight R. Kennedy invited me to come see him. We talked alone.

The Cuban crisis, R. Kennedy began, continues to quickly worsen. We have just received a report that an unarmed American plane was shot down while carrying out a reconnaissance flight over Cuba. The military is demanding that the President arm such planes and respond to fire with fire. The US government will have to do this.

I interrupted R. Kennedy and asked him, what right American planes had to fly over Cuba at all, crudely violating its sovereignty and accepted international norms? How would the USA have reacted if foreign planes appeared over its territory?

"We have a resolution of the Organization of American States that gives us the right to such overflights," R. Kennedy quickly replied.

I told him that the Soviet Union, like all peace-loving countries, resolutely rejects such a "right" or, to be more exact, this kind of true lawlessness, when people who don't like the social-political situation in a country try to impose their will on it—a small state where the people themselves established and maintained [their system]. "The OAS resolution is a direct violation of the UN Charter," I added, "and you, as the Attorney General of the USA, the highest American legal entity, should certainly know that."

R. Kennedy said that he realized that we had different approaches to these problems and it was not likely that we could convince each other. But now the matter is not in these differences, since time is of the essence. "I want," R. Kennedy stressed, "to lay out the current alarming situation the way the president sees it. He wants N.S. Khrushchev to know this. This is the thrust of the situation now."

"Because of the plane that was shot down, there is now strong pressure on the president to give an order to respond with fire if fired upon when American reconnaissance planes are flying over Cuba. The US can't stop these flights, because this is the only way we can quickly get information about the state of construction of the missile bases in Cuba, which we believe pose a very serious threat to our national security. But if we start to fire in response—a chain reaction will quickly start that will be very hard to stop. The same thing in regard to the essence of the issue of the missile bases in Cuba. The USA government is determined to get rid of those bases—up to, in the extreme case, of bombing them, since, I repeat, they pose a great threat to the security of the USA. But in response to the bombing of these bases, in the course of which Soviet specialists might suffer, the Soviet government will undoubtedly respond with the same against us, somewhere in Europe. A real war will begin, in which millions of Americans and Russians will die. We want to avoid that any way we can, I'm sure that the government of the USSR has the same wish. However, taking time to find a way out [of the situation] is very risky (here R. Kennedy mentioned as if in passing that there are many unreasonable heads among the generals, and not only among the generals, who are 'itching for a fight'). The situation might get out of control, with irreversible consequences."

"In this regard," R. Kennedy said, "the president considers that a suitable basis for regulating the entire Cuban conflict might be the letter N.S. Khrushchev sent on October 26 and the letter in response from the President which was sent off today to N.S. Khrushchev through the US Embassy in Moscow. The most important thing for us," R. Kennedy stressed, "is to get as soon as possible the agreement of the Soviet government to halt further work on the construction of the missile bases in Cuba and take measures under international control that would make it impossible to use these weapons. In exchange the government of the USA is ready, in addition to repealing all measures on the "quarantine," to give the assurances that there will not be any invasion of Cuba and that other countries of the Western Hemisphere are ready to give the same assurances—the US government is certain of this."

"And what about Turkey?" I asked R. Kennedy.

"If that is the only obstacle to achieving the regulation I mentioned earlier, then the president doesn't see any unsurmountable difficulties in resolving this issue," replied R. Kennedy. "The greatest difficulty for the president is the public discussion of the issue of Turkey. Formally the deployment of missile bases in Turkey was done by a special decision of the NATO Council. To announce now a unilateral decision by the president of the USA to withdraw missile bases from Turkey—this would damage the entire structure of NATO and the US position as the leader of NATO, where, as the Soviet government knows very well, there are many arguments. In short, if such a decision were announced now it would seriously tear apart NATO."

"However, President Kennedy is ready to come to agree on that question with N.S. Khrushchev, too. I think that in order to withdraw these bases from Turkey," R. Kennedy said, "we need 4–5 months. This is the minimal amount of time necessary for the US government to do this, taking into account the procedures that exist within the NATO framework. On the whole Turkey issue," R. Kennedy added, "if Premier N.S. Khrushchev agrees with what I've said, we can continue to exchange opinions between him and the president, using him, R. Kennedy and the Soviet ambassador.

However, the president can't say anything public in this regard about Turkey," R. Kennedy said again. R. Kennedy then warned that his comments about Turkey are extremely confidential; besides him and his brother, only 2–3 people know about it in Washington.

"That's all that he asked me to pass on to N.S. Khrushchev," R. Kennedy said in conclusion. "The president also asked N.S. Khrushchev to give him an answer (through the Soviet ambassador and R. Kennedy) if possible within the next day (Sunday) on these thoughts in order to have a business-like, clear answer in principle. [He asked him] not to get into a wordy discussion, which might drag things out. The current serious situation, unfortunately, is such that there is very little time to resolve this whole issue. Unfortunately, events are developing too quickly. The request for a reply tomorrow," stressed R. Kennedy, "is just that—a request, and not an ultimatum. The president hopes that the head of the Soviet government will understand him correctly."

I noted that it went without saying that the Soviet government would not accept any ultimatums and it was good that the American government realized that. I also reminded him of N.S. Khrushchev's appeal in his last letter to the president to demonstrate state wisdom in resolving this question. Then I told R. Kennedy that the president's thoughts would be brought to the attention of the head of the Soviet government. I also said that I would contact him as soon as there was a reply. In this regard, R. Kennedy gave me a number of a direct telephone line to the White House.

In the course of the conversation, R. Kennedy noted that he knew about the conversation that television commentator Scali had yesterday with an Embassy adviser on possible ways to regulate the Cuban conflict [one and a half lines whited out]

I should say that during our meeting R. Kennedy was very upset; in any case, I've never seen him like this before. True, about twice he tried to return to the topic of "deception" (that he talked about so persistently during our previous meeting), but he did so in passing and without any edge to it. He didn't even try to get into fights on various subjects, as he usually does, and only persistently returned to one topic: time is of the essence and we shouldn't miss the chance.

After meeting with me he immediately went to see the president, with whom, as R. Kennedy said, he spends almost all his time now.

27/X-62 A. DOBRYNIN

Source: Russian Foreign Ministry archives, translation from copy provided by NHK (Japanese Television), reprinted in Richard Ned Lebow and Janice Gross Stein, *We*

All Lost the Cold War (Princeton, NJ: Princeton University Press, 1994), appendix, pp. 523–526, with minor revisions. The National Security Archives, The George Washington University. Available at: http://www.gwu.edu/~nsarchiv/NSAEBB/ NSAEBB313/Doc01.pdf. Accessed December 1, 2011.

Memorandum from Attorney General Kennedy to Secretary of State Rusk, October 30, 1962

At the request of Secretary Rusk, I telephoned Ambassador Dobrynin at approximately 7:15 p.m. on Saturday, October 27th. I asked him if he would come to the Justice Department at a quarter of eight.

We met in my office. I told him first that we understood that the work was continuing on the Soviet missile bases in Cuba. Further, I explained to him that in the last two hours we had found that our planes flying over Cuba had been fired upon and that one of our U-2's had been shot down and the pilot killed. I said these men were flying unarmed planes.

I told him that this was an extremely serious turn in events. We would have to make certain decisions within the next 12 or possibly 24 hours. There was a very little time left. If the Cubans were shooting at our planes, then we were going to shoot back. This could not help but bring on further incidents and that he had better understand the full implications of this matter.

He raised the point that the argument the Cubans were making was that we were violating Cuban air space. I replied that if we had not been violating Cuban air space then we would still be believing what he and Khrushchev had said—that there were no long-range missiles in Cuba. In any case I said that this matter was far more serious than the air space over Cuba and involved peoples all over the world.

I said that he had better understand the situation and he had better communicate that understanding to Mr. Khrushchev. Mr. Khrushchev and he had misled us. The Soviet Union had secretly established missile bases in Cuba while at the same time proclaiming, privately and publicly, that this would never be done. I said those missile bases had to go and they had to go right away. We had to have a commitment by at least tomorrow that those bases would be removed. This was not an ultimatum, I said, but just a statement of fact. He should understand that if they did not remove those bases then we would remove them. His country might take retaliatory action but he should understand that before this was over, while there might be dead Americans there would also be dead Russians.

He asked me then what offer we were making. I said a letter had just been transmitted to the Soviet Embassy which stated in substance that the missile bases should be dismantled and all offensive weapons should be removed from Cuba. In return, if Cuba and Castro and the Communists ended their subversive activities in other Central and Latin American countries, we would agree to keep peace in the Caribbean and not permit an invasion from American soil.

He then asked me about Khrushchev's other proposal dealing with the removal of the missiles from Turkey. I replied that there could be no quid pro quo—no deal of this kind could be made. This was a matter that had to be considered by NATO and that it was up to NATO to make the decision. I said it was completely impossible for NATO to take such a step under the present threatening position of the Soviet Union. ~~If some time elapsed and per your instructions, I mentioned four or five months—I said I was sure that these matters could be resolved satisfactory.~~ [Deleted in original]

Per your instructions I repeated that there could be no deal of any kind and that any steps toward easing tensions in other parts of the world largely depended on the Soviet Union and Mr. Khrushchev taking action in Cuba and taking it immediately.

I repeated to him that this matter could not wait and that he had better contact Mr. Khrushchev and have a commitment from him by the next day to withdraw the missile bases under United Nations supervision for otherwise, I said, there would be drastic consequences.

Source: U.S. Department of State, *Foreign Relations of the United States 1961–1963,* Vol. XI: *The Cuban Missile Crisis and Its Aftermath* (Washington, DC: Government Printing Office, 1996), Document 96, http://www.state.gov/www/about_state/history/frusXI/76_100.html.

4. Meeting between U.S. Attorney General Robert F. Kennedy and Soviet Ambassador Anatoly Dobrynin, October 28, 1962

With a settlement in sight, on 28 October Soviet officials in Moscow used private exchanges between Ambassador Anatoly Dobrynin and Robert F. Kennedy as a conduit for additional assurances and understandings. Khrushchev sent a message to the president's brother, which Dobrynin passed on the same day, reporting back immediately to Moscow.

Telegram from Soviet Foreign Minister Andrey Gromyko to Ambassador Dobrynin, October 28, 1962

CIPHERED TELEGRAM
EXTRAORDINARY
WASHINGTON
SOVIET AMBASSADOR

Quickly get in touch with R. Kennedy and tell him that you passed on to N.S. Khrushchev the contents of your conversation with him. N.S. Khrushchev sent the following urgent response.

The thoughts which R. Kennedy expressed at the instruction of the President find understanding in Moscow. Today, an answer will be given by radio to the President's message of October 27, and that response will be the most favorable. The main thing which disturbs the President, precisely the issue of the dismantling under international control of the rocket bases in Cuba—meets no objection and will be explained in detail in N.S. Khrushchev's message.

Telegraph upon implementation.

[handwritten]

(A. Gromyko)

Source: Russian Foreign Ministry Archives (AVP RF), copy courtesy of The National Security Archive, The George Washington University. Translation by Mark H. Doctoroff. Available online at Cold War International History Project Virtual Archive, http://legacy.wilsoncenter.org/va2/index.cfm?topic_id=1409&fuseaction= home.document&identifier=5034E33A-96B6-175C-9C8D8C35D3CCF5BE &sort=collection&item=Cuban%20Missile%20Crisis.

Telegram from Ambassador Dobrynin to Soviet Ministry of Foreign Affairs, October 28, 1962

TOP SECRET
Making Copies Prohibited
Copy No. 1
CIPHERED TELEGRAM

R. Kennedy, with whom I met, listened very attentively to N.S. Khrushchev's response. Expressing thanks for the report, he said that he would quickly return to the White House in order to inform the President about the "important response" of the head of the Soviet government. "This is a great relief," R. Kennedy added further, and it was evident that he expressed his words somehow involuntarily. "I," said R. Kennedy, "today will finally be able to see my kids, for I have been entirely absent from home."

According to everything it was evident that R. Kennedy with satisfaction, it is necessary to say, really with great relief met the report about N.S. Khrushchev's response.

In parting, R. Kennedy once again requested that strict secrecy be maintained about the agreement with Turkey. "Especially so that the correspondents don't find out. At our place for the time being even [White House Press Secretary Pierre] Salinger does not know about it." (It was not entirely clear why he considered it necessary to mention his name, but he did it).

I responded that in the Embassy no one besides me knows about the conversation with him yesterday. R. Kennedy said that in addition to the current correspondence and future exchange of opinions via diplomatic channels, on important questions he will maintain contact with me directly, avoiding any intermediaries.

Before departing, R. Kennedy once again gave thanks for N.S. Khrushchev's quick and effective response.

Your instructions arrived here 1.5 hours after the announcement via radio about the essence of N.S. Khrushchev's response. I explained to R. Kennedy that the tardiness was caused by a delay of telegrams at the telegraph station.

28.X.62 A. DOBRYNIN

Source: Russian Foreign Ministry Archives (AVP RF), copy courtesy of The National Security Archive, The George Washington University. Translation by Mark H. Doctoroff. Available online at Cold War International History Project Virtual Archive, http://legacy.wilsoncenter.org/va2/index.cfm?topic_id=1409& fuseaction=home.document&identifier=5034E405-96B6-175C-9C201F3 F4D387E4B&sort=collection&item=Cuban%20Missile%20Crisis.

5. Chairman Nikita Khrushchev to President John F. Kennedy, Moscow, October 28, 1962

In response to U.S. Attorney General Robert Kennedy's discussions with Soviet ambassador Anatoly Dobrynin on October 27, Soviet premier Nikita Khrushchev dispatched a letter to President John F.

Kennedy, accepting the U.S. offer to remove missiles from Turkey. He promised to keep this arrangement secret. On October 29 Dobrynin forwarded Khrushchev's letter to Robert Kennedy. The president, however, thought the matter so sensitive that he refused to accept this letter, as he preferred that no formal written record of their bargain exist. One day later, his brother Robert therefore returned it to Ambassador Dobrynin.

DEAR MR. PRESIDENT,

Ambassador Dobrynin has apprised me of his conversation with Robert Kennedy which took place on October 27. In this conversation Robert Kennedy said that it is somewhat difficult for you at the present time to publicly discuss the question of eliminating the US missile bases in Turkey because of the fact that the stationing of those bases in Turkey was formalized through a NATO Council decision.

Readiness to agree on this issue that I raised in my message to you of October 27 was also emphasized. In this context Robert Kennedy said that removal of those bases from Turkey would take 4 to 5 months. Furthermore, a wish was expressed that exchanges of views on this matter between you and I should continue through Robert Kennedy and the Soviet Ambassador, and that these exchanges should be considered confidential.

I feel I must state to you that I do understand the delicacy involved for you in an open consideration of the issue of eliminating the US missile bases in Turkey. I take into account the complexity of this issue and I believe you are right about not wishing to publicly discuss it. I agree that our discussion of this subject be pursued confidentially through Robert Kennedy and the Soviet Ambassador in Washington. You may have noticed that in my message to you on October 28, which was to be published immediately, I did not raise this question—precisely because I was mindful of your wish conveyed through Robert Kennedy. But all the proposals that I presented in that message took into account the fact that you had agreed to resolve, [sic] the matter of your missile bases in Turkey consistent with what I had said in my message of October 27 and what you stated through Robert Kennedy in his meeting with Ambassador Dobrynin on the same day.

I express my great appreciation to you for having instructed your brother R. Kennedy to convey those thoughts.

I hope, Mr. President, that agreement on this matter, too, shall be a no small step advancing the cause of relaxation of international tensions and the tensions between our two powers. And that in turn can provide a good impetus to resolving other issues concerning both the security of Europe and the international situation as a whole.

Mr. President, the crisis that we have gone through may repeat again. This means that we need to address the issues which contain too much explosive material. Not right away, of course. Apparently, it will take some time for the passions to cool down. But we cannot delay the solution to these issues, for continuation of this situation is frought [sic] with many uncertainties and dangers.

Sincerely,

N. Khrushchev

Source: U.S. Department of State, *Foreign Relations of the United States 1961– 1963,* Vol. VI: *Kennedy-Khrushchev Exchanges* (Washington, DC: Government Printing Office, 1996), Document 70, http://www.state.gov/www/about_state/ history/volume_vi/exchanges.html.

6. Meeting between U.S. Attorney General Robert F. Kennedy and Soviet Ambassador Anatoly Dobrynin, October 30, 1962

On October 30, 1962, Attorney General Robert F. Kennedy met once again with the Soviet ambassador, Anatoly Dobrynin. He refused to accept a letter from Khrushchev, delivered the previous day, setting down in writing the understanding that NATO missiles would be removed from Turkey in exchange for the dismantling of those in Cuba. He promised, however, that the United States would ensure that the Jupiter missiles in both Italy and Turkey were taken out within four or five months. Kennedy's notes for this meeting survive, and Dobrynin sent an account of it to Moscow.

Robert F. Kennedy, Notes for Meeting with Ambassador Dobrynin, October 30, 1962

Read letter—Studied it over night.
No quid pro quo as I told you.
The letter makes it appear that there was.

You asked me about missile bases in Turkey. I told you we would be out of them—4 or 5 months. That still holds....You have my word on this & that is sufficient.

Take back your letter—Reconsider it & if you feel it is necessary to write letters then we will also write one which you cannot enjoy.

Also if you should publish any document indicating a deal then it is off & also if done afterward will further affect the relationship.

Source: Robert F. Kennedy Papers, John F. Kennedy Presidential Library, Boston. Reprinted in Arthur M. Schlesinger, Jr., *Robert Kennedy and His Times,* 2 vols. (Boston: Houghton Mifflin, 1978), 1:546.

Telegram from Ambassador Dobrynin to the Soviet Foreign Ministry, October 30, 1962

Today Robert Kennedy invited me to meet with him. He said that he would like to talk about N.S. Khrushchev's letter to the President yesterday.

The President, Robert Kennedy said, confirms the understanding [do-govorion-nost] with N.S. Khrushchev on the elimination of the American missile bases in Turkey (Robert Kennedy confirmed that one speaks of an understanding). Corresponding measures will be taken towards fulfilling this understanding within the period of time indicated earlier, in confidential observance of NATO guidelines, but of course without any mention that this is connected to the Cuban events.

We, however, said Robert Kennedy, are not prepared to formulate such an understanding in the form of letters, even the most confidential letters, between the President and the head of the Soviet government when it concerns such a highly delicate issue. Speaking in all candor, I myself, for example, do not want to risk getting involved in the transmission of this sort of letter, since who knows where and when such letters can surface or be somehow published—not now, but in the future—and any changes in the course of events are possible. The appearance of such a document could cause irreparable harm to my political career in the future. This is why we request that you take this letter back.

It is possible, Robert Kennedy continued, that you do not believe us and through letters you want to put the understanding in writing. The issue of Soviet missile bases in Cuba has unfortunately introduced a real element of uncertainty and suspicion even into confidential channels of contact. We will however live up to our promise, even if it is given in this oral form. As you know, it was in precisely the same oral form that the President made his promise to N.S. Khrushchev regarding the removal of a certain number of American soldiers from Thailand. That promise was kept. So too will this promise be kept.

As a guarantee, Robert Kennedy added, I can only give you my word. Moreover I can tell you that two other people besides the President know about the existing understanding: they are [Secretary of State Dean] Rusk and [advisor on Soviet affairs Llewellyn] Thompson. If you do not believe me, discuss it with them, and they will tell you the same thing. But it is better not to transfer this understanding into a formal, albeit confidential, exchange of letters (as can be noted, the greatest suspicion in the two Kennedy brothers was elicited by the part of Khrushchev's letter which speaks directly of a link between the Cuban events and the bases in Turkey). We hope that N.S. Khrushchev will understand us correctly. In regard to this Robert Kennedy insistently asked to take the letter back without delay.

I told Robert Kennedy that everything said above I would report to N.S. Khrushchev, emphasizing in doing so that even the President and he, Robert Kennedy, could be sure of the fact that the Soviet government is regarding the understanding that has been reached as strictly secret and not for publication. At the same time, in order to confirm Robert Kennedy's statement about the understanding, I asked him again about whether the President really confirms the understanding with N.S. Khrushchev on the elimination of American missile bases in Turkey.

Robert Kennedy said once again that he confirmed it, and again that he hoped that their motivations would be properly understood in Moscow. Taking what they explained into account, I believed it conditionally possible—before receiving any instructions from Moscow—to take this letter [back], since a categorical refusal to do so would, in my opinion, only weaken Robert Kennedy's firm statements on the understanding that has been reached. Moreover, leaving the letter with him, after he had clearly expressed the President's desire not to exchange letters, could scarcely be in the interests of doing business [in the future].

In conclusion Robert Kennedy said that, in his opinion, the events connected with the Cuban issue have been developing quite favorably, and that he hoped that everything would eventually be settled. He added that, on the Turkish issue and other highly confidential issues he was prepared to maintain a direct contact with me as earlier, emphasizing in doing so that the point was the possible oral considerations of the President and the head of the Soviet government N.S. Khrushchev on the exchange of letters on such delicate issues as missile bases in Turkey, or issues which need to be handled more by the State Department than by him personally, taking into account the delicacy of his situation as the President's brother and as Attorney General of the United States. I do not want, Robert Kennedy added, to claim for myself the function of the State Department, but my "solitary diplomacy" may be needed several more times, and we will be meeting with each other periodically.

I answered to Robert Kennedy that I was prepared to maintain contact with him on highly important issues in the future, passing over the heads, as he himself suggested, of all intermediaries. Robert Kennedy confirmed this. From what Robert Kennedy said it was clear that the President is trying now to avoid exchanging any documents on issues of a highly delicate nature like Turkey which could leave a trace anywhere, but that he favors the continuation of a confidential exchange of opinions between the heads of the two governments.

We believe it expedient to visit Robert Kennedy once again and to issue a statement, in referring to our mission, that the Soviet government and N.S. Khrushchev personally are prepared to take into account the President's desire for maintaining the secrecy of the oral understanding on the removal of the American missile bases from Turkey. It is also expedient to tell of our willingness, if the President is also prepared for this, to continue the confidential exchange of opinions between the heads of the governments on many important unresolved issues, on whose resolution the lessening of international tension, and of the tension between our two countries in particular, is to a very great degree dependent.

I request instructions.

30.X.62 A.DOBRYNIN

Source: Russian Foreign Ministry Archives (AVP RF), copy obtained by NHK (Japanese Television), provided to CWIHP, and on file at The National Security Archive, The George Washington University. Translation by John Henriksen, Harvard University. Available at: http://legacy.wilsoncenter.org/va2/index.cfm?topic_id=1409&fuseaction=home.document&identifier=5034EB58-96B6-175C-9E56519C864C5063&sort=rights&item=cwihp. Accessed January 1, 2012.

7. Letters between Cuban leader Fidel Castro and Soviet Premier Nikita Khrushchev, October 26–31, 1962

As the Cuban Missile Crisis intensified and was then resolved, Cuban Prime Minister Fidel Castro and Soviet premier Nikita Khrushchev exchanged a series of letters, in which Castro showed himself far more bellicose than Khrushchev. Fearing that a U.S. invasion of Cuba was inevitable, on October 26 Castro begged Khrushchev to open hostilities with a nuclear first strike against the United States. When he sent Kennedy two letters, on October 26 and 27, suggesting terms on which the ongoing crisis might be settled, Khrushchev did not consult Castro, an omission that infuriated the Cuban leader. On October 27, Khrushchev wrote to Castro, defending his proposals to Kennedy as the best outcome for Cuba, one that would keep Cuba secure against any future U.S. invasion. Not yet aware that Soviet rather than Cuban military personnel had been responsible for shooting down a U.S. U-2 reconnaissance plane over Cuba on October 27, he also warned Castro against attacking U.S. airplanes. On October 28, Castro asserted Cuba's right to shoot down U.S. aircraft and warned that he was unwilling to accept any outside inspections of Cuban territory in connection with the recent Soviet agreement to remove the missiles in question from the island. Khrushchev replied at length, justifying the recent agreement as one that was in Cuba's best interests, warning that a nuclear war would have brought destruction to Cuba and denying that he had failed to consult Castro during the crisis. His persuasions failed to mollify the deeply resentful Castro, who claimed that not just the Cubans, but also the Soviet soldiers stationed there, had been prepared to fight to the bitter end against the United States. Once again, Castro complained that Soviet officials had not consulted him when negotiating with their U.S. counterparts.

Fidel Castro to Nikita Khrushchev, October 26, 1962

Dear Comrade Khrushchev,

From an analysis of the situation and the reports in our possession, I consider that the aggression is almost imminent within the next 24 or 72 hours.

There are two possible variants: the first and likeliest one is an air attack against certain targets with the limited objective of destroying them; the second, less probable although possible, is invasion. I understand that this variant would call for a large number of forces and it is, in addition, the most repulsive form of aggression, which might inhibit them.

You can rest assured that we will firmly and resolutely resist attack, whatever it may be.

The morale of the Cuban people is extremely high and the aggressor will be confronted heroically.

At this time I want to convey to you briefly my personal opinion.

If the second variant is implemented and the imperialists invade Cuba with the goal of occupying it, the danger that that aggressive policy poses for humanity is so great that following that event the Soviet Union must never allow the circumstances in which the imperialists could launch the first nuclear strike against it.

I tell you this because I believe that the imperialists' aggressiveness is extremely dangerous and if they actually carry out the brutal act of invading Cuba in violation of international law and morality, that would be the moment to eliminate such danger forever through an act of clear legitimate defense, however harsh and terrible the solution would be for there is no other.

It has influenced my opinion to see how this aggressive policy is developing, how the imperialists, disregarding world public opinion and ignoring principles and the law, are blockading the seas, violating our airspace and preparing an invasion, while at the same time frustrating every possibility for talks, even though they are aware of the seriousness of the problem.

You have been and continue to be a tireless defender of peace and I realize how bitter these hours must be, when the outcome of your superhuman efforts is so seriously threatened. However, up to the last moment we will maintain the hope that peace will be safeguarded and we are willing to contribute to this as much as we can. But at the same time, we are ready to calmly confront a situation which we view as quite real and quite close.

Once more I convey to you the infinite gratitude and recognition of our Cuban people to the Soviet people who have been so generous and fraternal with us, as well as our profound gratitude and admiration for you, and wish you success in the huge task and serious responsibilities ahead of you.

Fraternally,

Fidel Castro

Source: The Cuban Missile Crisis, 1962: The 40th Anniversary. The National Security Archive, The George Washington University. Available at: http://www.gwu.edu/~nsarchiv/nsa/cuba_mis_cri/621026%20Castro%20Letter%20to%20Khrushchev.pdf. Accessed December 1, 2011.

Nikita Khrushchev to Fidel Castro, October 28, 1962

Dear Comrade Fidel Castro,

Our October 27 message to President Kennedy allows for the question to be settled in your favor, to defend Cuba from an invasion and prevent war from breaking out. Kennedy's reply, which you apparently also know, offers assurances that the United States will not invade Cuba with its own forces, nor will it permit its allies to carry out an invasion. In this way the president of the United States has positively answered messages of October 26 and 27, 1962.

We have now finished drafting our reply to the president's message. I am not going to convey it here, for you surely know the text, which is now being broadcast over the radio.

With this motive I would like to recommend to you now, at this moment of change in the crisis, not to be carried away by sentiment and to show firmness. I must say that I understand your feelings of indignation toward the aggressive actions and violation of elementary norms of international law on the part of the United States.

But now, rather than law, what prevails is the senselessness of the militarists at the Pentagon. Now that an agreement is within sight, the Pentagon is searching for a pretext to frustrate this agreement. This is why it is organizing the provocative flights. Yesterday you shot down one of these, while earlier you didn't shoot them down when they overflew your territory. The aggressors will take advantage of such a step for their own purposes.

Therefore, I would like to advise you in a friendly manner to show patience, firmness and even more firmness. Naturally, if there's an invasion it will be necessary to repulse it by every means. But we mustn't allow ourselves to be carried away by provocations, because the Pentagon's unbridled militarists, now that the solution to the conflict is in sight and apparently in your favor, creating a guarantee against the invasion of Cuba, are trying to frustrate the agreement and provoke you into actions that could be used against you. I ask you not to give them the pretext for doing that.

On our part, we will do everything possible to stabilize the situation in Cuba, defend Cuba against invasion and assure you the possibilities for peacefully building a socialist society.

I send you greetings, extensive to all your leadership group.

N. Khrushchev

Source: The Cuban Missile Crisis, 1962: The 40th Anniversary. The National Security Archive, The George Washington University. Available at: http://www.gwu.edu/~nsarchiv/nsa/cuba_mis_cri/19621028khrlet.pdf. Accessed December 1, 2011.

Fidel Castro to Nikita Khrushchev, October 28, 1962

Dear Comrade Khrushchev,

I have just received your letter.

The position of our government concerning your communication to us is embodied in the statement formulated today, whose text you surely know.

I wish to clear up something concerning the antiaircraft measures we adopted. You say: "Yesterday you shot down one of these [planes], while earlier you didn't shoot them down when they overflew your territory."

Earlier isolated violations were committed without a determined military purpose or without a real danger stemming from those flights.

This time that wasn't the case. There was the danger of a surprise attack on certain military installations. We decided not to sit back and wait for a surprise attack, with our detection radar turned off, when the potentially aggressive planes flying with impunity over targets could destroy them totally. We didn't think we should allow that after all the efforts and expenses incurred and, in addition, because it would weaken us greatly, militarily and morally. For that reason, on October 24 the Cuban forces mobilized 50 antiaircraft batteries, our entire reserve then, to provide support to the Soviet forces' positions. If we sought to avoid the risk of a surprise attack, it was necessary for Cuban artillerymen to have orders to shoot. The Soviet command can furnish you with additional reports of what happened to the plane that was shot down.

Earlier, airspace violations were carried out de facto and furtively. Yesterday the American government tried to make official the privilege of violating our airspace at any hour of the day and night. We cannot accept that, as it would be tantamount to giving up a sovereign prerogative. However, we agree that we must avoid an incident at this precise moment that could seriously harm the negotiations, so we will instruct the Cuban batteries not to open fire, but only for as long as the negotiations last and without revoking the declaration published yesterday about the decision to defend our airspace. It should also be taken into account that under the current tense conditions incidents can take place accidentally.

I also wish to inform you that we are in principle opposed to an inspection of our territory.

I appreciate extraordinarily the efforts you have made to keep the peace and we are absolutely in agreement with the need for struggling for that goal. If this is accomplished in a just, solid and definitive manner, it will be an inestimable service to humanity.

Fraternally,

Fidel Castro Ruz

Source: The Cuban Missile Crisis, 1962: The 40th Anniversary. The National Security Archive, The George Washington University. Available at: http://www.gwu.edu/~nsarchiv/nsa/cuba_mis_cri/19621028caslet.pdf. Accessed December 1, 2011.

Nikita Khrushchev to Fidel Castro, October 30, 1962

Dear Comrade Fidel Castro,

We have received your letter of October 28 and the reports on the talks that you as well as President Dorticós have had with our ambassador.

We understand your situation and take into account the difficulties you now have during this first transitional stage after the liquidation of maximum tension that arose due to the threat of attack on the part of the U.S. imperialists, which you expected would occur at any moment.

We understand that certain difficulties have been created for you as a result of our having promised the U.S. government to withdraw the missile base from Cuba, since it is viewed as an offensive weapon, in exchange for the U.S. commitment to abandon plans for an invasion of Cuba by U.S. troops or those of its allies in the western hemisphere, and lift the so-called "quarantine," that is, bring the [naval] blockade of Cuba to an end. This led to the liquidation of the conflict in the Caribbean zone which, as you well realize, was characterized by the clash of two superpowers and the possibility of being transformed into a thermonuclear world war using missiles.

As we learned from our ambassador, some Cubans have the opinion that the Cuban people want a declaration of another nature rather than the declaration of the withdrawal of the missiles. It's possible that this kind of feeling exists among the people. But we, political and government figures, are leaders of a people who doesn't know everything and can't really comprehend all that we leaders must deal with. Therefore, we should march at the head of the people and then the people will follow us and respect us.

Had we, yielding to the sentiments prevailing among the people, allowed ourselves to be carried away by certain passionate sectors of the population and refused to come to a reasonable agreement with the U.S. government, then a war could have broken out, in the course of which millions of people would have died and the survivors would pinned the blame on the leaders for not having taken the necessary measures to prevent this war of annihilation.

Preventing the war and an attack on Cuba depended not just on the measures adopted by our governments but also on an estimate of the actions of the enemy's forces deployed near you. Accordingly, the overall situation had to be considered.

In addition, there are opinions that you and we, as they say, failed to engage in consultations concerning these questions before adopting the decisions known to you.

For this reason we believed that we consulted with you, dear Comrade Fidel Castro, receiving your cables, each one more alarming than the next, and finally your cable of October 27, saying you were nearly certain that an attack on Cuba would be launched. You believed it was merely a question of time, that the attack would take place within the next 24 or 72 hours. Upon receiving this alarming cable from you and aware of your courage, we viewed it as a very well-founded alarm.

Wasn't this consultation on your part with us? I have viewed this cable as a signal of extreme alarm. Under the conditions created, also bearing in mind the information that the unabated warmongering group of U.S. militarists wanted to take advantage of the situation that had been created and launch an attack on Cuba, if we had continued our consultations, we would have wasted time and the attack would have been carried out.

We came to the conclusion that our strategic missiles in Cuba became an ominous force for the imperialists: they were frightened and because of their fear that our rockets could be launched, they could have dared to liquidate them by bombing them and launching an invasion of Cuba. And it must be said that they could have knocked them all out. Therefore, I repeat, your alarm was absolutely well-founded.

In your cable of October 27 you proposed that we be the first to launch a nuclear strike against the territory of the enemy. You, of course, realize where that would have led. Rather than a simple strike, it would have been the start of a thermonuclear world war.

Dear Comrade Fidel Castro, I consider this proposal of yours incorrect, although I understand your motivation.

We have lived through the most serious moment when a nuclear world war could have broken out. Obviously, in that case, the United States would have sustained huge losses, but the Soviet Union and the whole socialist camp would also have suffered greatly. As far as Cuba is concerned, it would be difficult to say even in general terms what this would have meant for them. In the first place, Cuba would have been burned in the fire of war. There is no doubt that the Cuban people would have fought courageously or that they would have died heroically. But we are not struggling against imperialism in order to die, but to take advantage of all our possibilities, to lose less in the struggle and win more to overcome and achieve the victory of communism.

Now, as a result of the measures taken, we reached the goal sought when we agreed with you to send the missiles to Cuba. We have wrested from the United States the commitment not to invade Cuba and not to permit their Latin American allies to do so. We have wrested all this from them without a nuclear strike.

We consider that we must take advantage of all the possibilities available to defend Cuba, strengthen its independence and sovereignty, defeat military aggression and prevent a nuclear world war in our time.

And we have accomplished that.

Of course, we made concessions, accepted a commitment, acting according to the principle that a concession on one side be answered by a concession on the other side. The United States also made a concession. It made the commitment before all the world not to attack Cuba.

That's why when we compare aggression on the part of the United States and thermonuclear war with the commitment of a concession in exchange for a concession, the upholding of the inviolability of the Republic of Cuba and the prevention of a world war, I think that the total outcome of this reckoning, of this comparison, is perfectly clear.

Naturally, in defending Cuba as well as the other socialist countries, we can't rely on a U.S. government veto. We have adopted and will continue to adopt in the future all the measures necessary to strengthen our defense and build up our forces, so that we can strike back if needed. At present, as a result of our weapons supplies, Cuba is stronger than ever. Even after the dismantling of the missile installations you will have powerful weapons to throw back the enemy, on land, in the air and on the sea, in the approaches to the island. At the same time, as you will recall, we have said in our message to the president of the United States dated October 28, that at the same time we want to assure the Cuban people that we stand at their side and we will not forget our responsibility to help the Cuban people. It is clear to everyone that this is an extremely serious warning to the enemy on our part.

You also stated during the rallies that the United States can't be trusted. That, of course, is correct. We also view your statements on the conditions of the talks with the United States as correct. The shooting down of a U.S. plane over Cuba turned out to be a useful measure because this operation ended without complications. Let it be a lesson for the imperialists.

Needless to say, our enemies will interpret the events in their own way. The Cuban counterrevolution will also try to raise its head. But we think you will completely dominate your domestic internal enemies without our assistance. The main thing we have secured is preventing aggression on the part of your foreign enemy at present.

We feel that the aggressor came out the loser. He made preparations to attack Cuba but we stopped him and forced him to recognize before world public opinion that he won't do it at the current stage. We view this as a great victory. The imperialists, of course, will not stop their struggle against communism. But we also have our plans and we are going to adopt our measures. This process of struggle will continue so long as there are two political and social systems in the world, until one of these—and we know it will be our communist system—wins and triumphs throughout the world.

Comrade Fidel Castro, I have decided to send this reply to you as soon as possible. A more detailed analysis of everything that has happened will be made in the letter I'll send you shortly. In that letter I will make the broadest analysis of the situation and give you my evaluation of the outcome of the end of the conflict.

Now, as the talks to settle the conflict get underway, I ask you to send me your considerations. For our part, we will continue to report to you on the development of these talks and make all necessary consultations.

I wish you success, Comrade Fidel Castro. You will no doubt have success. There will still be machinations against you, but together with you, we will adopt all the measures necessary to paralyze them and contribute to the strengthening and development of the Cuban Revolution.

Nikita Krushchev

Source: The Cuban Missile Crisis, 1962: The 40th Anniversary. The National Security Archive, The George Washington University. Available at: http://www.gwu.edu/~nsarchiv/nsa/cuba_mis_cri/621030%20Letter%20to%20Castro.pdf. Accessed December 1, 2011.

Fidel Castro to Nikita Khrushchev, October 31, 1962

Dear Comrade Khrushchev,

I received your letter of 30 October. You understand that we indeed were consulted before you adopted the decision to withdraw the strategic missiles. You base yourself on the alarming news that you say reached you from Cuba and, finally, my cable of October 27. I don't know what news you received; I can only respond for the message that I sent you the evening of October 26, which reached you the 27th.

What we did in the face of the events, Comrade Khrushchev, was to prepare ourselves and get ready to fight. In Cuba there was only one kind of alarm, that of battle stations.

When in our opinion the imperialist attack became imminent I deemed it appropriate to so advise you and alert both the Soviet government and command—since there were Soviet forces committed to fight at our side to defend the Republic of Cuba from foreign aggression—about the possibility of an attack that we could not prevent but could resist.

I told you that the morale of our people was very high and that the aggression would be heroically resisted. At the end of the message I reiterated to you that we awaited the events calmly.

Danger couldn't impress us, for danger has been hanging over the country for a long time now and in a certain way we have grown used to it.

The Soviet troops which have been at our side know how admirable the stand of our people was throughout this crisis and the profound brotherhood that was created among the troops from both peoples during the decisive hours. Countless eyes of Cuban and Soviet men who were willing to die with supreme dignity shed tears upon learning about the surprising, sudden and practically unconditional decision to withdraw the weapons.

Perhaps you don't know the degree to which the Cuban people was ready to do its duty toward the nation and humanity.

I realized when I wrote them that the words contained in my letter could be misinterpreted by you and that was what happened, perhaps because you didn't read them carefully, perhaps because of the translation, perhaps because I meant to say so much in too few lines. However, I didn't hesitate to do it. Do you think, Comrade Khrushchev, that we were selfishly thinking of ourselves, of our generous people ready to sacrifice themselves, and not at all in an unconscious manner, but fully assured of the risk they ran?

No, Comrade Khrushchev. Few times in history, and it could even be said that never before, because no people had ever faced such a tremendous danger, was a people so willing to fight and die with such a universal sense of duty.

We knew, and do not presume that we ignored it, that we would have been annihilated, as you insinuate in your letter, in the event of nuclear war. However, that didn't prompt us to ask you to withdraw the missiles, that didn't prompt us to ask you to yield. Do you believe that we wanted that war? But how could we prevent it if the invasion finally took place? The fact is that this event was possible, that imperialism was obstructing every solution and that its demands were, from our point of view, impossible for the USSR and Cuba to accept.

And if war had broken out, what was one to do with the insane people who unleashed the war? You yourself have said that under current conditions such a war would inevitably have escalated quickly into a nuclear war.

I understand that once aggression is unleashed, one shouldn't concede to the aggressor the privilege of deciding, moreover, when to use nuclear weapons. The destructive power of this weaponry is so great and the speed of its delivery so great that the aggressor would have a considerable initial advantage.

And I did not suggest to you, Comrade Khrushchev, that the USSR should be the aggressor, because that would be more than incorrect, it would be immoral and contemptible on my part. But from the instant the imperialists attack Cuba and while there are Soviet armed forces stationed in Cuba to help in our defense in case of attack from abroad, the imperialists would by this act become aggressors against Cuba and against the USSR, and we would respond with a strike that would annihilate them.

Everyone has his own opinions and I maintain mine about the dangerousness of the aggressive circles in the Pentagon and their preference for a preventive strike. I did not suggest, Comrade Khrushchev, that in the midst of this crisis the Soviet Union should attack, which is what your letter seems to say; rather, that following an imperialist attack, the USSR should act without vacillation and should never make the mistake of allowing circumstances to develop in which the enemy makes the first nuclear strike against the USSR. And in this sense, Comrade Khrushchev, I maintain my point of view, because I understand it to be a true and just evaluation of a specific situation. You may be able to convince me that I am wrong, but you can't tell me that I am wrong without convincing me.

I know that this is a delicate issue that can only be broached in circumstances such as these and in a very personal message.

You may wonder what right I have to broach this topic. I do so without worrying about how thorny it is, following the dictates of my conscience as a revolutionary duty and inspired by the most unselfish sentiments of admiration and affection for the USSR, for what she represents for the future of humanity and by the concern that she should never again be the victim of the perfidy and betrayal of aggressors, as she was in 1941, and which cost so many lives and so much destruction. Moreover, I spoke not as a troublemaker but as a combatant from the most endangered trenches.

I do not see how you can state that we were consulted in the decision you took.

I would like nothing more than to be proved wrong at this moment. I only wish that you were right.

There are not just a few Cubans, as has been reported to you, but in fact many Cubans who are experiencing at this moment unspeakable bitterness and sadness.

The imperialists are talking once again of invading our country, which is proof of how ephemeral and untrustworthy their promises are. Our people, however, maintain their indestructible will to resist the aggressors and perhaps more than ever need to trust in themselves and in that will to struggle.

We will struggle against adverse circumstances, we will overcome the current difficulties and we will come out ahead, and nothing can destroy the ties of friendship and the eternal gratitude we feel toward the USSR.

Fraternally,

Fidel Castro

Source: The Cuban Missile Crisis, 1962: The 40th Anniversary. The National Security Archive, The George Washington University. Available at: http://www.gwu.edu/~nsarchiv/nsa/cuba_mis_cri/621031%20Letter%20to%20Khrushchev.pdf. Accessed December 1, 2011.

Chronology

1823	Monroe Doctrine warns European powers against further territorial acquisitions or interventions in Latin America.
April 1898	The United States and Spain declare war on each other.
December 1898	Spain cedes Cuba to the United States under the Treaty of Paris.
1902	Cuba gains independence, but the Platt Amendment gives the United States the right to intervene in Cuban affairs.
1904	Roosevelt Corollary to the Monroe Doctrine asserts the right of the United States to intervene in the affairs of Latin American nations in order to keep them "stable, orderly and prosperous."
1933	Cuba abrogates the Platt Amendment. President Franklin D. Roosevelt withholds recognition of Ramón Grau's government for a year.
1940–1944	First presidential administration of Fulgencio Batista
1950–1958	Second presidential administration of Fulgencio Batista
1953	Fidel Castro leads an unsuccessful revolution against Batista.
1956	Fidel Castro begins a second rebellion against Batista.
1958	The United States withdraws military aid from Batista.

January 1, 1959	Fidel Castro establishes revolutionary government of Cuba.
February 1959	Castro becomes prime minister of Cuba.
April 1959	Castro visits the United States.
May 1959	Cuban Agrarian Reform Law forbids foreign land ownership and expropriates farm holdings over 1,000 acres.
October 1959	Soviet representative Aleksandr Alekseev arrives in Cuba.
February 1960	Soviet Politburo member Anastas Mikoyan visits Cuba, signs Soviet-Cuban trade agreement.
March 1960	President Dwight D. Eisenhower authorizes a program to fund and train Cuban exiles to overthrow Castro's government.
May 1960	Cuba and the Soviet Union resume diplomatic relations.
July 1960	The United States suspends Cuban sugar import quota. Soviet premier Nikita Khrushchev pledges that Cuba falls under the protection of the Soviet nuclear umbrella.
September 1960	Khrushchev and Castro meet and embrace at the United Nations in New York. Soviet arms shipments begin arriving in Cuba.
October 1960	Cuba nationalizes $1 billion of private American investments in Cuba. The United States imposes a complete economic embargo on Cuba (except for cigars, some foods, and medicines).
December 19, 1960	Cuba aligns itself with the Soviet Union and the communist bloc.
January 3, 1960	The United States ends diplomatic relations with Cuba.
January 20, 1961	John F. Kennedy becomes U.S. president.
April 14, 1961	U.S. B-26 bombers piloted by Cuban exiles attack Cuban airbases.
April 16, 1961	Castro announces he himself is a communist.
April 17–19, 1961	The CIA-backed invasion of Cuba by Cuban exiles ends in failure.

June 3–4, 1961	Kennedy and Khrushchev meet in Vienna.
August 13, 1961	Soviet and East German forces erect the Berlin Wall, dividing East and West Berlin.
November 30, 1961	Kennedy authorizes Operation MONGOOSE to destabilize Castro's government.
December 1, 1961	Castro declares he is a Marxist-Leninist.
January 1962	The Organization of American States excludes Cuba from participation in its activities.
February 1962	Kennedy imposes a full trade embargo—including cigars and food, though not medicines—on Cuba.
April 1962	15 U.S. Jupiter nuclear missiles in Turkey become operational.
May 1962	Khrushchev decides to offer to install nuclear-capable missiles in Cuba.
	Alekseev is appointed Soviet ambassador to Cuba.
July-October 1962	Over 100 Soviet shipments of troops and military equipment reach Cuba.
September 4, 1962	Kennedy states publicly that the United States will not tolerate Soviet offensive weapons in Cuba.
October 2, 1962	Transport of U.S. goods to Cuba is banned.
October 14, 1962	A U-2 surveillance flight over Cuba photographs nuclear-capable missile installations.
October 16, 1962	Kennedy receives photographic evidence of nuclear-capable missile bases on Cuba; summons meeting of Executive Committee (ExComm) of the National Security Council, his senior foreign policy advisers, which meets every day from then to October 28.
October 18, 1962	Kennedy meets Soviet foreign minister Andrey Gromyko, who denies the presence of any Soviet nuclear-capable missiles on Cuba.
October 22, 1962	Kennedy announces publicly that the United States knows Soviet nuclear-capable missiles have been installed on Cuba, demands their withdrawal, and imposes a naval quarantine on the island.
	U.S. forces move to DEFCON-3: high nuclear alert.

October 23, 1962	*Alexandrovsk,* a Soviet ship bearing 68 nuclear warheads, reaches Cuba just before the quarantine becomes operative.
October 24, 1962	The U.S. naval quarantine of Cuba becomes operative. Soviet ships stop at the quarantine line and go no further, while Kennedy delays boarding.
October 25, 1962	U.S. forces move to DEFCON-2: highest nuclear alert short of war.
	U.S. ambassador Adlai Stevenson presents photographic evidence of Soviet nuclear-capable missile installations on Cuba to the United Nations.
October 26, 1962	Khrushchev writes to Kennedy, offering to remove the missiles in exchange for a pledge not to invade Cuba. Castro urges Khrushchev to mount a nuclear first strike against the United States.
October 27, 1962	Khrushchev sends a second letter, requesting that the United States remove Jupiter missiles from Turkey. Soviet surface-to-air batteries shoot down a U-2 reconnaissance plane over Cuba. U.S. warships confront nuclear-armed Soviet Foxtrot submarine B-59 in the West Atlantic. Kennedy replies to the first Khrushchev letter, accepting its terms. Robert Kennedy secretly meets Soviet ambassador Anatoly Dobrynin and offers to remove Jupiter missiles from Turkey and Italy within 4–5 months.
October 28, 1962	Khrushchev accepts U.S. terms in letter read over Radio Moscow. Khrushchev writes private third letter to Kennedy setting out terms of agreement on Jupiter missiles.
October 30, 1962	Robert F. Kennedy hands back Khrushchev's private third letter to Kennedy to Ambassador Dobrynin.
November–December 1962	Soviet nuclear-capable missiles and some other weapons are removed from Cuba. Castro refuses to allow on-site inspections. Eighteen thousand Soviet troops remain in Cuba.
November 1962	Mikoyan visits Cuba in an effort to mollify Castro.
November 21, 1962	Kennedy lifts the naval quarantine of Cuba.

April–May 1963	Castro visits the Soviet Union.
May 1963	Khrushchev renews the Soviet nuclear guarantee of Cuba's security.
April 1963	Final Jupiter missiles are removed from Italy and Turkey.
August 5, 1963	The United States, Britain, and the Soviet Union sign the Partial Test Ban Treaty.
November 22, 1963	Kennedy is assassinated in Dallas, Texas, by an American Castro sympathizer.
October 1964	Khrushchev is ousted from power by Soviet Politburo.
December 1976	Fidel Castro becomes president of Cuba.
September 1991	Soviet president Mikhail Gorbachev withdraws all Soviet troops from Cuba.
July 31, 2006	Castro transfers his responsibilities to his brother Raúl Castro.
February 2008	Castro resigns as president of Cuba and Raúl takes over.

Bibliography

Acosta, Tomás Diez. *October 1962: The "Missile" Crisis as Seen from Cuba.* New York: Pathfinder, 2002.

Allison, Graham, and Philip Zelikow. *Essence of Decision: Explaining the Cuban Missile Crisis.* 2nd ed. New York: Longman, 1999.

Allyn, Bruce J., James G. Blight, and David A. Welch. *Cuba on the Brink: Castro, the Cuban Missile Crisis, and the Soviet Collapse.* New York: Pantheon, 1993.

Alterman, Eric. *When Presidents Lie: A History of Official Deception and Its Consequences.* New York: Viking, 2004.

Argote-Freyre, Frank. *Fulgencio Batista: From Revolutionary to Strongman.* New Brunswick, NJ: Rutgers University Press, 2006.

Attwood, William. *The Twilight Struggle: Tales of the Cold War.* New York: Harper and Row, 1987.

Ausland, John C. *Kennedy, Khrushchev, and the Berlin-Cuba Crisis 1961–1964.* Oslo, Norway: Scandinavian University Press, 1996.

Balfour, Sebastian. *Castro.* 3rd ed. Harlow, England: Longmans, 2009.

Barrass, Gordon S. *The Great Cold War: A Journey through the Hall of Mirrors.* Stanford, CA: Stanford University Press, 2009.

Benjamin, Jules R. *The United States and the Origins of the Cuban Revolution: An Empire of Liberty in an Age of National Liberation.* Princeton, NJ: Princeton University Press, 1990.

Beschloss, Michael R. *The Crisis Years: Kennedy and Khrushchev 1960–1963.* New York: Edward Burlingame Books, 1991.

Bethell, Leslie, ed. *Cuba: A Short History.* Cambridge: Cambridge University Press, 1993.

Bissell, Richard M., Jr., with Jonathan E. Lewis and Francis Pudlo. *Reflections of a Cold Warrior: From Yalta to the Bay of Pigs.* New Haven, CT: Yale University Press, 1996.

Blight, James G., and Philip Brenner. *Sad and Luminous Days: Cuba's Struggle with the Superpowers after the Missile Crisis.* Lanham, MD: Rowman and Littlefield, 2002.

Blight, James G., and Peter Kornbluh, eds. *Politics of Illusion: The Bay of Pigs Invasion Reexamined.* Boulder, CO: Lynne Rienner, 1998.

Blight, James G., and Janet M. Lang. *The Fog of War: Lessons from the Life of Robert S. McNamara.* Lanham, MD: Rowman and Littlefield, 2005.

Blight, James G., and David A. Welch, eds. *Intelligence and the Cuban Missile Crisis.* London: Frank Cass, 1998.

Blight, James G., and David A. Welch. *On the Brink: Americans and Soviets Reexamine the Cuban Missile Crisis.* New York: Hill and Wang, 1989.

Bohning, Don. *The Castro Obsession: U.S. Covert Operations against Cuba, 1959–1965.* Washington, DC: Potomac Books, 2005.

Bolender, Keith. *Voices from the Other Side: An Oral History of Terrorism against Cuba.* New York: Pluto Press, 2010.

Brenner, Philip. *From Confrontation to Negotiation: U.S. Relations with Cuba.* Boulder, CO: Westview Press, 1988.

Breuer, William B. *Vendetta: Fidel Castro and the Kennedy Brothers.* New York: John Wiley, 1997.

Brewer, Stewart. *Borders and Bridges: A History of U.S.-Latin American Relations.* Westport, CT: Praeger, 2006.

Brugioni, Dino. *Eyeball to Eyeball: The Inside Story of the Cuban Missile Crisis.* Edited by Robert F. McCort. New York: Random House, 1991.

Brune, Lester H. *The Cuba-Caribbean Missile Crisis of October 1962: A Review of Issues and References.* Claremont, CA: Regina Books, 1996.

Bundy, McGeorge. *Danger and Survival: Choices about the Bomb in the First Fifty Years.* New York: Random House, 1988.

Castro, Fidel. *The Declarations of Havana.* New York: Verso, 2008.

Castro, Fidel, and Ignacio Ramonet. *My Life: A Spoken Autobiography.* Translated by Andrew Hurley. New York: Scribner, 2007.

Chang, Laurence, and Peter Kornbluh, eds. *The Cuban Missile Crisis, 1962: A National Security Archive Documents Reader.* New York: New Press, 1992.

Chun, Clayton K. S. *Thunder over the Horizon: From V-2 Rockets to Ballistic Missiles.* Westport, CT: Praeger, 2005.

Cimbala, Stephen J. *Coercive Military Strategy.* College Station: Texas A & M University Press, 1998.

Cimbala, Stephen J. *Military Persuasion in War and Policy: The Power of Soft.* Westport, CT: Praeger, 2002.

Cline, Ray S. *Secrets, Spies and Scholars: Blueprint of the Essential CIA.* Washington, DC: Acropolis Books, 1976.

Coltman, Leycester. *The Real Fidel Castro*. New Haven, CT: Yale University Press, 2003.

Dallek, Robert. *An Unfinished Life: John F. Kennedy, 1917–1963*. New York: Back Bay Books, 2004.

Dent, David W. *The Legacy of the Monroe Doctrine: A Reference Guide to U.S. Involvement in Latin America and the Caribbean*. Westport, CT: Greenwood Press, 1999.

DePalma, Anthony. *The Man Who Invented Castro: Cuba, Castro, and Herbert L. Matthews of the New York Times*. New York: PublicAffairs, 2006.

Dinerstein, Herbert S. *The Making of a Missile Crisis: October 1962*. Baltimore, MD: Johns Hopkins University Press, 1976.

Dobbs, Michael. *One Minute to Midnight: Kennedy, Khrushchev, and Castro on the Brink of Nuclear War*. New York: Knopf, 2008.

Dobrynin, Anatoly. *In Confidence: Moscow's Ambassador to America's Six Cold War Presidents (1962–1986)*. Rev. ed. Seattle: University of Washington Press, 2001.

Dominguez, Esteban Morales, and Gary Prevost. *United States–Cuban Relations: A Critical History*. Lanham, MD: Lexington Books, 2008.

Dominguez, Jorge I. *To Make a World Safe for Revolution: Cuba's Foreign Policy*. Cambridge, MA: Harvard University Press, 1989.

Elliston, Jon, ed. *Psywar on Cuba: The Declassified History of U.S. Anti-Castro Propaganda*. New York: Ocean Press, 1999.

Eubank, Keith. *The Missile Crisis in Cuba*. Malabar, FL: Krieger Publishing, 2000.

Farber, Samuel. *The Origins of the Cuban Revolution Reconsidered*. Chapel Hill: University of North Carolina Press, 2006.

Feklisov, Alexander. *The Man Behind the Rosenbergs*. Translated by Catherine Dop. New York: Enigma Books, 2001.

Foner, Philip S. *A History of Cuba and Its Relations with the United States*. New York: International Publishers, 1962.

Foner, Philip S. *The Spanish-Cuban-American War and the Birth of American Imperialism, 1895–1902*. New York: Monthly Review Press, 1972.

Frankel, Max. *High Noon in the Cold War: Kennedy, Khrushchev, and the Cuban Missile Crisis*. New York: Ballantine Books, 2004.

Freedman, Lawrence. *Kennedy's Wars: Berlin, Cuba, Laos, and Vietnam*. New York: Oxford University Press, 2000.

Fuente, Alejandro de la. *A Nation for All: Race, Inequality, and Politics in Twentieth-Century Cuba*. Chapel Hill: University of North Carolina Press, 2001.

Fursenko, Aleksandr, and Timothy Naftali. *Khrushchev's Cold War: The Inside Story of an American Adversary*. New York: Norton, 2006.

Fursenko, Aleksandr, and Timothy Naftali. *One Hell of a Gamble: Khrushchev, Castro, and Kennedy, 1958–1964.* New York: Norton, 1997.

Gaddis, John Lewis. *The Cold War: A New History.* New York: Penguin, 2006.

Gaddis, John Lewis. *We Now Know: Rethinking Cold War History.* New York: Oxford University Press, 1997.

Gaddis, John Lewis, Philip H. Gordon, Ernest R. May, and Jonathan Rosenberg. *Cold War Statesmen Confront the Bomb: Nuclear Diplomacy Since 1945.* New York: Oxford University Press, 1999.

García, Maria Cristina. *Havana USA: Cuban Exiles and Cuban Americans in South Florida, 1959–1994.* Berkeley: University of California Press, 1996.

Garthoff, Raymond L. *A Journey Through the Cold War: A Memoir of Containment and Coexistence.* Washington, DC: Brookings Institution, 2001.

Garthoff, Raymond L. *Reflections on the Cuban Missile Crisis.* Washington, DC: Brookings Institution, 1987.

Gellman, Irving. *Roosevelt and Batista: Good Neighbor Diplomacy in Cuba, 1933–1945.* Albuquerque: University of New Mexico Press, 1973.

George, Alice L. *Awaiting Armageddon: How Americans Faced the Cuban Missile Crisis.* Chapel Hill: University of North Carolina Press, 2006.

Gibson, David R. *Talk at the Brink: Deliberation and Decision During the Cuban Missile Crisis.* Princeton, NJ: Princeton University Press, 2012.

Gilderhus, Mark T. *The Second Century: U.S.-Latin American Relations Since 1889.* Wilmington, DE: Scholarly Resources, 2000.

Gleijeses, Piero. *Conflicting Missions: Havana, Washington, and Africa, 1959–1976.* Chapel Hill: University of North Carolina Press, 2002.

Goduti, Philip A., Jr. *Kennedy's Kitchen Cabinet and the Pursuit of Peace: The Shaping of American Foreign Policy, 1961–1963.* Jefferson, NC: McFarland Press, 2009.

Gott, Richard. *Cuba: A New History.* New Haven, CT: Yale University Press, 2004.

Grandin, Greg, and Gilbert M, Joseph, eds. *A Century of Revolution: Insurgent and Counterinsurgent Violence during Latin America's Long Cold War.* Durham, NC: Duke University Press, 2010.

Grenier, Guillermo J., and Lisandro Pérez. *The Legacy of Exile: Cubans in the United States.* Boston, MA: Allyn and Bacon, 2003.

Gribkov, Anatoli I., and Smith, William Y. *Operation ANADYR: U.S. and Soviet Generals Recount the Cuban Missile Crisis.* Edited by Alfred Friendly, Jr. Chicago, Berlin, Tokyo, and Moscow: edition q, 1994.

Grow, Michael. *U.S. Presidents and Latin American Interventions: Pursuing Regime Change in the Cold War.* Lawrence: University Press of Kansas, 2008.

Haney, Patrick J., and Walt Vanderbush. *The Cuban Embargo: The Domestic Politics of An American Foreign Policy.* Pittsburgh, PA: University of Pittsburgh Press, 2005.

Haslam, Jonathan. *Russia's Cold War: From the October Revolution to the Fall of the Wall.* New Haven, CT: Yale University Press, 2011.

Hennessy, Alastair, and George Lambie, eds. *The Fractured Blockade: West European-Cuban Relations during the Revolution.* London: Macmillan Caribbean, 1993.

Hersh, Seymour M. *The Dark Side of Camelot.* Boston: Little, Brown, 1997.

Higgins, Trumbull. *The Perfect Failure: Kennedy, Eisenhower, and the CIA at the Bay of Pigs.* New York: Norton, 1987.

Hilsman, Roger. *The Cuban Missile Crisis: The Struggle over Policy.* Westport, CT: Praeger, 1996.

Hilsman, Roger. *To Move a Nation: The Politics of Foreign Policy in the Administration of John F. Kennedy.* Garden City, NY: Doubleday, 1967.

Hinckle, Warren, and William W. Turner. *The Fish is Red: The Story of the Secret War Against Castro.* New York: Harper and Row, 1981.

Horowitz, Louis. *The Long Night of Dark Intent: A Half Century of Cuban Communism.* New Brunswick, NJ: Transaction Books, 2008.

Huchthausen, Peter A. *October Fury.* Hoboken, NJ: John Wiley, 2002.

Huggins, Martha K. *Political Policing: The United States and Latin America.* Durham, NC: Duke University Press, 1998.

Isaacson, Walter, and Evan Thomas. *The Wise Men: Six Friends and the World they Made.* New York: Simon and Schuster, 1986.

Johnson, Dominic D. P. *Overconfidence and War: The Havoc and Glory of Positive Illusions.* Cambridge, MA: Harvard University Press, 2004.

Johnson, Dominic D. P., and Dominic Tierney. *Failing to Win: Perceptions of Victory and Defeat in International Politics.* Cambridge, MA: Harvard University Press, 2006.

Johnson, John J. *A Hemisphere Apart: The Foundations of United States Policy Toward Latin America.* Baltimore, MD: Johns Hopkins University Press, 1990.

Jones, Howard. *The Bay of Pigs.* New York: Oxford University Press, 2008.

Jordan, David C. *Revolutionary Cuba and the End of the Cold War.* Lanham, MD: University Press of America, 1993.

Kaplan, Fred. *1959: The Year That Changed Everything.* New York: John Wiley, 2009.

Kaplowitz, Donna Rich. *Anatomy of a Failed Embargo: U.S. Sanctions Against Cuba.* Boulder, CO: Lynne Rienner, 1998.

Karabell, Zachary. *Architects of Intervention: The United States, the Third World, and the Cold War, 1946–1962*. Baton Rouge: Louisiana State University Press, 1999.

Kempe, Frederick. *Berlin 1961: Kennedy, Khrushchev, and the Most Dangerous Place on Earth*. New York: Putnam, 2011.

Kennedy, Robert F. *Thirteen Days: A Memoir of the Cuban Missile Crisis*. New York: Norton, 1969, 1999.

Khrushchev, Nikita. *Khrushchev Remembers*. Edited by Edward Crankshaw. Translated by Strobe Talbott. Boston: Little, Brown, 1970.

Khrushchev, Nikita. *Khrushchev Remembers: The Glasnost Tapes*. Edited and translated by Jerrold L. Schechter and Vyacheslav V. Luchkov. Boston: Little, Brown, 1990.

Khrushchev, Nikita. *Khrushchev Remembers: The Last Testament*. Edited by Edward Crankshaw and Jerrold L. Schechter. Translated by Strobe Talbott. Boston: Little, Brown, 1974.

Khrushchev, Sergei N. *Nikita Khrushchev and the Creation of a Superpower*. Edited by William Taubman, Sergei Khrushchev, and Abbott Gleason. New Haven, CT: Yale University Press, 2000.

Kolko, Gabriel. *Confronting the Third World: United States Foreign Policy, 1945–1980*. New York: Pantheon, 1980.

Kornbluh, Peter, ed. *Bay of Pigs Declassified: The Secret CIA Report on the Invasion of Cuba*. New York: New Press, 1998.

Latham, Michael E. *Modernization as Ideology: American Social Science and "Nation Building" in the Kennedy Era*. Chapel Hill: University of North Carolina Press, 2000.

Lebow, Richard Ned, and Janice Gross Stein. *We All Lost the Cold War*. Princeton, NJ: Princeton University Press, 1994.

Lechuga, Carlos M. *In the Eye of the Storm: Castro, Kennedy, Khrushchev, and the Missile Crisis*. Translated by Mary Todd. Melbourne, Victoria, Australia: Ocean Press, 1995.

Leffler, Melvyn P. *For the Soul of Mankind: The United States, the Soviet Union, and the Cold War*. New York: Hill and Wang, 2007.

Leffler, Melvyn P., and Odd Arne Westad, eds. *The Cambridge History of the Cold War*. 3 vols. Cambridge: Cambridge University Press, 2010.

Leonard, Thomas M. *Castro and the Cuban Revolution*. Westport, CT: Greenwood Press, 1999.

Lipman, Jana K. *Guantánamo: A Working-Class History between Empire and Revolution*. Berkeley: University of California Press, 2008.

Longley, Kyle. *In the Eagle's Shadow: The United States and Latin America*. 2nd ed. Wheeling, IL: Harlan Davidson, 2009.

Lynch, Grayston L. *Decision for Disaster: Betrayal at the Bay of Pigs.* Washington, DC: Potomac Books, 1998.

Masud-Piloto, Felix Roberto. *From Welcomed Exiles to Illegal Immigrants: Cuban Migration to the U.S., 1959–1995.* Lanham, MD: Rowman and Littlefield, 1996.

May, Ernest R., and Philip D. Zelikow, eds. *The Kennedy Tapes: Inside the White House during the Cuban Missile Crisis.* Cambridge, MA: Harvard University Press, 1997.

McAuliffe, Mary S., ed. *CIA Documents on the Cuban Missile Crisis, 1962.* Washington, DC: Central Intelligence Agency, 1992. https://www.cia.gov/library/center-for-the-study-of-intelligence/csi-publications/books-and-monographs/Cuban%20Missile%20Crisis1962.pdf; also available at http://www.allworldwars.com/Cuban-Missile-Crisis-CIA-Documents.html

McKenna, Peter, and John M. Kirk, eds. *Competing Voices from Revolutionary Cuba.* Westport, CT: Greenwood Press, 2009.

McPherson, Alan. *Intimate Ties, Bitter Struggles: The United States and Latin America Since 1945.* Washington, DC: Potomac Books, 2006.

Medland, William J. *The Cuban Missile Crisis of 1962: Needless or Necessary.* New York: Praeger, 1988.

Montaner, Carlos Alberto. *Cuba, Castro, and the Caribbean: The Cuban Revolution and the Crisis in Western Conscience.* Translated by Nelson Duran. New Brunswick, NJ: Transactions Books, 1985.

Montaner, Carlos Alberto. *Journey to the Heart of Cuba: Life as Fidel Castro.* New York: Algora Publishers, 2001.

Morley, Morris H. *Imperial State and Revolution: The United States and Cuba, 1952–1986.* Cambridge: Cambridge University Press, 1987.

Morley, Morris, and Chris McGillion, eds. *Cuba, the United States, and the Post-Cold War World: The International Dimensions of the Washington-Havana Relationship.* Gainesville: University Press of Florida, 2005.

Morley, Morris, and Chris McGillion. *Unfinished Business: America and Cuba After the Cold War, 1989–2001.* Cambridge: Cambridge University Press, 2002.

Munton, Don, and David A. Welch. *The Cuban Missile Crisis: A Concise History.* New York: Oxford University Press, 2006.

Naftali, Timothy, Philip D. Zelikow, and Ernest R. May, eds. *John F. Kennedy: The Great Crises.* 3 vols. New York: Norton, 2001.

Nash, Philip. *The Other Missiles of October: Eisenhower, Kennedy, and the Jupiters, 1957–1963.* Chapel Hill: University of North Carolina Press, 1997.

Nathan, James A. *Anatomy of the Cuban Missile Crisis.* Westport, CT: Greenwood Press, 2001.

Newsom, David D. *The Soviet Brigade in Cuba: A Study in Political Diplomacy.* Bloomington: University of Indiana Press, 1987.

O'Brien, Michael. *Rethinking Kennedy: An Interpretive Biography.* New York: St. Martin's Press, 2005.

Paterson, Thomas G. *Contesting Castro: The United States and the Triumph of the Cuban Revolution.* New York: Oxford University Press, 2004.

Paterson, Thomas G., ed. *Kennedy's Quest for Victory: American Foreign Policy, 1961–1963.* New York: Oxford University Press, 1989.

Pavia, Peter. *The Cuba Project: Castro, Kennedy, Dirty Business, Double Dealing, and the FBI's Tamale Squad.* New York: Palgrave Macmillan, 2006.

Pedraza, Silvia. *Political Disaffection in Cuba's Revolution and Exodus.* New York: Cambridge University Press, 2007.

Pérez, Louis A., Jr. *Cuba and the United States: Ties of Singular Intimacy.* 2nd ed. Athens: University of Georgia Press, 1997.

Pérez, Louis A. *Cuba: Between Reform and Revolution.* 4th ed. New York: Oxford University Press, 2011.

Pérez, Louis A., Jr. *Cuba in the American Imagination: Metaphor and the Imperial Ethos.* Chapel Hill: University of North Carolina Press, 2008.

Pérez-Stable, Marifeli. *The Cuban Revolution: Origins, Course, and Legacy.* New York: Oxford University Press, 1993.

Pérez-Stable, Marifeli. *The United States and Cuba: Intimate Enemies.* New York: Routledge, 2011.

Polmar, Norman, and John D. Gresham. *DEFCON-2: Standing on the Brink of Nuclear War during the Cuban Missile Crisis.* New York: John Wiley, 2006.

Press, Daryl G. *Calculating Credibility: How Leaders Evaluate Military Threats.* Ithaca, NY: Cornell University Press, 2005.

Priestland, Jane, ed. *Cuba under Castro: The Declassified British Documents.* 5 vols. London: Archival Publications, 2003.

Rabe, Stephen G. *Eisenhower and Latin America: The Foreign Policy of Anticommunism.* Chapel Hill: University of North Carolina Press, 1988.

Rabe, Stephen G. *The Most Dangerous Area in the World: John F. Kennedy Confronts Communist Revolution in Latin America.* Chapel Hill: University of North Carolina Press, 1999.

Rasenberger, Jim. *The Brilliant Disaster: JFK, Castro, and America's Doomed Invasion of Cuba's Bay of Pigs.* New York: Scribner, 2011.

Reid-Henry, Simon. *Fidel and Che: A Revolutionary Friendship.* London: Sceptre, 2008.

Roy, Joaquin. *The Cuban Revolution (1959–2009): Relations with Spain, the European Union, and the United States.* New York: Palgrave Macmillan, 2009.

Russo, Gus, and Stephen Molton. *Brothers in Arms: The Kennedys, the Castros, and the Politics of Murder.* New York: Bloomsbury, 2008.

Sáenz-Rovner, Eduardo. *The Cuban Connection: Drug Trafficking, Smuggling, and Gambling in Cuba from the 1920s to the Revolution.* Translated by Russ Davidson. Chapel Hill: University of North Carolina Press, 2008.

Salinger, Pierre. *P.S., A Memoir.* New York: St. Martin's Press, 1995.

Schlesinger, Arthur M., Jr. *Journals, 1952–2000.* Edited by Andrew Schlesinger and Stephen Schlesinger. New York: Penguin, 2007.

Schlesinger, Arthur M., Jr. *Robert Kennedy and His Times.* Boston: Houghton Mifflin, 1978.

Schlesinger, Arthur M., Jr. *A Thousand Days: John F. Kennedy in the White House.* Boston: Houghton Mifflin, 1965.

Schoultz, Lars. *Beneath the United States: A History of U.S. Policy toward Latin America.* Cambridge, MA: Harvard University Press, 1998.

Schoultz, Lars. *That Infernal Little Cuban Republic: The United States and the Cuban Revolution.* Chapel Hill: University of North Carolina Press, 2009.

Schwab, Peter. *Cuba: Confronting the U.S. Embargo.* New York: St. Martin's Press, 1999.

Scott, L. V. *Macmillan, Kennedy and the Cuban Missile Crisis: Political, Military and Intelligence Aspects.* New York: St. Martin's Press, 1999.

Scott, Len. *The Cuban Missile Crisis and the Threat of Nuclear War: Lessons From History.* New York: Continuum Books, 2007.

Skwiot, Christine. *The Purposes of Paradise: U.S. Tourism and Empire in Cuba and Hawai'i.* Philadelphia, PA: University of Pennsylvania Press, 2010.

Smith, Gaddis. *The Last Years of the Monroe Doctrine, 1945–1993.* New York: Hill and Wang, 1994.

Smith, Joseph. *The United States and Latin America: A History of American Diplomacy, 1776–2000.* New York: Routledge, 2005.

Smith, Peter H. *Talons of the Eagle: Dynamics of U.S.-Latin American Relations.* 3rd ed. New York: Oxford University Press, 2007.

Smith, Robert Freeman. *The United States and Cuba: Business and Diplomacy, 1917–1960.* New York: Bookman Associates, 1961.

Smith, Wayne S. *The Closest of Enemies: A Personal and Diplomatic Account of U.S.-Cuban Relations Since 1957.* New York: Norton, 1987.

Solomon, Daniel F. *Breaking Up with Cuba: The Dissolution of Friendly Relations between Washington and Havana, 1956–1961.* Jefferson, NC: McFarland Press, 2011.

Sorensen, Theodore C. *Counselor: A Life at the Edge of History.* New York: Harper, 2008.

Sorensen, Theodore C. *Kennedy.* With new preface. New York: Harper, 2009.

Staten, Clifford L. *The History of Cuba.* Westport, CT: Greenwood Press, 2003.

Stern, Sheldon M. *Averting 'The Final Failure': John F. Kennedy and the Secret Cuban Missile Crisis Meetings.* Stanford, CA: Stanford University Press, 2003.

Stern, Sheldon M. *The Week the World Stood Still: Inside the Secret Cuban Missile Crisis.* Stanford, CA: Stanford University Press, 2005.

Strauss, Michael J. *The Leasing of Guantanamo Bay.* Westport, CT: Praeger Security International, 2009.

Suchlicki, Jaime. *Cuba: From Columbus to Castro and Beyond.* 5th ed. Washington, DC: Potomac Books, 2002.

Swedin, Eric G. *When Angels Wept: A What-If History of the Cuban Missile Crisis.* Washington, DC: Potomac Books, 2010.

Sweig, Julia E. *Cuba: What Everyone Needs to Know.* New York: Oxford University Press, 2009.

Sweig, Julia E. *Friendly Fire: Losing Friends and Making Enemies in the Anti-American Century.* New York: PublicAffairs, 2006.

Sweig, Julia E. *Inside the Cuban Revolution: Fidel Castro and the Urban Underground.* Cambridge, MA: Harvard University Press, 2002.

Szulc, Tad. *Fidel: A Critical Portrait.* New York: William Morrow, 1986.

Taffet, Jeffrey F. *Foreign Aid as Foreign Policy: The Alliance for Progress in Latin America.* New York: Routledge, 2007.

Taubman, William S. *Khrushchev: The Man and His Era.* New York: Norton, 2003.

Thomas, Evan. *Robert Kennedy: His Life.* New York: Simon and Schuster, 2000.

Thompson, Robert Smith. *The Missiles of October: The Declassified Story of John F. Kennedy and the Cuban Missile Crisis.* New York: Simon and Schuster, 1992.

United States Department of State. *Foreign Relations of the United States 1958–1960,* Vol. VI: *Cuba.* Washington, DC: Government

Printing Office, 1991. http://digicoll.library.wisc.edu/cgi-bin/FRUS/FRUS-idx?id=FRUS.FRUS195860v06

United States Department of State. *Foreign Relations of the United States 1961–1963,* Vol. VI: *Kennedy-Khrushchev Exchanges.* Washington, DC: Government Printing Office, 1996. http://www.state.gov/www/about_state/history/volume_vi/volumevi.html

United States Department of State. *Foreign Relations of the United States 1961–1963,* Vol. X: *Cuba, 1961–1962.* Washington, DC: Government Printing Office, 1997. http://www.state.gov/www/about_state/history/frusX/

United States Department of State. *Foreign Relations of the United States 1961–1963,* Vol. XI: *The Cuban Missile Crisis and Its Aftermath.* Washington, DC: Government Printing Office, 1996. http://www.state.gov/www/about_state/history/frusXI/

Uslu, Nasuh. *The Turkish-American Relationship between 1947 and 2003: The History of a Distinctive Alliance.* New York: Nova Science Publishers, 2003.

Von Tunzelmann, Alex. *Red Heat: Conspiracy, Murder, and the Cold War in the Caribbean.* New York: Henry Holt, 2011.

Waldron, Lamar, with Thom Hartmann. *Ultimate Sacrifice: John and Robert Kennedy, the Plan for a Coup in Cuba, and the Murder of JFK.* New York: Carroll and Graf, 2005.

Weisbrot, Robert. *Maximum Danger: Kennedy, the Missiles, and the Crisis of American Confidence.* Chicago: Ivan R. Dee, 2001.

Welch, Richard E., Jr. *Response to Revolution: The United States and the Cuban Revolution, 1959–1961.* Chapel Hill: University of North Carolina Press, 1985.

Weldes, Jutta. *Constructing National Interests: The United States and the Cuban Missile Crisis.* Minneapolis: University of Minnesota Press, 1999.

Westad, Odd Arne. *The Global Cold War: Third World Interventions and the Making of Our Times.* New York: Cambridge University Press, 2005.

White, Mark J. *The Cuban Missile Crisis.* London: Macmillan, 1996.

White, Mark J. *The Kennedys and Cuba: The Declassified Documentary History.* Chicago: Ivan R. Dee, 1999.

White, Mark J. *Missiles in Cuba: Kennedy, Khrushchev, Castro and the 1962 Crisis.* Chicago: Ivan R. Dee, 1997.

Wright, Thomas C. *Latin America in the Era of the Cuban Revolution.* Rev. ed. Westport, CT: Praeger, 2001.

Zubok, Vladislav M. *A Failed Empire: The Soviet Union in the Cold War from Stalin to Gorbachev.* Chapel Hill: University of North Carolina Press, 2007.

Zubok, Vladislav, and Constantine Pleshakov. *Inside the Kremlin's Cold War: From Stalin to Khrushchev.* Cambridge, MA: Harvard University Press, 1996.

Web Sites

Cold War International History Project: Virtual Archive 2.0 The Cold War in Latin America, Cuba in the Cold War, The Cuban Missile Crisis, and US-Cuban Relations. http://legacy.wilsoncenter.org/va2/index.cfm?topic_id=1409&fuseaction=HOME.browse&sort=Subject&item=Soviet%20Union,%20relations%20with%Cubanet. http://www.cubanet.org

The Cuban Missile Crisis, 40 Years Later. National Public Radio. http://www.npr.org/news/specials/cuban_missile/

CubanMissileCrisis.Info. http://cubanmissilecrisis.info/index.htm

Federation of Atomic Scientists Intelligence Resource Program: The Cuban Missile Crisis. http://www.fas.org/irp/imint/cuba.htm

GlobalSecurity.Org: The Cuban Missile Crisis. http://www.globalsecurity.org/military/ops/cuba-62.htm

HistoryofCuba.Com. http://www.historyofcuba.com/cuba.htm

John F. Kennedy Presidential Library and Museum: The Cuban Missile Crisis. http://www.jfklibrary.org/JFK/JFK-in-History/Cuban-Missile-Crisis.aspx

Miller Center of Public Affairs, University of Virginia: John F. Kennedy—Presidential Recordings. http://millercenter.org/scripps/archive/presidentialrecordings/kennedy

Mount Holyoke College: Resources for the Study of International Relations and Foreign Policy: Documents Relating to the Bay of Pigs Invasion and the Cuban Missile Crisis. http://www.mtholyoke.edu/acad/intrel/cuba.htm

National Security Archive: The Bay of Pigs. http://www.gwu.edu/~nsarchiv/bayofpigs/

National Security Archive: The Cuban Missile Crisis. http://www.gwu.edu/~nsarchiv/nsa/cuba_mis_cri/docs.htm

No Time to Talk: The Cuban Missile Crisis. http://www.october1962.com/

NuclearFiles.Org:CubanMissileCrisis.http://www.nuclearfiles.org/menu/
key-issues/nuclear-weapons/history/cold-war/cuban-missile-crisis/

Films and Television

ABC News Nightline: The JFK Tapes (1994). ABC.

American Experience: Fidel Castro (2005). PBS.

Castro's Cuba (2004). PBS.

Che (2008). Directed by Stephen Soderbergh. Starring Julia Ormond and Benicio del Toro.

Cuba: The 40 Years War (2002). Directed by Peter Melaragno.

The Cold War (1998). BBC/CNN. Directed by Jeremy Isaacs.

Fidel! (1974). Micromedia. Directed by Sam Landau.

Fidel (2002). Starring Victor Huggo Martin, Gael García Bernal, and David Attwood.

Fidel Castro: A Life of Revolution (2008). Canadian Broadcasting Corporation. Directed by Terence McKenna.

The Fog of War: Eleven Lessons from the Life of Robert S. McNamara (2004). Sony. Directed by Errol Morris.

K-19: The Widow Maker (2002). Starring Harrison Ford and Liam Neeson.

Kennedy (1983). NBC. Starring Martin Sheen, Blair Brown, and E. G. Marshall.

Kennedy and Castro: The Secret History (2003). NBC.

The Missiles of October (1974). Starring William Devane, Ralph Bellamy, and Howard Da Silva.

Thirteen Days (2001). Starring Kevin Costner, Bruce Greenwood, and Roger Donaldson.

CD-ROM

Cuban Missile Crisis: CIA-NSA-NSC-State Dept. Files: Audio Recordings. BACM Research: PaperlessArchives.Com. 2008.

About the Editor and Contributors

Editor

Dr. Priscilla Roberts
Associate Professor of History,
School of Humanities
Honorary Director, Centre of
American Studies
University of Hong Kong
Pokfulam, Hong Kong

Contributors

Dr. Valerie Adams
School of Letters and Sciences
Arizona State University—
Polytechnic Campus
Mesa, Arizona

Lacie A. Ballinger
Collections Manager
Fort Worth Museum of Science
and History
Fort Worth, Texas

Dr. Günter Bischof
Department of History
University of New Orleans
New Orleans, Louisiana

Dr. Paul R. Camacho
Director Emeritus, William Joiner
Center for the Study of War and
Social Consequences
University of Massachusetts
Boston, Massachusetts

Dr. Barry Carr
Department of History and
Institute of Latin American Studies
La Trobe University
Melbourne, Australia

Dr. Don M. Coerver
Department of History
Texas Christian University
Fort Worth, Texas

Dr. Jérôme Dorvidal
CRESOI Department of History
University of La Réunion
Réunion Island, Indian Ocean

Dr. Beatrice de Graaf
Centre for Terrorism and
Counterterrorism
Campus The Hague
Leiden University
Netherlands

Dr. Steven W. Guerrier
Department of History
James Madison University
Harrisonburg, Virginia

Dr. Magarditsch Hatschikjan
Institute of East European History
University of Cologne
Cologne, Germany

Dr. Brian Madison Jones
Department of History
Johnson C. Smith University
Charlotte, North Carolina

Dr. Jeffrey Larsen
Senior Policy Analyst
Science Applications International
Corporation
Colorado Springs, Colorado

Dr. Mark Atwood Lawrence
Department of History
University of Texas at Austin
Austin, Texas

Arturo Lopez-Levy
Josef Korbel School of
International Studies
University of Denver
Denver, Colorado

Dr. Lise Namikas
Department of History
Louisiana State University
Baton Rouge, Louisiana

Dr. Caryn E. Neumann
Lecturer in Integrative Studies
History Department
Miami University of Ohio
Oxford, Ohio

Dr. Christian Nuenlist
Lecturer in Contemporary History
University of Zurich
Zurich, Switzerland

Dr. Michael Share
Independent Scholar

Dr. James F. Siekmeier
Assistant Professor of History
West Virginia University
Morgantown, West Virginia

Dr. Daniel E. Spector
Emeritus Professor of History
University of Alabama
Birmingham, Alabama

Dr. David Tal
Kahanoff Chair in Israeli Studies
Department of History
University of Calgary
Calgary, Canada

Dr. Spencer C. Tucker
Senior Fellow
Military History, ABC-CLIO,
 LLC

Dr. Josh Ushay
Independent Scholar

Dr. Robert Anthony Waters, Jr.
Department of History
Ohio Northern University
Ada, Ohio

Dr. Paul Wingrove
Department of Politics
University of Greenwich
Greenwich
United Kingdom

Index